'In this lively and engaging book, Jerome Creach introduces contemporary Christians to the book of Psalms and encourages them to use the psalms for both study and worship. At a time when many churches are losing touch with the psalms, he convincingly shows that they are at the spiritual heart of the Bible.'
John Barton, Emeritus Oriel and Laing Professor of the Interpretation of Holy Scripture, University of Oxford

'This book is the product of some thirty years' experience of teaching and writing for both the Church and academy. It enters a competitive market, but Jerome Creach's passion for the psalms has resulted in an eminently readable introduction.'
Sue Gillingham, Professor of the Hebrew Bible, University of Oxford

'This introduction to the Psalms, by a scholar who has been studying them and praying them for decades, amply demonstrates their potential to feed our worship and revolutionize the way we pray.'
John Goldingay, Professor Emeritus of Old Testament, Fuller Theological Seminary, California

'Jerome Creach's book will be of great help and interest to Christians beginning study of the Psalms who are looking for a serious engagement with scholarship within a context of faithful reading. It is a valuable resource for ministry students and any Christian who wants to go deeper with the psalms. It combines detailed analysis of the material itself, such as the discussion on what poetry is, with an attention always to the significance of the Psalter for its own time and for ours.'
Jenni Williams, Vicar of St Matthew with St Luke, and former Tutor in Old Testament, Wycliffe Hall, Oxford

T0366499

Jerome F. D. Creach is the Robert C. Holland Professor of Old Testament at Pittsburgh Theological Seminary. He is the author of *The Destiny of the Righteous in the Psalms* (Chalice Press, 2008) and *Yahweh as Refuge and the Editing of the Hebrew Psalter* (JSOTSup 217; Sheffield Academic Press, 1996) as well as numerous articles and essays on the Psalms. He is also the author of *Violence in Scripture* (Interpretation: Resources for the Use of Scripture in the Church; Westminster John Knox Press, 2013).

Discovering Biblical Texts
Content, interpretation, reception

Comprehensive, up-to-date and student-friendly introductions to the books of the Bible: their structure, content, theological concerns, key interpretative debates and historical reception.

Also available:

Ian Boxall, *Discovering Matthew* (2014)
Ruth B. Edwards, *Discovering John* (second edition, 2014)
Iain Provan, *Discovering Genesis* (2015)
Anthony C. Thiselton, *Discovering Romans* (2016)

DISCOVERING THE PSALMS

Content, interpretation, reception

Jerome F. D. Creach

First published in Great Britain in 2020

Society for Promoting Christian Knowledge
36 Causton Street
London SW1P 4ST
www.spck.org.uk

British Library Cataloguing-in-Publication Data
A catalogue record for this book is available from the British Library

ISBN 978–0–281–07320–7
eBook ISBN 978–0–281–07321–4

Typeset by Manila Typesetting Company

Subsequently digitally printed in Great Britain

eBook by Manila Typesetting Company

Produced on paper from sustainable forests

In memory of James Luther Mays (1921–2015)

Contents

Acknowledgements   xii

Abbreviations   xiv

Introduction: The role of the Psalms in the life of the Church   1

    The nature and purpose of this book   5

    A preview of the book   7

Part 1
ISSUES IN READING THE PSALMS AND THE PSALTER

1 **What is a psalm?**   11

    Titles for the book   11

    How many psalms?   13

    Anatomy of a psalm   14

    Collections and clusters of psalms   22

    The structure of the book   24

2 **It's poetry!**   28

    What is poetry and why is it important?   28

    Important terms   31

    What makes the Psalms poetry?   32

3 **Did David write the Psalms?**   48

    Claims of Davidic authorship   48

    Questioning David as author of the Psalms   52

    Psalm 72 as turning point in Davidic authorship   54

    Figurative readings of David in the Psalms   55

    If not David, then who?   56

    Recovering David in the Psalms   58

Contents

4 A psalm for every occasion: types of psalms   61
  Psalms study in the twentieth century   61
  Hermann Gunkel and the rise of form criticism   63
  Types of psalms   64
  Conclusion   79

5 Settings for performance of the Psalms   80
  Cultic setting of the Psalms   80
  Imagining the Psalms in worship   87
  Specific theories of cultic settings   92
  Re-use of cultic psalms   96

Part 2
READING THE PSALMS TOGETHER

6 Going by the book: the Psalter as a guide to reading
  the psalms   101
  Signs of coherence   103
  Going further: the theological shape of the Psalter 105
  Conclusion   119

7 The theology of the Psalms, Part 1: 'The LORD reigns!' 120
  God's kingship as the centre of the Psalms   121
  Administration of the LORD's reign   128

8 The theology of the Psalms, Part 2: What is the human
  being?   135
  One who trusts   137
  Right behaviour: Psalms 15 and 24   141
  David as righteous   144

Part 3
THE PSALMS AS PRAYERS

9 The tradition of psalmic prayer, Part 1: Opening fully
  to God   149
  Neglect of the Psalms in Christian prayer   150
  The nature of psalmic prayer: out of the depths   152

Contents

The identity of those who pray the Psalms   155

The elements of psalmic prayer   158

A broader identity in prayer   162

Conclusion   164

10 The tradition of psalmic prayer, Part 2: Psalms that pray
for vengeance   **165**

Why do we need prayers of vengeance?   166

Guidelines for praying psalms of vengeance   167

Three 'model' prayers   168

The imprecatory psalms and the meaning of 'vengeance'   179

Conclusion: The Psalms and Jesus Christ   **183**

Jesus' identity as Son of God and Messiah   184

Baptism, Transfiguration and trial   184

Suffering and death   186

Resurrection of the 'son of David'   188

Works cited   190

Copyright acknowledgements   199

Index of Scripture references and ancient authors   201

Index of modern authors   209

Index of subjects   211

Acknowledgements

This book is the result of three decades of reading, studying and reflecting on the Psalms. During that time I have been fortunate to learn from great teachers and to form friendships around the study of the Psalter that have made life much richer. I begin this work by thanking some of those who have shaped my thinking, corrected my ideas and supported my work.

I am grateful to my colleagues at Pittsburgh Theological Seminary for their commitment to and appreciation for scholarship that serves the Church as well as the academy. Thanks especially to President David Esterline, Dean Heather Vacek and members of the Board of Directors for supporting this type of scholarship. I am also grateful to Holly McKelvey, the faculty's administrative assistant for her constant help in day-to-day collection of resources, copying, and editing.

I must express my thanks to Philip Law of SPCK who invited me to write this volume and to the editorial staffs of SPCK and Eerdmans for their professional work on the manuscript. I am particularly appreciative of the work of Mollie Barker who read the manuscript closely for style and accuracy. As to the content of the book itself, many colleagues have helped me understand more fully the riches of the Psalms and have opened my eyes to angles of vision on the Psalter I would not have otherwise had. I am indebted to them for much that appears in these chapters, as the discussion and the footnotes will show. There are too many to name them all, but I must mention a few who have been particularly helpful to me during my work on this project: William Bellinger, William P. Brown, Nancy deClaissé-Walford, Erhard Gerstenberger, Susan Gillingham, Adam Hensley, Rolf Jacobson, Clint McCann, Patrick D. Miller, James Nogalski, Beth LaNeel Tanner and Dennis Tucker. These scholars have helped me see the Psalms more clearly and, in many cases, have revealed to me how much I still have to learn. I also wish to thank the many other scholars who have participated in the Book of Psalms Section at the Society of Biblical Literature over the past 25 years. The annual meeting has been a marvellous context for discussions of the Psalms.

The writing of this book occurred in the midst of many other joys and challenges of life, and I am thankful to my family for supporting and encouraging me to complete this project when other matters were pressing. As always, I must thank my wife Page for being the first line of support. More than that general support, however, I am grateful for the many conversations we have had about biblical texts and their meaning, for the multitude of times she has raised critical and theological questions that have directed my thoughts about the Psalms to make them more relevant and fruitful. Thanks also to my children, Adair (and husband Chris) and Davis. They have been a source of joy and blessing during the writing of this book. They have also expanded my understanding of poetry and so contributed indirectly to the second chapter of the book.

Finally, the most important influences on my reading of the Psalms have been two teachers who have now passed from this life into the next. One is Marvin E. Tate, who first introduced me to the scholarly study of the Psalms, especially to issues related to their poetic qualities. The other is my *Doktorvater*, James Luther Mays. I cannot express how profoundly he shaped my thinking about the Psalms and just about everything else in the Bible. He was a pre-eminent scholar and a master teacher, and he continues to teach, inform, correct and inspire my thinking about the Psalter. I dedicate this book to his memory.

Abbreviations

11QPs[a]	*Psalms Scroll* (Dead Sea Scrolls)
b. Ber.	*Berakhot* (Babylonian Talmud)
b. Sanh.	*Sanhedrin* (Babylonian Talmud)
CEB	Common English Bible
CEV	Contemporary English Version
IBT	Interpreting Biblical Texts
ICC	International Critical Commentary
JPS	Jewish Publication Society
JSOTSup	Journal for the Study of the Old Testament Supplement Series
KJV	King James Version
NIV	New International Version
NRSV	New Revised Standard Version
RSV	Revised Standard Version
SBL	Society of Biblical Literature
SBLDS	Society of Biblical Literature Dissertation Series
TLOT	*Theological Lexicon of the Old Testament.* Ed. Ernst Jenni and Claus Westermann. Trans. Mark E. Biddle. 3 vols. Peabody, MA: Hendrickson, 1997.

Introduction: The role of the Psalms in the life of the Church

In his book *A Case for the Psalms: Why they are essential*, N. T. Wright declares that the Psalms are at the 'heart of the Bible', and they have been the 'lifeblood of Christians' from the earliest times.[1] He is surely correct on both points. The New Testament confirms the Psalms' status as the heart of the Bible. New Testament authors quoted from the Psalms more than any other Old Testament book, and they found in the Psalms important confirmation of Jesus' identity as the Son of God, the anointed, who came to usher in God's kingdom.

On the second point, Wright echoes interpreters through the centuries who have recognized the crucial role the Psalms play in the life of Christians. Writing in the fourth century, John Chrysostom observed that the Psalms provided words for every vigil, and inspiration for every hymn, and they served as key elements in every Christian liturgy and devotional practice. To this sweeping assessment he added, 'O marvellous wonder! Many who have made but little progress in literature, nay, who have scarcely mastered its first principles, have the Psalter by heart.'[2]

Chrysostom's comment that ordinary people in his day committed the Psalter to memory affirms the idea that the Psalms have always been the 'lifeblood' of Christian faith. We are not exaggerating if we say that Christians throughout the ages have heard and read the Psalms more than any other book of the Bible. A few examples illustrate the fact:

- Since ancient times, worshippers have heard the words of Psalm 34.8(9) in the invitation to partake of the Lord's Supper: 'O taste and see that the LORD is good.'
- They have also recited Psalm 26.6 to remind themselves how to prepare their heart for the table: 'I wash my hands in innocence'.

---

1 N. T. Wright, *A Case for the Psalms: Why they are essential* (San Francisco, CA: HarperOne, 2013; UK edn: *Finding God in the Psalms* (London: SPCK, 2014)), p. 1.

2 Cited in J. M. Neale and R. F. Littledale, *A Commentary on the Psalms: From primitive and mediaeval writers; and from the various office-books and hymns of the Roman, Mozarabic, Ambrosian, Gallican, Greek, Coptic, Armenian, and Syriac rites, vol. 1: Psalms 1–38* (3rd edn; London: Joseph Masters, 1874), p. 1.

- For Lent and Easter, Psalms have always accompanied the Gospel readings to help worshippers ponder the saving work of God through Jesus Christ (Psalms 2, 110 and 118 being quite prominent).[3]
- Benedictine monks have for nearly fifteen hundred years recited the whole book of Psalms every week.
- This focus on the Psalms for devotional reading continues in almost all Christian liturgical traditions, as their guides to prayer and devotion feature the Psalms in every service.[4]

But why the Psalms? What makes them so unique and gives them this special place in Christian life and thought?

The Psalms' unique status is due in part to the book's character as a compendium of all parts of Scripture. Martin Luther called the Psalms 'a little Bible', and for good reason. It contains psalms that speak of God as creator and marvel at the wonders of the creation like Genesis 1 and 2 (Pss. 8; 19; 104). Other psalms rehearse God's victory over Pharaoh and the period of wilderness wandering, and so echo the narratives of Exodus and Numbers (Pss. 78; 105—106; 136). Still other psalms speak, like the Hebrew prophets, against empty ritual and sacrifice (Pss. 40.6; 50.8–15). When the book highlights the LORD's anointed, the Davidic king, it anticipates the life and ministry of Jesus (Pss. 2; 72; 110). Thus, the Psalms touch the content and themes of nearly every part of the Bible and therefore have a unique place in the theological claims of Scripture.

Perhaps more than their contribution to Christian theology, however, the Psalms occupy their place among Christians because they express the heights and depths of human emotion more than any other part of Scripture. Wright touches on this feature of the Psalms when he says:

> They are full of passion and power, horrendous misery and unrestrained jubilation, tender sensitivity and powerful hope. Anyone at all whose heart is open to new dimensions of human experience . . . anyone who wants a window into the bright lights and dark corners of the human soul – anyone open to the beautiful expression of a larger vision of reality

---

3 See William L. Holladay, *The Psalms through Three Thousand Years: Prayerbook of a cloud of witnesses* (Minneapolis, MN: Fortress Press, 1993), pp. 166–8.

4 See for example, *Upper Room Worship Book: Music and liturgies for spiritual formation* (comp. and ed. Elise S. Esliger; Nashville, TN: Upper Room Books, 2006).

should react to these poems like someone who hasn't had a good meal for a week or two. It's all there.[5]

Again, Wright echoes voices from the past. Athanasius of Alexandria (c. 296–373 CE) declared that each psalm 'holds up a mirror' to the human heart.[6] Similarly, John Calvin said the Psalms are 'an anatomy of all parts of the soul'.[7] It seems that this character of deep expression of human need and longing gives the Psalms their power, and makes the Psalms a crucial resource for Christian prayer and theology.

The profound expression of human emotion perhaps also explains why the Psalms' influence has gone so far beyond the worship and devotion of the Church and synagogue. Perhaps more than any other book of the Bible, the Psalms have become regular material for the voices of those in popular culture who also strive to communicate the depths of human emotion and struggle.

In the early 1980s Irish rock band U2 was gaining acclaim as a group of musicians who spoke to the tragedies, inequities and anxieties of their generation. During a late-night recording session for their album *War*, lead singer Bono was searching for lyrics to put to a tune that was in his head. He opened a Bible and found the words he needed in the Psalms:

I waited patiently for the LORD;
    he inclined to me and heard my cry.
He drew me up from the desolate pit,
    out of the miry bog,
and set my feet upon a rock,
    making my steps secure.
He put a new song in my mouth,
    a song of praise to our God.
Many will see and fear,
    and put their trust in the LORD.
(Ps. 40.1–3(2–4))

---

5 Wright, *A Case for the Psalms*, p. 2.

6 Cited in Ellen T. Charry, *Psalms 1–50: Sighs and songs of Israel* (Brazos Theological Commentary on the Bible; Grand Rapids, MI: Brazos Press, 2015), p. xviii; Athanasius, 'Letter to Marcellinus', in *Athanasius: The life of Antony and the Letter to Marcellinum* (ed. Robert C. Gregg; Classics of Western Spirituality; New York, NY: Paulist Press, 1980), pp. 101–47.

7 John Calvin, *Commentary on the Psalms* (Edinburgh: Calvin Translation Society, 1845), vol. 1, p. xxxvii.

They named their stylized version of the psalm '40' after the number of the psalm. It was the last song on the album, and for nearly a decade they concluded each concert with '40'. Since U2's bold embrace of psalm lyrics other artists have followed, finding in the Psalms words that express the depths of the soul. Musical acts as diverse as R.E.M. ('Everybody Hurts'),[8] Megadeth ('Shadow of Deth')[9] and The Notorious B.I.G. ('You're Nobody ('til Somebody Kills You)')[10] have quoted from or alluded to the Psalms in popular songs.

As Wright says, when it comes to the human condition, 'It's all there' (in the Psalms). As the use of the Psalms in popular culture suggests, however, the greatest power of the Psalms may be in their accent on complaint and petition. Although praise and thanksgiving are prominent in their lyrics, they lead with lament. The Psalms cry to God for help from the threat of enemies, the betrayal of friends, and a host of human failures and disappointments. The popular artists listed above are but a sample of those who long for a deeper connection to the human experience and long to have a connection with One who is greater than the traumas of human existence. That is a primary reason Christians for centuries have turned to this book. It is also why the Psalms are so crucial. In a time when the Church is struggling to speak authentically to the world around it, and when much prayer and devotion is a shallow expression of prosperity religion, the Psalms are a breath of fresh air, an honest voice in the midst of so much inauthentic faith. For this reason in part Eugene Peterson declares that the Psalms are essential 'tools for prayer'.[11] Wright speaks more broadly of their role for Christians, making the bold assertion that 'The Psalms are the steady, sustained subcurrent of healthy Christian living'.[12]

Despite the continuing popularity of the Psalms, they, like the rest of Scripture, are at risk of being lost to a new generation. This book intends to introduce the Psalms to those who are discovering them for the first time, and make them more accessible to those who already read and interpret them. As we explore the Psalms, however, we recognize that there are numerous challenges:

---

8 'Everybody Hurts' appears on the album *Automatic for the People*, Warner Bros. Records, 1992; the lyrics of various psalms appear in the video for 'Everybody Hurts'; see <https://www.youtube.com/watch?v=5rOiW_xY-kc>.

9 'Shadow of Deth' appears on the album *The System Has Failed*, Sanctuary Records, 2004.

10 'You're Nobody ('til Somebody Kills You)' appears on the album *Life After Death*, Bad Boy Records and Arista Records, 1997.

11 Eugene H. Peterson, *Answering God: The Psalms as tools for prayer* (San Francisco, CA: HarperSanFrancisco, 1989).

12 Wright, *A Case for the Psalms*, p. 23.

1 The book of Psalms is one of the most complex books in the Bible with a long history of development. Thus, we need an orientation to its contents and the process of its formation to read it faithfully. The earliest psalms may date to the time of Israel's United Monarchy in the tenth century BCE.[13] The Psalms grew and developed for centuries, however, and came into the form we now know during the Persian period (539–333 BCE) or perhaps even later.

2 The book may seem strange to contemporary readers, and we need to bridge historical and cultural gaps between its world and ours. For example, the psalmist speaks of God as a king (Ps. 93.1) and of the heavens as a 'tent' that God spread out in creation (Ps. 104.2). These ways of thinking are foreign to many modern Western readers.

3 For Christians, the particular contents of the prayers in the Psalms may seem inappropriate. The psalmist often calls on God for help with enemies and asks God to bring vengeance on the opponents. The Church has always insisted, nevertheless, that the Psalms are there to teach us to pray. So, understanding this tradition of praying the Psalms requires some serious work on our part.

4 The book has a long history of being read and interpreted, and much of that history is lost to contemporary readers. One goal of this volume is to illuminate various ways Christians (and to some extent Jews) have read the Psalms as part of Scripture.

The nature and purpose of this book

This book attempts to introduce numerous dimensions of the Psalms. In these chapters I intend to orient you to the structure, content and theology of the Psalms and to invite you to ponder what place this marvellous part of Scripture might play in your own life of prayer, worship and devotion. I am writing from the perspective of a Christian biblical scholar and theologian primarily for a Christian audience, though I hope others from different perspectives may also benefit from the book.

This volume occupies a particular place in resources for the study of the Psalms. In the past 25 years there has been a surge of such publications. We now have a wealth of commentaries and introductory works that lead us into

---

13 See Frank Moore Cross Jr and David Noel Freedman, *Studies in Ancient Yahwistic Poetry* (Biblical Resource Series; Grand Rapids, MI: Eerdmans, 1997), p. 85.

and through the Psalter. Most introductory works fall into one of three categories. Some are technical works whose primary questions come from modern scholarship. The premier work of this type is Hermann Gunkel's *Einleitung in die Psalmen* published in 1933 and translated into English as *An Introduction to the Psalms* (trans. James D. Nogalski; Macon, GA: Mercer University Press, 1998). True to the German scholarly concept of 'introduction', this book does not invite us into the content of the Psalms so much as it lays out issues for understanding the contexts the Psalms occupied in Ancient Israel. A fine but more recent expression of this type of approach is Klaus Seybold, *Introducing the Psalms*. You will notice that I cite both of these works here.

A second type of introduction is a general work that gives an orientation to the main issues in interpreting the Psalms. Some excellent examples of this type are William H. Bellinger Jr, *Psalms: A guide to studying the psalter* (2nd edn; Grand Rapids, MI: Baker Academic, 2012) and William P. Brown, *Psalms* (IBT; Nashville, TN: Abingdon Press, 2010). These works cover issues such as the genre and social setting of the Psalms, the Psalms as poetry and the Psalms as a book.

The final type of introduction is the theological handbook or guidebook. Works in this category contain essays that give an orientation to the theological content of the Psalter. Two examples stand out: James Luther Mays, *The Lord Reigns: A theological handbook to the Psalms* (Louisville, KY: Westminster John Knox Press, 1994) and J. Clinton McCann Jr, *A Theological Introduction to the Psalms: The Psalms as Torah* (Nashville, TN: Abingdon Press, 1993).

This book falls somewhere between the general introduction and the theological handbook and it includes some of the features of both. I will introduce the content and structure of the Psalms and explore primary issues of interpretation such as the Psalms as poetry, the genres and social settings of the Psalms, and the Psalms as a book. I will also invite you to ponder the theological character of the Psalms and the way Christians especially have drawn from them for prayer and worship. You will notice, however, that I frequently cite the works I have just listed and those of many more scholars. I have learned and continue to learn much from them. As a student of the Psalms I am part of a community of scholars and ministers who desire to understand this book more deeply and fully for the sake of God's work in the world. In this book I frequently say 'we' have covered or explored a topic. Part of what I mean by 'we' is that I am speaking with an awareness of how much I have learned from these many colleagues. Most importantly, however, when I say 'we' I am including you, the reader. I invite you also to enter this community of readers who love the Psalms. Enter here and explore the riches of this book that has been at the centre of the life of the Church for two thousand years!

A preview of the book

In the following chapters we will explore the Psalms from a variety of perspectives, but all with the goal of understanding the book more fully as Christian Scripture. My hope is that as you read you will discover the 'varied and resplendent riches' of the Psalms, just as myriads of readers have done for centuries.[14]

I have arranged the chapters in three parts. Part 1 includes discussions of basic features of psalms and the Psalter along with essays on trends in the study of the Psalms. Chapter 1 covers the main characteristics of the contents of the Psalter such as what makes up a single psalm, how psalms appear in clusters and groups, and the structure of the biblical book. It will be helpful to read this chapter first since it provides a general introduction to what we are reading and it anticipates the chapters that follow. Chapter 2 explores the poetic quality of the Psalms: what makes the Psalms poetry, and why is that important for our reading of them? The third chapter addresses the age-old question of authorship: did David write the Psalms; if not David, then who; and what do we mean by 'authorship' in the first place? Chapters 4 and 5 discuss the important historical and social questions that the method called 'form criticism' seeks to answer: what are the literary forms or genres of the Psalms (Chapter 4), and what settings (ceremonies, celebrations and worship events) likely provide the backdrop for the earliest use of the Psalms (Chapter 5)? You may find it helpful to read these two chapters together since they address essentially two aspects of the same issue.

Part 2 consists of three chapters that explore ways to read the Psalms all together. Chapter 6 examines the literary characteristics of the Psalter as a whole and possible meanings we may derive from the book's structure. Chapter 6 follows the discussion of the Psalms' earliest setting in worship (Chapters 4 and 5) with a treatment of various psalms' setting in the book and in the canon of Christian Scripture. Chapter 7 asks about the theology of the Psalms: are there claims about God and God's way with the creation that appear in such frequency and importance in the Psalms that they allow us to say that the book coheres around those claims? Just as Chapter 6 addresses the question of literary unity, Chapter 7 examines a unity of belief

---

14 Calvin, *Commentary on the Book of Psalms*, vol. 1, p. xxxvi.

and conviction about the God who is the main subject of the Psalms.[15] Chapter 7 is concerned about more than coherence, however. The primary issue here is what the Psalms say about God, what God does and how God deals with God's creatures. This is the question of theology in the classic sense of the term: 'words about God' (*logos*=word/*theos*=God). Chapter 8 then asks the next logical question: 'What is the human being in relation to God?'

Part 3 includes two chapters on ways Christians pray the psalms, or perhaps *should* pray the Psalms. More than any other part of the book, Chapters 9 and 10 encourage particular Christian practices of prayer and devotion. The Conclusion highlights some of the ways Christians have read and used the Psalms to enhance faith and deepen belief in Jesus Christ. It presents a sample of ways in which New Testament authors presented the Psalms as a witness to the life and ministry of Jesus Christ.

A few other notes will help you as you read: I refer to the voice in the Psalms as the 'psalmist'. This is a common way of speaking about the one who speaks, sings or prays the Psalms and it does not imply any particular identity. The traditional idea that David wrote and spoke the Psalms is important for the interpretation of the book, but it is a complex idea historically and theologically and one that we will discuss in Chapter 3. One thing is clear, however: whoever first spoke or wrote any of the psalms, scribes collected and preserved them to be words for any person who desires to call on God and to praise God. Therefore, in this book I alternate between calling the psalmist 'he' and 'she' to acknowledge this fact.

When the verse numbers of a psalm are different in Hebrew and English, I give the English verse number(s) first, with the Hebrew verse number(s) in parentheses (e.g. Ps. 6.3(4)). See Chapter 1 for further explanation of the verse numbers in the Psalms.

When I refer to a Hebrew word of phrase, I transliterate the Hebrew by using a simple translation system.

Most importantly, this book constantly refers to and quotes from the Psalms. So have a Bible open as you read. I hope you read this book closely but, more than that, I hope you will read the Psalms and learn to meditate on them day and night (Ps. 1.2–3)!

---

15 On the idea that God is the main subject of the Psalms see Patrick D. Miller, *The Lord of the Psalms* (Louisville, KY: Westminster John Knox Press, 2013), pp. xi–xiv.

Part 1

ISSUES IN READING THE PSALMS AND THE PSALTER

1
What is a psalm?

The word 'psalm' refers to a religious poem or song from Ancient Israel. Psalms were part of the Israelites' public worship and private prayer. Therefore, it should not be a surprise that psalms appear in Old Testament narrative reports of Israelites praising God (Exod. 15.1–8) or calling on God for help (Jonah 2). The Hebrew prophets frequently include psalms to help convey their messages of judgement or hope (Isa. 44.23) or to plead with God on behalf of the people (Jer. 8.18—9.3). These and all other psalms in the Old Testament share many literary and stylistic features. The term 'psalm', however, has a special meaning when it applies to the poems and songs in the book we call 'The Psalms'. This book is a deposit of religious poems and songs that now forms a distinct part of the canon for Jews and Christians. Although the poems in this book are in many ways like the prayers and songs that appear in narrative and prophetic sections of the Old Testament, they are part of a unique collection that became a distinct canonical book. The Church recognizes this book as perhaps its greatest spiritual resource and one of the most important sources of theology as well.

The distinctive place the book of Psalms occupies in Christian Scripture and tradition is due in part to its identity as a collection of model prayers and songs that give believers words to say in prayer and worship. While the psalm-like passages in narrative books appear as the prayers of particular characters – Moses (Deut. 33) and Hannah (1 Sam. 2.1–10), for example – those in the Psalms are uniquely *our* prayers. Even if we read them as people have for centuries as prayers of David, it is clear that David does not own them. Rather, he is our example and he offers the words to us to take up as our own.

Titles for the book

The expression 'book of Psalms' appears first in Acts 1.20 in Peter's first address to the disciples after the Ascension of Jesus. By that time 'Psalms' had already become an accepted title for the collection and Christians recognized it as a canonical book (see Luke 24.44). 'Psalm' comes from a Greek term, *psalmos*, that refers to a song with musical accompaniment. The verbal root from which the word derives (*psallo*) means 'to play a stringed instrument with the fingers'. This title appeared for the first time on a Greek manuscript in the fourth century CE (Codex Vaticanus). This Greek title, however, translates the Hebrew term *mizmor*, which appears in the titles of many individual psalms. The Hebrew word also refers to a song accompanied by stringed music. So, this most familiar title for the book refers to the collection of psalms as a songbook. Many interpreters have therefore called the Psalms 'the hymnal of the Second Temple'.

Another common title for the book is Psalter, from the Greek word *psalterion*. This term refers to the lyre, the instrument David played to soothe Saul's troubled spirit (1 Sam. 16.14–23) and the favourite of musicians in the Jerusalem Temple (1 Chron. 15.16, 21, 28; 16.5). A fifth-century manuscript, Codex Alexandrinus, uses this expression as the title for the Psalms, most likely because those who wrote the document thought these poems were songs meant for singing or performing.[1]

The Hebrew tradition gives a title that describes more the content than the purpose of the psalms in the book. It calls the collection *sepher tehillim*, which means 'book of praises'. The Jewish philosopher Philo and the Jewish historian Josephus, both in the first century CE, translated this expression with the Greek word meaning 'hymns'. It is curious that the Hebrew scribes and these two early interpreters used words that highlight praise as the purpose and character of the Psalms. Most of the psalms are in fact prayers that complain to God and petition God for help. So, in what sense is this book a 'book of praises'? This label may come from the fact that the Psalter moves from complaints and prayers for help, which dominate the first part of the book, to psalms of praise that conclude it (Pss. 146—150).[2] Or 'praises' may intend to capture the Psalter's variegated expressions of faith, including doubt and lament, in a way that acknowledges all of it as appropriate address to God and in some sense as praise.

What is certain is that the titles of this book reflect the various uses of the Psalms for Jews and Christians. The Psalms are liturgy, song and prayer. In all their uses they give words for us to respond to God's salvation with praise and thanksgiving and to cry to God for help when we are in trouble or grieving. As a book of Scripture, they also provide a rich resource for theology.

---

1 Klaus Seybold, *Introducing the Psalms* (trans. Graeme Dunphy; Edinburgh: T&T Clark, 1990), p. 1.

2 Claus Westermann, *Praise and Lament in the Psalms* (Atlanta, GA: John Knox Press, 1981), highlights the significance of this movement.

How many psalms?

Those who read the Psalms in English encounter 150 individual psalms. The answer to the question 'How many psalms?', however, is much more complex than our English translations let on. There are two dimensions to the problem. First, the Hebrew and Greek versions of the Psalms both have 150 psalms, but they come to that number in different ways. The primary Hebrew manuscript, known as the Leningrad Codex (which dates to 1008 CE; some now call it the St Petersburg Codex), has the arrangement of psalms that English translators follow today. Thus, the Hebrew tradition seems to present the same 150 psalms that we find in the Bible. The Greek version of the Hebrew Scriptures, sometimes called the Septuagint, however, divides some of the psalms differently. Assuming that the Hebrew order is the standard, the Greek version:

- combines Psalms 9 and 10 into one psalm;
- combines Psalms 114 and 115 into one psalm;
- divides Psalm 116 into two psalms (vv. 1–9, 10–19);
- divides Psalm 147 into two psalms (vv. 1–11, 12–20).

In addition, the Greek version includes an additional psalm (Ps. 151) that does not appear in the Leningrad Codex. A note attached to this psalm indicates it is 'outside the number'. This note perhaps indicates an awareness that the final poem is not canonical.[3] Thus, the familiar number of psalms appears in both traditions, but the Hebrew and Greek versions do not agree at every point on where one psalm ends and another begins. To complicate matters more, there are some psalms that appear as separate poems in both Hebrew and Greek even though they clearly read as one psalm. The best example is Psalms 42—43. Furthermore, some psalms material appears in more than one psalm. Psalm 14 is essentially the same as Psalm 53; Psalm 40.13–17(14–18) is also Psalm 70; and Psalm 108 is a combination of parts of Psalms 57 and 60. Each of these psalms is distinct, but the fact that some psalms material reappears complicates the question of how many psalms we have in the Psalter.

The second problem is that some ancient and medieval Hebrew manuscripts divide some of the psalms differently from the Leningrad Codex and the Greek version, and they even vary in the final number of psalms. Some of

---

3   See the discussion by Nancy deClaissé-Walford, Rolf A. Jacobson and Beth LaNeel Tanner, *The Book of Psalms* (New International Commentary on the Old Testament; Grand Rapids, MI: Eerdmans, 2014), pp. 3–7.

these manuscripts have as few as 147 psalms and others as many as 154.[4] This problem stems in part from the fact that scribes who copied manuscripts by hand were more likely to divide some psalms into two and combine others. With the invention of moveable type in 1517 the order and number of psalms in the Psalter stabilized into what we now have in our Bibles.[5] Most of the psalms in the collection develop clearly from beginning to end and divide naturally from the psalms around them. Nevertheless, the process of arriving at the 150 individual psalms we have in our Bible was not simple. The process of preserving and transmitting the Psalms should caution us against making definitive statements about the significance of the number and ordering of the psalms in the book.

Anatomy of a psalm

Most readers approach the Psalms one psalm at a time. The most familiar aspects of the Psalms are the particular verses such as 'The LORD is my shepherd' (Ps. 23.1) and 'The stone that the builders rejected has become the chief cornerstone' (Ps. 118.22). The individual psalms contain many other features, however, that may be less familiar and yet are important for understanding them. To explore the various elements of individual psalms we will begin with Psalm 6 as an example:

> *To the leader: with stringed instruments; according to*
> *The Sheminith. A Psalm of David.*

¹ O LORD, do not rebuke me in your anger,
   or discipline me in your wrath.
² Be gracious to me, O LORD, for I am languishing;
   O LORD, heal me, for my bones are shaking with terror.
³ My soul also is struck with terror,
   while you, O LORD – how long?
⁴ Turn, O LORD, save my life;
   deliver me for the sake of your steadfast love.
⁵ For in death there is no remembrance of you;
   in Sheol who can give you praise?

---

4   William Yarchin, 'Is there an authoritative shape for the book of Psalms? Profiling the manuscripts of the Hebrew Psalter', paper presented at the Sixteenth World Congress of Jewish Studies, Hebrew University, Jerusalem, 2013.

5   deClaissé-Walford, Jacobson and Tanner, *Psalms*, p. 5.

⁶ I am weary with my moaning;
  every night I flood my bed with tears;
  I drench my couch with my weeping.
⁷ My eyes waste away because of grief;
  they grow weak because of all my foes.
⁸ Depart from me, all you workers of evil,
  for the LORD has heard the sound of my weeping.
⁹ The LORD has heard my supplication;
  the LORD accepts my prayer.
¹⁰ All my enemies shall be ashamed and struck with terror;
  they shall turn back, and in a moment be put to shame.

The heading

The first item in Psalm 6 is a heading: 'To the leader: with stringed instruments; according to The Sheminith. A Psalm of David.' As scribes preserved the psalms, they often put information about the psalm at the beginning in a heading or superscription like this one. Nearly three-quarters of the psalms have such a heading. The headings are not part of the psalm proper, however, and they do not have a verse number in English. The lack of a verse number in English creates in some psalms a different verse number from that in the modern Hebrew edition used by scholars to translate the Psalms.[6] In the case of Psalm 6, the edited Hebrew Bible counts the heading as verse 1. As a result, the verse numbers for Psalm 6 in Hebrew and English are off by one. Verse 1 in English is verse 2 in Hebrew, and so on. Where such differences occur we will refer to verses in English and put the Hebrew verse number in parentheses (e.g. Ps. 6.2(3)).

The heading of Psalm 6 has four distinct elements. Most scholars interpret the first three as musical directives, though their exact meaning and significance are not clear.

1. The expression 'to the leader' translates a word that includes a Hebrew root meaning 'supervise'. In Ezra 3.8 the word refers to the Levites leading the work of the Temple. Therefore, many scholars have concluded that the form of the word in Psalm 6 refers to a music leader in the Jerusalem Temple (so RSV: 'choirmaster').

---

6 *Biblia Hebraica Stuttgartensia* (ed. A. Alt, O. Eissfeldt, P. Kahle et al.; Stuttgart: Deutsche Bibelgesellschaft, 1967) is an edited version of the Leningrad Codex (*c.*1008 CE).

15

2. The second expression, 'with stringed instruments' (Hebrew *binginoth*), consists of a preposition (*b*) meaning 'with' and a plural noun (*neginoth*) that refers to musical instruments like the lyre. In almost all its occurrences in the Old Testament this form of the word signifies musical accompaniment (Isa. 38.20).

3. The third element in the heading of Psalm 6, 'according to The Sheminith', is more difficult to interpret. In Hebrew it consists of two words. The first is a preposition (*'al*) that often expresses a norm and means something like 'according to'.[7] The word that follows is an ordinal number in Hebrew with the definite article, 'the eighth'. Although the basic meaning of the expression is clear, we have little idea what the expression signifies. Does 'the eighth' refer to an eighth in some musical sense (a musical key, a certain beat), or is this the name of a tune or a practice of performance? The Greek version translates woodenly 'according to the eighth', and some modern translations such as the Common English Bible (CEB) have followed that example. The New Revised Standard Version (NRSV) seems wise, however, in simply transliterating the expression 'according to The Sheminith'. Other expressions of this type also appear in the Psalms, and the significance of each of them remains a mystery. For example, the heading of Psalm 8 includes 'according to The Gittith'. The word *gittith* means 'winepresses', and the Greek version renders this literally 'according to the Winepresses'. This does not help us much since we don't know what 'winepresses' signify in this case. The Aramaic version takes this to refer to a musical instrument from Gath and so includes that place-name in the translation. The fact that the earliest translators seemed to be guessing at the meaning of these terms should signal caution for us in trying to understand them. This applies to other expressions such as 'according to Muth-labben' in the heading of Psalm 9.

4. The final element of the heading of Psalm 6 is the most common one in the Psalter: 'A Psalm of David'. This expression seems fairly straightforward, but it also is shrouded in mystery. 'A Psalm' names the poem according to an ancient genre category. As we noted above, 'psalm' (Hebrew *mizmor*) refers to a song with musical accompaniment. Other genre labels appear in the headings of other psalms. For example, some headings identify their psalm as a *shiggaion* (Ps. 7), a *miktam* (Pss. 16; 56—60), a *maskil* (Pss. 32; 42; 44; 45), a song (Pss. 46;

---

7 Ronald J. Williams, *Hebrew Syntax: An outline* (2nd edn; Toronto: University of Toronto Press, 1976), §290.

65—68) or a prayer (Pss. 17; 86; 90). Most translators simply transliterate the Hebrew word if its meaning is not certain. Presumably the ancient scribes tried to distinguish one type of poem from another with these labels. It is not clear, however, how they distinguished a 'psalm' from either a *maskil*, a *miktam* or a 'prayer'. To illustrate the problem, consider the character of Psalms 7 and 17 and the labels that appear on the two. Psalm 17 has the label 'A Prayer'. This certainly fits since the psalm addresses God directly in first-person style. Yet, Psalm 7 also addresses God directly in first-person style and seems to fit in every way what we would call a prayer, but has the label *shiggaion*. What makes Psalm 7 a *shiggaion* and Psalm 17 a prayer? Psalm 16 has the same basic features as Psalms 7 and 17, but that poem bears the label *miktam*. To further complicate the matter, the common label 'psalm' (*mizmor*) appears on many poems that have the same content as prayers and *miktam*s. Also, some psalms have more than one of these labels in their headings (e.g. Pss. 75; 92; 142) while others have no label at all (e.g. Pss. 103; 138). So, like some of the musical directives in the headings of psalms, we have lost the significance of these identifiers of psalm type as scribes preserved the psalms and passed them on to us.

Perhaps the most important part of the heading is the name 'David'. David's name appears in the heading of Psalm 6 and in 73 other psalms. The appearance of his name on these psalms is one of the keys to the tradition that David authored the entire book (Mark 12.35–37; Acts 4.25–26). Yet the words 'of David' alone do not necessarily suggest David authored Psalm 6, much less the entire Psalter. These words could mean David spoke or wrote the poem, but they could also mean that someone wrote it in honour of David, or that David sponsored the writing.[8] The original meaning of 'of David' could have been any of these. We will explore this subject more in Chapter 3.

To understand more fully the tradition of Davidic authorship of the Psalms we must consider another element of the headings that appears in 12 psalms (Pss. 3; 18; 34; 51; 52; 54; 56; 57; 59; 60; 63; 142).[9] The superscription of each of these psalms includes a note that gives a setting in the life of David. Perhaps the most familiar of these 'historical' notes appears in the heading of Psalm 51: 'A Psalm of David, when the prophet Nathan came to him, after he had gone in to Bathsheba.' The heading of Psalm 51 and the similar headings in other psalms connect the psalm to an event that appears in the narratives in 1 and

---

8 See the discussion in Bernhard W. Anderson, *Out of the Depths: The Psalms speak for us today* (rev. and exp. edn; Philadelphia, PA: Westminster Press, 1983), pp. 28–31.

9 This list sometimes includes Ps. 7, but its heading has a sentence about David with different syntax from that of the others. Also, the reference to 'Cush, a Benjaminite' does not match anything we know from the narratives about David's life.

2 Samuel and/or 1 Chronicles. The superscription here presents the psalm as David's prayer in response to Nathan's judgement on him after his affair with Bathsheba. The psalm shares several expressions with the story in 2 Samuel 11–12: 'Against you, you alone, have I sinned' (Ps. 51.4(6)) is very similar to David's confession to Nathan, 'I have sinned against the LORD' (2 Sam. 12.13); 'and done what is evil in your sight' (Ps. 51.4(6)) is similar to 2 Samuel 11.27b, 'But the thing that David had done displeased the LORD' (in both cases the Hebrew reads literally 'in your/the LORD's eyes').

Several other names besides 'David' appear in psalm headings. Most of these are names of Levites who were installed as musicians and worship leaders for the sanctuary in Jerusalem (see 1 Chron. 16) as David established plans for the Temple (1 Chron. 22). Psalms 42—49 and 84, 85, 87 and 88 are 'psalms of the Korahites'. According to 1 Chronicles 26.1–19, David appointed the Korahites as gatekeepers for the Temple. Psalms 50 and 73—83 are 'psalms of Asaph'. In 1 Chronicles 16.4 Asaph is identified as chief among the 'ministers before the ark of the LORD', and the narrative reports that he and his family were the head musicians (1 Chron. 16.7–42; 25.1–31). Psalms 88 and 89 identify two individuals, Heman (Ps. 88) and Ethan (Ps. 89), who are also named elsewhere as musicians in the Temple (see 1 Chron. 15.17, 19; 16.41–42; 25.1).[10] 'Solomon' appears in the headings of Psalms 72 and 127.[11] The superscription of Psalm 90 identifies it as a prayer of Moses. It is the only psalm with 'Moses' in its heading.

Scattered throughout the psalm headings are a variety of other items that mainly give information about occasions for reading these psalms. The heading of Psalm 30 includes 'A Song at the dedication of the temple'. The heading of Psalm 92 indicates it is 'A Song for the Sabbath Day'. Psalm 102 introduces the poem as 'A prayer of one afflicted, when faint and pleading before the LORD'. Psalms 120—134 hold together around a common identity and purpose. In each of these psalms the superscription reads, 'A Song of Ascents'. 'Ascent' here probably refers to 'going up' to the Jerusalem Temple (see 2 Chron. 36.23).

The body of a psalm

The body of the psalm expresses themes and subjects through poetry. The poetry of the Psalms unfolds in a series of **lines**, and **measures** or **strophes**.

---

10 These two also appear in a list of sages as part of the testimony to the wisdom of Solomon (1 Kings 4.31).

11 The words 'of Solomon' in the heading of Psalm 72 may not intend to attribute the psalm to Solomon, as our discussion will show.

The poetic line is the basic unit of these poems, and a line typically consists of two or three smaller statements. A single line may represent a verse in the English Bible, but not necessarily. Scholars typically call an individual segment of a poetic line a **colon** (plural **cola**).[12] The cola in a poetic line make statements that are semantically parallel. That is, they have clauses that are similar in content and language, and together the cola express a complete thought. For example, Psalm 6.1(2) is a poetic line with two cola:

Colon 1: O LORD, do not rebuke me in your anger
Colon 2: Or discipline me in your wrath

These cola have two important parallels that help communicate the psalmist's petition: rebuke/discipline and anger/wrath. We might consider the words 'anger' and 'wrath' as nearly synonymous. The difference in meaning is not that significant. 'Rebuke' and 'discipline', however, represent either two different kinds of actions or two actions that occur in a logical sequence (i.e. discipline follows rebuke). So, the psalmist pleads with God to restrain God's response to sinfulness by naming with these two words the range of actions God might take. Many other types of parallel statements are possible.

Measures, or strophes, are sections of a psalm in which an idea develops over two or more lines. Psalm 6.6–7(7–8) is a good example of a strophe. These two verses are distinct from what goes before and after them. The strophe develops in two poetic lines that contain five cola. The first colon states the basic problem: 'I am weary with my moaning' (v. 6a(7a)). The next two cola expound on this statement with synonymous parallels: I flood my bed with tears/I drench my couch with weeping (vv. 6a–b(7a–b)). Then the psalmist continues the description of grief with a line that has two statements about the condition of his eyes: My eyes waste away because of grief/they grow weak because of foes (v. 7(8)). We will explore the nature of the poetry of the Psalms further in Chapter 2.

A number of psalms in the Psalter have an arrangement and structure that follows the Hebrew alphabet. These 'acrostic' psalms start each successive line or section with a word that begins with successive letters of the alphabet. For example, Psalm 111 begins (after the initial *hallelu-yah*) 'I will give thanks to the LORD with my whole heart' (v. 1a). The verb 'I will give thanks' begins

---

12 James Kugel, *The Idea of Biblical Poetry* (New Haven, CT, and London: Yale University Press, 1981), pp. 2–3; Robert Alter, *The Art of Biblical Poetry* (New York, NY: Basic Books, 1985), prefers the expression 'verset'; see pp. 8–9.

with aleph, the first Hebrew letter. The next line (v. 1b), 'in the company of the upright', begins with the letter beth. The poem continues with lines that begin with gimmel, dalet, hey, and so on through the 22 letters of the Hebrew alphabet.

We cannot see this alphabetic structure in English, but we may detect in our translations of the acrostic psalms a somewhat artificial unity. The acrostic psalms rarely sustain and develop an idea over multiple lines (compare Ps. 111 with Ps. 114.1–6). The goal of composition was to make statements that led with successive letters of the alphabet. The scribes who composed these psalms perhaps thought of the exercise as an attempt to make a complete point conceptually, one that represented everything from aleph to tau (or 'from a to z'). Other examples of acrostic psalms include Psalms 25 and 112. The most impressive example is the massive Psalm 119, which has 176 verses, and is by far the longest psalm in the Psalter. This psalm has 22 eight-line sections (known as 'octads'). In each section each of the eight lines begins with a particular Hebrew letter. The psalm as a whole is a reflection on the blessings of meditating on Torah, God's instruction. The psalm's repeated emphasis on Torah's benefits, with the alphabetic structure, acts like a mantra for the reader. It does not so much develop ideas in strophes as it repeats the same point to emphasize and inculcate the idea that Torah encompasses everything. The alphabetic arrangement provides the framework for the experience of reading.[13]

Selah is another interesting feature of the body of a psalm. The Hebrew word *selah* appears throughout the book of Psalms, often at natural breaks between strophes and sometimes within a strophe. Like the musical directives in the psalm headings, the meaning of this term remains a mystery. The origin of the word is not certain. It may come from a root meaning 'to lift up', as of one's voice (*salal*; see Ps. 68.4(5)). Many scholars have interpreted selah as a musical or liturgical directive of some kind, but what exactly it signalled is only a guess. Was it a cue to shout, sing or perform some ritual movement? St Jerome thought it was equivalent to 'Amen' or 'Shalom'. Worshippers may thus have shouted 'Selah!' as a way of confirming the contents of what preceded it.[14] Perhaps 'lift up' referred to the sound or volume of temple music.[15] So perhaps

---

13 Jon D. Levenson, 'The Sources of Torah: Psalm 119 and the modes of revelation in Second Temple Judaism', in *Ancient Israelite Religion: Essays in honor of Frank Moore Cross* (ed. Patrick D. Miller Jr, Paul D. Hanson and S. Dean McBride Jr; Philadelphia, PA: Fortress Press, 1987), pp. 559–74.

14 Jerome, *Nicene and Post-Nicene Fathers of the Christian Church*, Second Series, vol. 6: *Jerome: Letters and Select Works* (ed. Philip Schaff and Henry Wace; Buffalo, NY: The Christian Literature Company, 1893), letter 28.

15 See the discussion in Charles Augustus and Emily Grace Briggs, *A Critical and Exegetical Commentary on the Book of Psalms* (ICC; Edinburgh: T&T Clark, 1906), vol. 1, pp. lxxxvii–lxxxviii.

it was a signal to the temple musicians to strike up the band, akin to the words 'Hit it!'? Scholars have considered these ideas as they have puzzled over the meaning and significance of the word *selah*, but they have very little information to advance any hypothesis. One scholar has developed the unique theory that selah marked a break in the performance of psalms, at which point worshippers recited or heard a worship leader read a part of the story of David.[16] There is no evidence for this theory. It simply illustrates how inventive scholars can be when there is nothing to go on. Other than the general notion that this word signals some liturgical movement, selah remains a mystery.

Colophon

A colophon is a scribal note at the end of a poem (e.g. Hab. 3.19). There is only one colophon in the Psalter, in Psalm 72.20: 'The prayers of David son of Jesse are ended.' This note perhaps originally concluded the collection of Davidic psalms, Psalms 51—72. Now it marks a major juncture in the Psalter, roughly at the midpoint of the collection. We will explore the importance of the colophon further in Chapters 3 and 6.

Translation

The words of Psalm 6 that we have considered above are taken from NRSV. Like most of the Old Testament, the Psalms appeared first in Hebrew. So our reading and presentation of the Psalms in English depend on the work of scholars who have made these poems accessible to us. Translators typically begin with the Psalms as they appear in the Leningrad Codex, which dates to 1008 CE and is the oldest copy of the complete Old Testament in Hebrew. Then they consider differences between this manuscript and others, such as the psalms manuscripts found among the Dead Sea Scrolls, to determine what the original wording likely was.[17]

Modern translators render the Hebrew Psalter into English words that are familiar to us. Publishers then take the work of translators and create edited Bibles that provide additional helps to reading. The most obvious aid they give is in the psalm numbers (we might call them 'chapters') and verse numbers. Ancient Hebrew manuscripts did not number the psalms and did not number lines or verses. This is an invention of scholars in England in the Middle Ages. Also, many translations add a descriptive label for each psalm that sums

---

16 Michael Goulder, *The Prayers of David (Psalms 51–72): Studies in the Psalter II* (JSOTSup 102; Sheffield: Sheffield Academic Press, 1990), pp. 144–5.

17 See especially the scroll known as 11QPs³ edited by James Sanders, *The Dead Sea Psalms Scroll* (Ithaca, NY: Cornell University Press, 1967).

up its content. For example, in some editions NRSV labels Psalm 6 a 'Prayer for Recovery from Grave Illness' and describes Psalm 148 as 'Praise for God's Universal Glory'. Similarly, the Contemporary English Version (CEV) dubs Psalm 41 'A prayer in time of sickness'. These labels can be a helpful guide to reading individual psalms, but they can also prejudice the reader concerning what she or he will encounter in the psalm and prevent a close reading. In the case of Psalm 6, it certainly seems the psalmist suffers illness when she says, 'O LORD, heal me, for my bones are shaking with terror' (v. 2(3)). The Psalms often use rich and evocative images, however, and the petition 'heal me' may signify divine aid that comes in a form other than bodily healing. Moreover, even if the psalmist is dealing with sickness, the psalm also speaks of the soul being struck with terror (v. 3(4)) and experiencing tremendous grief (v. 7(8)). It is best always to read the psalm closely and find in its words its main subject rather than receiving such information from the editorial helps of English translators.

Collections and clusters of psalms

Although there are 150 individual psalms in the Psalter, many psalms appear within small collections associated with a particular person, or in clusters that share a common vocabulary and theme. These collections and clusters are evidence of the process by which the psalms became a book. Although the history of writing and collecting psalms into the present form of the book is impossible to reconstruct with any confidence, these groupings are signs of its growth. These collections and clusters likely provided the building blocks for the Psalter as we now know it. They are therefore 'growth rings' of the present book.[18]

There are two large Davidic collections in the first half of the Psalter that form the starting point of the book: Psalms 3—41 and 51—72. Almost all of these psalms have 'of David' in their headings. Those who collected the psalms read each of the few psalms without a heading (Pss. 10; 33; 71) as part of the psalm that preceded it. So, for example, Psalm 71 begins with a confession of trust in the LORD ('In you, O LORD, I take refuge', v. 1(2)) that continues the style and vocabulary of the end of Psalm 70 ('But I am poor and needy; hasten to me, O God! You are my help and my deliverer; O LORD, do not delay!', v. 5). The heading of Psalm 72 identifies it as 'of Solomon', but the colophon at the end of the psalm may intend to say the psalm was a prayer for Solomon by

---

18 This is the language of Seybold, *Introducing the Psalms*, p. 18. Seybold uses this expression particularly to speak of the doxologies at the end of major collections and clusters of psalms.

David ('The prayers of David son of Jesse are ended'). Psalms 108—110 also have 'David' in their heading, and near the end of the Psalter there is another cluster of psalms that have 'David' in their titles (Pss. 138—145).

The other names in psalm headings we listed earlier have their own collections. Psalms 42—49 comprise a collection that identifies with the Korahites (see also the cluster of Pss. 84; 85; 87; 88). Psalms 73—83 (and see Ps. 50) make up a collection of 'psalms of Asaph'. Thus the groupings of psalms that identify with a particular person or family are:

Psalms 3—41: David;
Psalms 42—49: Korahites;
Psalms 51—72: David;
Psalms 50; 73—83: Asaph;
Psalms 84—85; 87; 88: Korahites.

As we noted earlier, Psalms 120—134 make up a unique grouping of psalms that holds together around the superscription 'A Song of Ascents'.[19] 'Ascent' here refers to 'going up', presumably to the Jerusalem Temple (see 2 Chron. 36.23). The collection as a whole celebrates the Temple and the city of Jerusalem (Pss. 122; 125; 126; 128; 129; 132; 133) and encourages worshippers on pilgrimage that God protects and blesses them (Pss. 121; 122; 134).

Psalms 93—100 have a thematic unity. These psalms focus on the LORD's kingship. Four times these psalms declare 'The LORD is king' (Pss. 93.1; 96.10; 97.1; 99.1) and they are replete with other language of God's kingship. As king, the LORD rules over the cosmos as its creator, and the elements of the cosmos give God praise (Pss. 93.1b–4; 95.4–5; 96.10–12; 97.2–5; 98.7–8; 99.1). As king, the LORD judges the world, and brings justice and equity to its inhabitants (Pss. 94.1–7; 96.13; 97.10–11; 98.9; 99.4). As king, the LORD shepherds the people of Israel and guides them by divine commands (Pss. 93.5; 95.6–7; 99.7; 100.3). See further Chapter 7 on the theology of the Psalms.

Several clusters of psalms have catchwords that tie them together. These psalms were perhaps originally unrelated to one another, but they have come together for liturgical purposes. Psalms 111—118 bind together with the expression 'Praise the LORD' (*hallelu-yah*) at the beginning or end of psalms in this grouping. Psalm 118 concludes this run of psalms with thanksgiving for God's goodness and deliverance (Ps. 118.1, 28–29). It celebrates God's 'steadfast love' and faithfulness, as do the psalms that precede it (e.g. Pss. 116.1–2;

---

19 The heading of Ps. 121 reads slightly differently, literally 'A psalm *for* ascents' (with the preposition *le*).

117.2). Similarly, Psalms 146—150 all begin and end with 'Praise the Lord' and so bring the Psalter to a close with a concatenation of praise.

Psalms 42—83 include four of the collections listed above, but as a larger group they have another unifying feature. They overwhelmingly prefer the general name for God (Elohim) rather than the personal name known by the letters YHWH that translators render 'Lord' (perhaps originally pronounced 'yahweh'). In addition to the numerous appearances of 'Elohim' in these psalms, we surmise that those who collected these psalms preferred it over 'Lord', because they changed 'YHWH' to 'Elohim' in Psalms 53 and 70 (which appear earlier as Pss. 14 and 40.13–17(14–18)).

The structure of the book

Since ancient times those reading and studying the Psalms have recognized that the 150 individual psalms came together to form a book, a distinct unit of Scripture. As such, they read the book as having a distinct purpose and theology as a collection. The arrangement of the psalms is one key to the meaning and purpose of its individual parts, and as a whole the book has meaning that transcends its parts. We will explore the structure of the book and its meaning in more detail in Chapter 6, but for now we will note the basic structural features of the Psalms.

Introductory psalms: Psalms 1 and 2

The first two psalms serve as an introduction to the book. Psalm 1 opens with the declaration 'Happy/Blessed (*'ashre*) are those . . .' and then proceeds to present a way of life that leads to permanence and success. This is the 'way of the righteous', which contrasts sharply with the 'way of the wicked' (1.4–6). The way of the righteous involves the person learning of God's designs and submitting to God's purposes by meditating constantly on Torah, the Lord's instruction. The psalm promises that those who choose this way will be 'like trees planted by streams of water' (1.3a). They will have staying power and their lives will prosper (1.3b).

Psalm 2 shares some key vocabulary with Psalm 1 and thus also presents a distinct way of life that leads to good fortune. The last line in the psalm begins with the same word with which Psalm 1 opened: 'happy'/'blessed' (*'ashre*, 2.12). Psalm 2, however, fills out the nature of a fruitful life in terms of submitting to the reign of God (2.4, 11). Those who choose such a life 'take refuge' in the Lord (2.12). That is, they trust in God rather than in their own wisdom or might, or in the power or accomplishments of human beings (Pss. 118.8–9;

146.3–4). The reader enters the Psalter with this injunction to rely on God, and encounters countless illustrations and testimonies to the character and wisdom of this life of dependence and faith. It becomes obvious in subsequent psalms, however, that those who live according to the prescription for blessing may not know such blessing immediately. From Psalm 3 onwards, the dominant expressions in the Psalter are complaint, petition, and protest over inequities and suffering.

Concluding psalms: Psalms 146—150

The final five psalms act as a conclusion. They tie together with the words 'Praise the LORD' at the beginning and end of each psalm. Though complaint dominates the Psalter, suffering and lament dissolve into doxology as the book closes.

Fivefold division

The Psalter has five main divisions or 'books'. The five book-divisions are as follows:

Book I = Psalms 1—41;
Book II = Psalms 42—72;
Book III = Psalms 73—89;
Book IV = Psalms 90—106;
Book V = Psalms 107—150.

The rabbis recognized this fivefold structure and commented that 'as Moses gave five books of laws to Israel, so David gave five books of psalms to Israel'.[20] Thus they saw in the Psalms the kind of instruction (Hebrew *torah*) in a divinely approved way of life that Moses gave in the Pentateuch. The fivefold division in imitation of the books of Moses affirms the role of Psalm 1 as introduction, with its emphasis on meditation on Torah as a primary practice of the righteous. Evidence for the five divisions is a set of doxologies that appear at the end of Psalms 41, 72, 89 and 106:

Blessed be the LORD, the God of Israel, from everlasting to everlasting. Amen and Amen.
(Ps. 41.13(14))

---

20 *The Midrash on Psalms* (trans. William G. Braude; Yale Judaica Series 13; New Haven, CT: Yale University Press, 1959), vol. 1, p. 5.

Blessed be the LORD, the God of Israel, who alone does wondrous things.
Blessed be his glorious name for ever; may his glory fill the whole earth.
Amen and Amen.
(Ps. 72.18–19)

Blessed be the LORD for ever. Amen and Amen.
(Ps. 89.52(53))

Blessed be the LORD, the God of Israel, from everlasting to everlasting.
And let all the people say, 'Amen.' Praise the LORD!
(Ps. 106.48)

English translations also typically signal the five major divisions of the Psalter with headings: Book I, Book II, Book III, Book IV and Book V. As we have observed, however, the division of the Psalter into five books derives from doxologies at the end of each division, not from an explicit identification of a 'book' division.

The scribes who created this fivefold structure perhaps intended the last verse of Psalm 145 as a final doxology: 'My mouth will speak the praise of the LORD, and all flesh will bless his holy name for ever and ever' (145.21). If so, then we might think of the book divisions slightly differently:

Introduction: Psalms 1—2;
Book I = Psalms 3—41;
Book II = Psalms 42—72;
Book III = Psalms 73—89;
Book IV = Psalms 90—106;
Book V = Psalms 107—145;
Conclusion: Psalms 146—150.

Within each individual book, and across the collection as a whole, a certain degree of organization is apparent, though there seems to be no explanation for the exact placement of each psalm. The order of the final form of the book shows the limitations of prior collections that went into making the whole. Nevertheless, there are indications of purposeful order. Psalms 15—24 make up a unique grouping within the first Davidic collection that seems to have an intentional organization. This section of the Psalter has a chiastic structure. The two psalms on the outer limits are parallel in content. These psalms, at each end of this group, contain an 'entrance liturgy', that is, a question-and-answer section concerning the identity of those who may ascend the Temple Mount and enter its gates (Pss. 15; 24.3–6). Psalms 16 and 23 both speak of God delivering the psalmist from death and being kept in God's presence (Pss. 16.9–11; 23.4, 6). Psalms 17—18 and 21—22 share a concern for the well-being of the king. At the centre is a psalm about the beauty and benefits of God's instruction or Torah.[21] This organization is one clue that the book is the result of scribes collecting and editing in order to communicate through the book a message that is larger than the sum of its parts. In Chapter 6 we will explore the larger organization and purpose of the book as a whole.

---

21 See William P. Brown, *Psalms* (IBT; Nashville, TN: Abingdon Press, 2010), pp. 97–107.

2
It's poetry!

Poetry grabs for the jugular.
(Eugene Peterson)

What is poetry and why is it important?

The Psalms are poetry. The point may seem obvious, but in the history of interpreting the Psalms it has been anything but obvious and in fact often controversial. The first problem is with the nature of poetry itself. The question of what makes poetry poetry has been the subject of debate at least since the time of Aristotle. Poetry has rhythm, but some narratives have rhythmic qualities as well. Many have described poetry in terms of how poetry is different from prose, either in kind or degree. Patrick Miller observes that poems 'walk around a thought' and 'create climaxes in a very few lines'.[1] Eugene Peterson says that 'Poets use words to drag us into the depth of reality itself. They do so not by reporting on how life is, but by pushing-pulling us into the middle of it.'[2] William Brown notes, 'Narratives can be summarized with synopses. Poetry, however, resists such reductions.'[3] All of this seems true, but it is difficult to distinguish exactly what makes something like the Psalms poetry as opposed to the prose that appears in other parts of the Old Testament.

A second issue is why it matters that the Psalms are poetry. Some readers may think attention to the poetic qualities of the Psalms is not necessary since the Church is more interested in the meaning of the words of Scripture than in their style. When it comes to the Bible, is not the most pressing issue how the words edify and instruct us? Understanding the devices of poetry may seem superfluous to the task of interpretation. Some Christians have declared that the form of the message is not important at all and that attention to form

---

1   Patrick D. Miller, *Interpreting the Psalms* (Philadelphia, PA: Fortress Press, 1986), p. 29.
2   Eugene H. Peterson, *Answering God: The Psalms as tools for prayer* (San Francisco, CA: Harper-SanFrancisco, 1989), p. 11.
3   William P. Brown, *Psalms* (IBT; Nashville, TN: Abingdon Press, 2010), p. 1.

denigrates the content.[4] This way of thinking seems short-sighted, however, since the meaning of a passage is bound to its mode of expression. 'Meaning and beauty, the semantic and aesthetic, are woven together into a whole', and both deserve attention.[5] Moreover, some theologians before the modern era insisted that poetry is the primary mode of expressing thoughts about God. The Renaissance poet Petrarch declared:

> One may almost say that theology actually is poetry, poetry concerning God. To call Christ a lion, now a lamb, now a worm, what pray is that if not poetical? And you will find thousands of such things in Scripture, so very many that I cannot attempt to enumerate them.[6]

Indeed, an appreciation of the poetic quality of the Psalms enhances our reading of them as Scripture. The Psalms' figurative language and deep emotional expressions are crucial signs of their theological character. So much of our current speech is 'bureaucratic jargon' that robs language of its power.[7] The Psalms, however, speak to the depths of human experience in language that defies propositional summaries. As Kathleen Norris says, poetry like that in the Psalms 'is not designed to convince the reader of a certain point of view' but 'to express truth that can be revealed only through' the kind of evocative language we find in poetic verse.[8]

Some Christian thinkers have also insightfully noted that the poetry of the Psalms gives them an 'incarnational' character. The language of the Psalms is indeed incarnational in at least two ways. First, it lays bare the human condition – suffering, abandonment, rejection, fear – with language and images that embody that condition. C. S. Lewis said of the poetry in the Psalms that 'it is a little incarnation, giving body to what had been before invisible and inaudible'.[9] It does this, and perhaps can only do this, through poetic language and images. We cannot express human experience of the kind that is at the heart of *the* Incarnation in banal or trite speech. It requires language that

---

4   See James Kugel, *The Idea of Biblical Poetry* (New Haven, CT, and London: Yale University Press, 1981), pp. 159–64.

5   Miller, *Interpreting the Psalms*, p. 30.

6   J. H. Robinson, ed. and trans., *Petrarch: The first modern scholar* (New York, NY: Putnam's, 1907), pp. 261–4; cited in Kugel, *Idea of Biblical Poetry*, p. 214.

7   See the discussion of John P. Burgess, *Why Scripture Matters: Reading the Bible in a time of church conflict* (Louisville, KY: Westminster John Knox Press, 1998), pp. 39–41.

8   Kathleen Norris, 'Incarnational language', *Christian Century* 114, no. 22 (30 July–6 August 1997), p. 699.

9   C. S. Lewis, *Reflections on the Psalms* (London: Geoffrey Bles, 1958), p. 12.

is at once 'visceral and sublime, evocative and intense'.[10] On the level of the individual before God and before his or her deepest fears such language is crucial as well. We find that language in the Psalms.

Second, through poetry the Psalms also reveal the nature of God, who saves and comforts people in the depths of the human condition. Poetry is necessary to speak adequately of who God is and what God does. Language that is logical, linear and analytical has its place in theology, but it can never capture fully the nature of God.[11] Consider, for example, the opening verse of Psalm 91, a great hymn that has spurred theological imagination for centuries:

> You who live in the shelter of the Most High,
>   who abide in the shadow of the Almighty,
> will say to the LORD, 'My refuge and my fortress;
>   my God, in whom I trust.'

John Calvin lists this verse as one of the great promises of God's providence (reading the second part of the verse as a statement: 'will live in the shadow of the Almighty'). He uses it to make the point that divine providence is not just universal but also individual, and God extends it to particular creatures. Yet, as Calvin discusses this, he draws on poetic language in his explanation. He cites Jesus' promise that not even a tiny sparrow falls without God's attention and care (Matt. 10.29).[12] Propositions sometimes fall flat in the light of the care of the Almighty. Although it is possible to extract propositions from the poetic verses in the Psalms, propositions fail to capture the full impact. It is impossible to define exactly what it means to 'live in the shelter of the Most High'. This verse speaks to the relationship we have with our creator, the one who protects and watches over us. It connotes a long history of experiences in which God has been there for us.

The same is true of the confession that begins Psalm 90. In *The Message* Eugene Peterson translates verses 1–2 as:

> God, it seems you've been our home forever . . .
> from 'once upon a time' to 'kingdom come' – you are God.

---

10 William P. Brown, *Seeing the Psalms: A theology of metaphor* (Louisville, KY: Westminster John Knox Press, 2002), p. 12.

11 Brown, *Seeing the Psalms*, p. 3.

12 John Calvin, *Institutes of the Christian Religion* (ed. John T. McNeill; trans. Ford Lewis Battles; Library of Christian Classics 20; Philadelphia, PA: Westminster Press, 1960), 1:17:6.

This illustrates well what poetry does. Words like 'home' are too rich in meaning and emotion for us to reduce them to bullet points. To be sure, it is possible to expound on what it means for God to be our 'dwelling-place' (NRSV). We might say, for example, that God 'shelters' us in the fellowship of believers, in the worship of the Church, and in God's protective presence that we explain further as divine providence. Ancient Israelites might have experienced God's 'shelter' in the Jerusalem Temple. Whether all of that covers the meaning of Psalm 90.1 is debatable. Regardless of whether it does, however, the psalm says it in one simple expression: 'Lord, you have been our dwelling-place'. Also, Peterson captures the essence of verse 2 in the phrases 'once upon a time' and 'kingdom come'. These words express time in a way that cannot be measured or calculated, and they speak to the heart in a way prose usually does not. That seems to be what Peterson means when he says, 'Poetry grabs for the jugular.' It engages us, not just in analytical or logical questions and issues, but also, and especially, in the places we are most vulnerable, where life with God is most crucial, painful and joyful.

Important terms

As we consider the poetic qualities of the Psalms a few terms are crucial. As James Kugel says, the most basic element of poetry in the Psalms is 'a relatively short sentence-form that consists of two brief clauses'.[13] We will refer to this short sentence in a psalm as a poetic line (see Chapter 1). A line expresses a complete idea or subject in brief form.[14] The following figure represents how a line of Hebrew poetry works:

The typical line in Hebrew poetry begins with a statement that calls for a slight pause at its end (here represented as /). The pause is slight because the second part of the line continues the thought and completes it, after which there is a longer pause (//).[15] For example, Psalm 96.1 is a line of poetry with two clauses:

O sing to the LORD a new song/sing to the LORD all the earth//

---

13 Kugel, *Idea of Biblical Poetry*, p. 1.

14 See F. W. Dobbs-Allsopp, *On Biblical Poetry* (Oxford: Oxford University Press, 2015), pp. 20–1, 42–94.

15 Kugel, *Idea of Biblical Poetry*, pp. 1–2.

Here the idea the line expresses is 'sing to the LORD'. A pair of imperatives leads this expression ('sing'). The line clearly has two parts, both of which begin with the imperative 'sing'. The second part of the line completes the thought and then there is a pause before the next line.

Most lines of Hebrew poetry have two divisions as we see in Psalm 96.1, though some have three or four. Scholars have used various labels for the divisions of a poetic line: colon, hemistich, verset, or simply A and B.[16] Here we will use the word 'colon' and its plural 'cola'.

A strophe is a section of multiple lines in which the psalm develops an idea that is broader than a single line can convey. Psalm 96 divides naturally into three strophes: verses 1–6, 7–9 and 10–13. Each strophe begins with an imperative ('sing'/'ascribe'/'say'), and the verses that follow it in each case develop the idea. For example, verses 1–2 call for worshippers to sing about God, bless God's name and tell of God's salvation. Verse 3 issues yet another invitation to 'declare' God's marvellous deeds. The final three verses of the strophe explain and declare further why God is worthy of praise and song.

What makes the Psalms poetry?

Many critics have tried to identify technical aspects of the Psalms (and other Hebrew poetry) that make them poetry. The most popular is **metre**, which creates a sustained rhythm throughout the lines of poetry. A popular pattern is 3:3. That is, each portion of the poetic line has three stresses. Although this is the metre of many lines in the Psalms, it is not the only one, and many lines do not have an exact balance of stresses in their cola.[17] Hebrew poetry does not have any uniform and consistent metre that allows us to identify metre as *the* identifying mark of poetry. In the absence of any sustained consistency of metre, two features of the poetry of the Psalms seem to mark it off from prose: **semantic parallelism** and figurative language, primarily **metaphor** and **simile**.

Semantic parallelism

The most clear and consistent feature of the poetry in the Psalms is semantic parallelism. That is, within a line of poetry a colon states something that is similar to the other colon (or cola) in that line. The words of a colon may sound

---

16 Kugel lists these terms in *The Idea of Biblical Poetry*, pp. 2–3, but he prefers the simple references A and B. Alter coined the expression 'verset'; see Robert Alter, *The Art of Biblical Poetry* (New York, NY: Basic Books, 1985), pp. 8–9.

17 Alter, *Art of Biblical Poetry*, pp. 8–9.

much like those of the other colon in the line, but they are not identical. To return to our example from Psalm 96.1, note the similarity of the two cola:

O sing to the LORD a new song/sing to the LORD all the earth//

'Sing to the LORD' appears in both cola, but the first colon includes what is to be sung ('a new song'). The second colon assumes the first, but now expands the call, telling 'all the earth' to sing.

In such repetition of ideas and in the overlapping of language the poetry in the Psalms creates powerful 'experiences' for the reader or hearer. Thus Miller says that poems 'walk around a thought, say it one way here, another there'.[18] To expand on Miller's ambulation metaphor, we might say that we don't watch this 'walking around a thought' from a distance. The nature of the Psalms' language is such that, as Peterson says, they 'drag us into reality', 'push and pull us' into the middle of it. Parallelism is the structural feature of the Psalms that accomplishes this, dragging us into its joys and concerns.

In 1753 Robert Lowth, a scholar at Oxford University, published the first modern study of Hebrew poetry that identified parallelism as the key feature of biblical verse. He referred to the phenomenon as 'the parallelism of the clauses'.[19] Lowth meant by this expression that within a poetic line there are individual clauses that work together to make a larger point. Lowth then classified the relationship between the various parallel clauses in three types: **synonymous**, **antithetical** and **synthetic**. Although there are severe limitations to these categories, they continue to inform the study of Hebrew poetry. We will begin with Lowth's categories as we consider how parallelism appears in the Psalms.

Lowth's categories of parallelism

Synonymous

There are few parallel lines in the Psalms that are identical. Nevertheless, there are many pairs of lines that seem to have roughly equivalent semantic and emotive impact on us as we read. For example, Psalm 59.1(2) begins a prayer with an address to God in two cola that are roughly equivalent:

---

18 Miller, *Interpreting the Psalms*, p. 29.
19 Robert Lowth, *Lectures on the Sacred Poetry of the Hebrews*, 2 vols (New York, NY: Garland, 1971 (original 1787)).

Deliver me from my enemies, O my God/protect me from those who rise up against me//

The next verse in the psalm has another pair of synonymous parallels:

Deliver me from those who work evil/from the bloodthirsty save me// (Ps. 59.2(3))

The parallel words are similar in meaning. Though we can distinguish nuances of meaning between 'deliver' and 'protect' (v. 1(2)), they are closely related. Also, the identity of the opponents as enemies/those who rise against (v. 1(2)) and those who work evil/the bloodthirsty (v. 2(3)) includes labels that are distinct yet overlapping in semantic quality. The power is in repetition of an idea in related but not identical language.

None of the examples given thus far shows an exact repetition. There is some movement between cola and therefore each successive colon adds something to the previous one. Even in the case of verbatim repetition, however, something new in terms of the impact appears in the repeated words. A familiar example of this power of repetition in American literature is the last lines of Robert Frost's poem 'Stopping by Woods on a Snowy Evening':

The woods are lovely, dark and deep,
but I have promises to keep,
and miles to go before I sleep,
and miles to go before I sleep.[20]

The last line continues to advance the feeling and emotion of the poem, even though it is identical to the line that precedes it. Because the poem uses such tightly configured lines, the conclusion leads the reader to ponder over the reference to 'miles to go before I sleep.' Does the final occurrence of 'sleep' refer to death? Even if we take both references to signify the same reality, the repetition adds a punch, an unmistakable accent to the idea of having miles to go before sleep.

This kind of verbatim repetition is rare in the Psalms, but when it does appear it has the same effect as the final line in Frost's poem. Psalm 90.17 is a line with three cola that has verbatim repetition in the final two, literally:

---

20 *The Norton Anthology of American Literature* (ed. Ronald Gottesman et al.; shorter edn; New York, NY: Norton, 1980), pp. 1294–5.

Let the favour of the Lord our God be upon us,
    and prosper the work of our hands –
    O prosper the work of our hands!

The last two cola are identical in Hebrew.[21] The entire psalm moves to this concluding petition for God to give purpose and meaning to the lives of God's people. Thus, the twofold 'prosper the work of our hands' brings the psalm to an end by driving home this final petition.

Antithetical

The 'antithetical' type of parallel is most common in the book of Proverbs, which often presents two 'ways' – behaviours or attitudes that are opposite. We may express the logic of this type of parallel by the words 'thesis' and 'antithesis'. The slogan for the book in Proverbs 1.7 contains such opposites:

The fear of the LORD is the beginning of knowledge (thesis)
Fools despise wisdom and instruction (antithesis)

The English word 'but' usually facilitates this relationship between the cola, whether or not there is a word in Hebrew that suggests such a translation. This type of contrast also appears in some psalms. Psalm 20.7(8) is a parade example:

Some take pride in chariots, and some in horses (thesis)
But our pride is in the name of the LORD our God (antithesis)

As is often the case, the Hebrew is even more compact than the translation shows, and it makes each word all the more powerful. We could translate Psalm 20.7(8) word for word as:

These in chariots, and these in horses,
    but we in the name of Yahweh our God take pride.

The next verse (8(9)) has another example that continues the antithetical formula:

---

21 The Masoretic Text (i.e. the Leningrad Codex) has an additional word at the end of the second colon. It is the same preposition with pronominal suffix that ends the first colon ('upon us'). Many scholars take this to be accidental repetition.

They will collapse and fall (thesis)
But we shall rise and stand upright (antithesis)

Notice also that these two pairs of antithetical parallels overlap as they convey their message. The first statement in verse 7(8) refers to the same negative reality as the first statement in verse 8(9): trust in chariots and horses (thesis 1) leads to calamity (thesis 2), but trust in God (antithesis 1) leads to stability and permanence (antithesis 2). In both antitheses 'we' reveals the faith of the one who speaks, certain that this way of trust will last.

Once again, the point of these lines is not a set of propositions or exact comparisons, but a truth that appears best in terse yet powerful parallels. Does the word 'They', in the phrase 'They will collapse', mean the horses or those who trust in them? Grammatically either is possible. The point is what the 'we' voice claims in both concluding statements: 'We trust' (see v. 7(8)); therefore 'we will stand' (v. 8(9)).

Synthetic

What Lowth called 'synthetic' parallelism is a catch-all expression.[22] He recognized that many cola in poetic lines do not fall into the categories of either synonymous or antithetical. These include the many poetic lines that include a petition for God's help followed by a reason for the petition:

Vindicate me, O LORD/for I have walked in integrity//
(Ps. 26.1)

This category also applies to lines that include a quotation, such as Psalm 115.2:

Why should the nations say/'Where is their God?'//

The second colon completes what started in the first colon, but the relationship is not synonymous or antithetical. The overly general nature of the label 'synthetic' thus points to a major limitation of Lowth's categories. There are so many types of parallels these categories do not capture that they are useful only as a starting point for understanding how Hebrew poetry actually communicates its message across poetic lines.

---

22 See the discussion in Kugel, *Idea of Biblical Poetry*, pp. 12–13.

Refining the categories

Although Lowth's labels of parallel clauses as 'synonymous' and 'antitheti-cal' have endured and continue to be useful to a point, they are so broad that they fail to describe what happens as one colon follows another. James Kugel criticizes these two categories as overly general, just as the label 'synthetic' fails to describe how parallel lines communicate their message. Furthermore, he argues that Lowth's categories obscure the primary relationship between parallel clauses. Namely, the second clause tends to amplify, strengthen and heighten the first. It has essentially a 'seconding' effect.[23] A popular formula for this relationship is:

A, and what is more, B.

The 'what is more' statements in the Psalms, however, are rich and varied. As our examples of synonymous parallels above show, some parallel clauses express similar ideas while others amplify or move the meaning into more concrete or extreme expressions. Therefore, some further descriptions of types of semantic parallels seem helpful.[24]

Intensification

Many of the parallel cola in the Psalms have a relationship in which the second colon amplifies the first. As Kugel indicates, this label describes what happens in many poetic lines in the Psalms, so 'intensification' could have numerous subcategories. The second and sometimes third colon in a sequence often in-tensifies the statement by heightening, focusing or specifying what the first colon said. Consider this line in Psalm 59.5(6):

Awake to punish all the nations/spare none of those who treacherously plot evil//

The first colon petitions God with a general request: 'punish all the nations'. The colon that follows makes a similar request but intensifies it in two ways. The general 'punish' in the first colon gives way to the more extreme 'spare none' in the second. The second colon then follows the designation 'nations' with a detailed and narrow description, 'those who treacherously plot evil'.

---

23 Kugel, *Idea of Biblical Poetry*, pp. 57–8.
24 I have borrowed the categories that follow from Alter, *Art of Biblical Poetry*, p. 29.

Psalm 61.4(5) presents another example:

Let me abide in your tent for ever/find refuge under the shelter of your wings//

Here the psalmist's words 'abide'/'find refuge' are very similar, though the second 'find refuge' uses a metaphor of hiding or finding shelter that we might well consider more intense. The second part of both these cola, however, shows movement that heightens the intensity and meaning of the statement. 'Tent' in the first colon becomes 'the shelter of your wings' in the second. 'Tent' itself is a metaphor for the place where the psalmist finds safety, under the cover of God's protection. 'Shelter of your wings', however, goes further to depict the protecting 'apparatus' that is part of the One who acts as host in the tent.[25] The same kind of intensification appears in the previous verse:

For you are my refuge/a strong tower against the enemy//
(v. 3(4))

This pair of cola shows another variety of the heightening that takes place in the relationship between the smallest poetic units. The terms 'refuge' and 'strong tower' are very close in meaning. The second line, however, adds 'against the enemy', thus defining further how God offers protection. Since the second colon assumes the verb-form 'you are', it adds this additional description while keeping its length the same as the first (in Hebrew there are four words in each colon; thus they are identical in length).

What we are calling 'intensification', as we have noted, represents a broad range of relationships between cola that have a 'seconding' effect. In some cases the seconding is something akin to the second colon clarifying or making concrete the words of the first. This is the case in Psalm 146.3:

Do not put your trust in princes/in mortals, in whom there is no help//

The injunction in the first colon is clear: 'do not trust in princes'. But why? The word 'princes' denotes human rulers or officials who may be corrupt or abuse their authority. These are potential reasons for not trusting in them. The

---

25 See the extensive discussion of this metaphor in Joel LeMon, *Yahweh's Winged Form in the Psalms: Exploring congruent iconography and texts* (Orbis Biblicus et Orientalis 242; Göttingen: Vandenhoeck & Ruprecht, 2010).

second colon gives a more basic reason, however, that effectively reduces the power of those called 'princes'. Namely, princes are human, and humans are by definition weak and limited creatures, as verse 4 elaborates: 'When their breath departs, they return to the earth; on that very day their plans perish.' Thus the second colon in verse 3 clarifies why one should not trust in princes. It is not that they are not trustworthy because they are part of an elite class. Rather it is because the elevation of them that so often occurs is unwarranted. As the psalm continues it makes clear that the 'God of Jacob' is the only possible object of hope and trust, the only one who has proven reliable (vv. 5–7).

Complementarity

Some lines of poetry have pairs of cola that present part of an idea in one colon and then the rest of the idea in the colon that follows. Together, the two parts of the poetic line create a complete picture of what the lines describe or say, a whole 'set'. We see such complementary cola particularly in passages that speak of the various parts of the world God created. For example, Psalm 95.4 says concerning God's sovereignty over the cosmos:

> In his hand are the depths of the earth/the heights of the mountains are his also//

The complementary pair, 'earth' and 'mountains', here refers to two prominent parts of the area beneath the heavens. 'Earth' denotes the more accessible areas, and 'mountains' the places that are higher and more remote. Yet, as this line suggests, both have parts that are difficult to explore or experience, thus '*depths* of the earth' and '*heights* of the mountains'.[26]

Psalm 95.5 continues this complementary expression with another that is even more evident in how the parts relate to each other:

> The sea is his, for he made it/and the dry land, which his hands have formed//

'Sea' and 'dry land' are the two primary parts of God's creation beneath the heavens, as Genesis 1.9–10 indicates. Here the two main divisions appear in

---

26 The Hebrew word translated 'depths' (*mehqere*) appears only here and many scholars believe it is a mistake. The verb *haqar*, however, means 'to investigate' and the noun form could refer to those places 'to be explored'. See Hans-Joachim Kraus, *Psalms 60–150: A continental commentary* (trans. Hilton C. Oswald; Minneapolis, MN: Fortress Press, 1993), p. 245.

two complementary cola and together they name a complete whole. The effect of the two cola, however, is not a list of parts of creation, but an enhanced statement of God as creator and sovereign lord over the created order: 'God owns this part, but that part as well' (see Ps. 95.4). 'He made this region, and that region also' (see Ps. 95.5).

Consequential statements

Robert Alter uses the term 'consequentiality' to describe parallel cola that have a logical or temporal sequence. Colon A makes a statement or petition, and colon B (and/or perhaps colon C as well) expresses the logical outcome or result of A's occurrence. In Psalm 69.2(3) the psalmist describes her trouble by using a sequence of verbs for being inundated:

> I sink in deep mire/where there is no foothold/
> I have come into deep waters/and the flood sweeps over me//

The first line has two synonymous parallels that give the basic circumstance: deep mire/no foothold. Then the psalmist relates the increasing trouble with two cola that have a temporal logic:

> I have come into deep waters/flood sweeps over me//

This kind of consequential parallelism appears in simple petitions like Psalm 35.2:

> Take hold of shield and buckler/and rise to help me//

The petition includes two imperatives that present two stages in the help the psalmist asks God to give. The first asks God to take up weapons, and the second asks God to use those weapons to defend the psalmist.

Some poetic lines that contain cola with a sequential relationship have a narrative-like quality. They tell a 'story', sometimes within a single line or over the span of several lines. Psalm 55.6–8(7–9) presents this type of sequence as the psalmist muses over the desire to escape an enemy:

> And I say, 'O that I had wings like a dove/I would fly away and be at rest//
> Truly, I would flee far away/I would lodge in the wilderness/
> I would hurry to find a shelter for myself/from the raging wind and tempest'//

We find within this section of poetic lines techniques of parallelism we have seen already. For example, there are synonymous parallels in the segment:

I would lodge/hurry to find shelter//

The section as a whole, however, moves temporally, as the psalmist wishes for wings to fly away and find shelter from trouble. The psalmist takes us on a journey that spells out the stages of fulfilment of the wish to 'fly away and be at rest': the verbs 'flee'/'lodge'/'find shelter' show this movement, from escape to resting in safety.

Psalm 51.5(6) presents a sequence in reverse order to make one of the most powerful confessions of sin in Scripture:

Indeed, I was born guilty/a sinner when my mother conceived me//

The two cola move us backwards in time, from birth to conception, in order to portray the magnitude of sinfulness.

A sequential relationship between cola is also obvious in the psalms that tell some part of Israel's story. Psalm 105.23–45 recalls the exodus story, from Israel's arrival in Egypt and enslavement (vv. 23–25) to God's sending of Moses and Aaron (v. 26) to the killing of the firstborn of Egypt (v. 36) and guiding Israel through the wilderness (vv. 37–45).

These are but a few of the types of parallels that appear regularly in the Psalms. The possible relationships between cola in poetic lines are nearly unlimited. Furthermore, we do well to remember Kugel's admonition that attempts to put these relationships between cola into neat categories do the poetry of the Psalms a disservice. We will read the Psalms most faithfully if we allow these examples to heighten our awareness of the dynamic movement within poetic lines.

Metaphor

Metaphor is the other major feature of the Psalms that suggests they are poetry and, as such, radically different from prose. Metaphor is one among many figures of speech we encounter in the Psalms, but metaphor is perhaps 'the supreme source of expressiveness in language'.[27] A metaphor is a figure of speech in which one thing is said to be another, which it obviously is not. The

---

27 H. Sperber, *Einführung in die Bedeutungslehre* (2nd edn; Leipzig: de Gruyter, 1930), p. 150.

power of metaphor, however, resides precisely in the equation of one thing to another. Some linguistic theorists label the concept or person that a metaphor illuminates the **tenor** of the metaphor. In our examples, the tenor is God, the LORD, who is the subject of the Psalms. The figure by which the psalmist speaks of God is said to be the **vehicle**. To take a familiar example, in the expression 'The LORD is my shepherd' (Ps. 23.1), 'shepherd' is the vehicle, the figure by which the psalmist speaks of the LORD. The tenor, or 'target domain' as some literary theorists label it, becomes better known and understood by the equation with the vehicle.

Part of the power of a metaphor is that it informs as well as inspires or delights the one who hears or reads it. Thus 'The LORD is my shepherd' gives new insight into who the LORD is and what the LORD is like. As Janet Soskice puts it, a metaphor organizes 'a network of associations' and a strong metaphor 'compels new possibilities of vision'.[28] For this to happen, the one who receives the metaphor must understand both fields that come together in it. Some understanding of shepherds is necessary for 'The LORD is my shepherd' to illuminate the nature of the LORD. Nevertheless, strong metaphors also create friction since the tenor and vehicle are not exact equivalents. We cannot list duties and characteristics of shepherds in the Ancient Near East and claim to grasp fully the line 'The LORD is my shepherd'. Part of the learning that occurs in the presence of a metaphor is precisely the dissonance the verse creates. In the case of Psalm 23.1 the metaphor maps a host of associations that we cannot exhaust by analysis. Furthermore, we cannot pinpoint any narrow set of shepherd characteristics that *explain* it. The image certainly has some association with those whose profession or family duty it was to care for sheep (1 Sam. 16.11; 17.15, 20, 28, 34–37). As Ancient Near Eastern literature and iconography show, however, 'shepherd' was a label monarchs desired for themselves.[29] Thus the label carried associations of care as well as power and authority. Most important for Ancient Israelites, the LORD had been and still was shepherd for the people. Psalm 78.52 declares, 'Then he led out his people like sheep, and guided them in the wilderness like a flock.' Also, Isaiah 40.1–11 draws from this image to give hope to the people of Judah who were exiles in Babylon. For those aware of such associations, therefore, '*my* shepherd' creates friction as well as familiarity.[30]

---

28 Janet Soskice, *Metaphor and Religious Language* (Oxford: Clarendon Press, 1985), pp. 57–8.

29 See Othmar Keel, *The Symbolism of the Biblical World: Ancient Near Eastern iconography and the book of Psalms* (trans. Timothy Hallet; Winona Lake, IN: Eisenbrauns, 1997), pp. 254–5.

30 Keel, *Symbolism of the Biblical World*, pp. 229–30.

The LORD is king

One of the most common metaphors for God in the Psalms is king. The Hebrew noun *melek* ('king') appears numerous times in vocative address to the LORD (e.g. Pss. 5.2; 10.16; 44.4; 47.2; 95.3). The related verb *malak* ('to be king' or 'to reign') also appears many times, especially in Psalms 93—100.[31] It is too simple to say that the sentence 'The LORD is king' casts human kingship on to the heavens. Divine kingship includes God's work as creator. God's reign includes the taming of chaos and the maintenance of order in the cosmos. Still, the Psalms use much language we associate with human rule to speak of God's reign over the world. God 'sits enthroned', albeit above the heavens (Pss. 2.4; 97.2).

The image of God as king gives rise to numerous other metaphors. As king, God exercises authority over all others, including the gods of the nations (Ps. 97.9). God convenes a council of divine beings to enact plans to create equity on earth. Psalm 82 testifies that the divine king found other gods wanting in this respect and cast them to the earth like mortals. As king, God acts as judge and arbiter of justice (Ps. 96.10). As king, God goes forth into battle for the sake of righteousness and justice, and wins victories (Ps. 98.1–2). Among the other sub-metaphors of the king metaphor are **shepherd** and **refuge**. Thus the Psalter displays a host of images of God that derive from this main metaphor that, in turn, is the basis of most of the petitions for God to act. The Psalms imagine God through this primary relational image, not primarily through abstract notions of what deity is and does. The basic metaphor of God's 'rule' and exercise of 'sovereignty' is a key to nearly every petition, prayer and word of praise.

Refuge

One of the richest and most frequent sub-metaphors for God as king is God as 'refuge' (see Judg. 9.7–15).[32] Although it derives from the image of God as king, it has substantial development and nuances of its own that make it more than merely an extension of the metaphor of king.

The inspiration for the image of God as refuge may have been experiences of warfare in which Israelites escaped an enemy by fleeing to a fortress or to a rocky height. The heading of Psalm 57 which includes this metaphor places it in the time when David was fleeing from Saul and hiding in a cave. Thus, David's situation fits this image of seeking protection from God in the face of an enemy threat.

---

31 See the discussion of James Luther Mays, *The Lord Reigns: A theological handbook to the Psalms* (Louisville, KY: Westminster John Knox Press, 1994), pp. 12–22.

32 See Jerome F. D. Creach, *Yahweh as Refuge and the Editing of the Hebrew Psalter* (JSOTSup 217; Sheffield: Sheffield Academic Press, 1996).

'To seek refuge' means to take cover or seek shelter. Among the associated expressions are the labels 'rock' and 'fortress' (Ps. 18.2(3)). The declaration that 'in you I take refuge' (Ps. 7.1(2)) confesses that in the LORD there is a kind of protection that no other 'shelter' provides. Thus the psalmist contrasts divine refuge with humanly conceived plans of escape from enemies such as 'fleeing to the mountains' (see Ps. 11.1).

One of the most picturesque extensions of this metaphor is the image of God having wings that cover the one seeking protection: 'in the shadow of your wings I will take refuge, until the destroying storms pass by' (Ps. 57.1(2)). This image may suggest yet another origin for the metaphor, that of the mother bird who protects her young under her pinions.[33] Or the reference to 'wings' may have found inspiration in the wings of the cherubim on the ark of the covenant in the Temple.

Regardless of the origin of the refuge imagery, the language of God as refuge is closely connected with the experience of God in the Temple, which is conceived as a fortress itself (Pss. 57.1(2); 61.4; 63.7(8)). The Temple was a place where worshippers found the safety of God's presence. So it is natural that the Temple also symbolized the 'refuge' of God (Ps. 43.2).

Simile: another powerful figure of speech

Although the metaphors in the Psalms are uniquely expressive in the way they equate one thing with another, there are also numerous powerful similes that have similarly potent impacts on a reader. The simile uses direct comparison to make its point, with words such as 'like' and 'as'. Because a simile declares one thing to be like another, and does not declare direct equivalency, many denigrate similes as weaker expressions than metaphors. Although this is generally true, the Psalms contain some exquisite similes that convey faith and theology as deeply as many metaphors.[34] Two examples illustrate the point.

As a deer longs for water

Psalm 42 begins with a simile that makes the psalm unique in the Psalter:

As a deer longs for flowing streams,
    so my soul longs for you, O God.
(v. 1(2))

---

33 For an extended discussion of each occurrence of this image, see LeMon, *Yahweh's Winged Form*.
34 See the discussion in Brown, *Seeing the Psalms*, pp. 7–8.

The word for 'flowing streams' refers to wadis, gullies that become streams after rain but are dry otherwise (see Ezek. 6.3). The image is rich and imaginative: the psalmist is like a deer that has wandered over a parched landscape and arrived at a dry wadi, and brays desperately at the lack of water. Although the psalm does not equate the psalmist with the deer, the image continues to develop and displays expressive power like the strongest metaphors in the Psalter. That longing for water is an emblem of the psalmist's longing to be in God's presence. As the psalm develops further, the simile of the deer combines with the metaphor of thirst: 'My soul thirsts for God, for the living God' (Ps. 43.2a(3a)).

The psalmist's desire to be in God's presence is the main subject of Psalms 42—43 and this theme dominates the movement of the poem. The initial declarations about thirsting for God (42.1–2a(2–3a)) give way to a question that represents the main problem: 'When shall I come and behold the face of God?' (42.2b(3b)). The taunting question 'Where is your God?' comes because the psalmist is not in the holy place and so God seems absent (42.3(4)). Memories of being among worshippers in the Temple fuel the pain (42.4(5)). Matching the memory of being there and keeping festival is the current awareness of distance from the holy place. Geographical references in 42.6(7) seem to locate the psalmist far in the north, on Mount Hermon where the waters of the Jordan begin.[35] The distance from God and from God's people is almost unbearable. It is captured in the notion that the psalmist 'thirsts' for God as a deer in desperate search of water.

Like a tree

In several psalms the psalmist speaks of those who trust in God as resembling a tree (Pss. 1.3; 52.8(9); 92.12–15(13–16)). The power of the image derives in part from the nature of trees in the local climate and landscape. In an arid region where trees are sparse, the psalmist portrays human frailty by speaking of the fleeting grasses and flowers that spring up quickly and just as quickly fade and die (Ps. 90.5–6). That too is a powerful image of the negative side of human experience. The comparison of the righteous person to a tree, however, is more complex. For a tree to flourish in the psalmist's world required an abundance of water, which was rare. A tree represented permanence and fruitfulness, outcomes that were only possible with proper nutrition capable of defying the harsh environment.

---

35 James Luther Mays, *Psalms* (Interpretation: A Bible commentary for teaching and preaching; Louisville, KY: Westminster John Knox Press, 1994), p. 174.

Like a good metaphor, this simile draws together a number of associated subjects. In the Ancient Near East trees grew in well-tended gardens that were themselves symbols of life and vitality (Gen. 2.15–17). In turn, Ancient Near Eastern people conceived of their temples as garden paradises where life flourished. Depictions of such worship-places feature streams of flowing water and plants of all kinds, including trees. It seems logical, therefore, that two of the appearances of this simile compare the faithful person to trees that grew in the Jerusalem Temple:

> But I am like a green olive tree
> > in the house of God.
> I trust in the steadfast love of God
> > for ever and ever.
> (Ps. 52.8(9))

> The righteous flourish like the palm tree,
> > and grow like a cedar in Lebanon.
> They are planted in the house of the LORD;
> > they flourish in the courts of our God.
> In old age they still produce fruit;
> > they are always green and full of sap,
> showing that the LORD is upright;
> > he is my rock, and there is no unrighteousness in him.
> (Ps. 92.12–15(13–16))

Both of these similes attribute stability and fruitfulness to trust in God, and they suggest that being in the Temple – near the divine Presence – is the primary key to the life of goodness and blessing. Both similes also develop the tree image in particular ways. Psalm 52.8(9) extends the description by identifying the person as an olive tree. With its incredibly long life (sometimes two thousand years!), the olive tree is a powerful image of resilience and fruitfulness. Psalm 92.12–15(13–16) compares the righteous person first to a palm and then to a cedar in Lebanon, one of the largest and most luxuriant trees in the region (v. 12(13)). The simile then morphs into a metaphor: 'They are planted in the house of the LORD' (v. 13(14)). The righteous are *like* these fabulous trees because they *are* planted in the house of the LORD.

Psalm 1.3 opens the Psalter with this image of the righteous person as 'like a tree'. The psalm develops the simile with a web of associations that rivals any metaphor in the book. It begins the description of the righteous with a line that appears almost exactly in Jeremiah 17.8: 'They shall be like a tree planted by water.' The Jeremiah passage presents the righteous person as being like a tree in a garden, by a water source, in contrast to the wicked human being who is like a 'shrub in the desert' (Jer. 17.6). In this way Jeremiah 17.5–8 is like a popular Ancient Egyptian text known as *The Instruction of Amenemope*, which also contrasts a plant in a garden with a plant in the wilderness.[36] Psalm 1.3 transforms this basic image, however, by adding words and phrases from other passages, all of which describe the Temple as a paradise where water flows in abundance and trees flourish. For example, it includes the term 'streams' (*pelagim*), which in some contexts connotes the water channels on the holy mountain where the Temple is located (Pss. 46.4(5); 65.9(10)). When it describes how the leaves of the tree do not wither, Psalm 1.3 quotes almost word for word from Ezekiel's vision of trees planted beside the stream that flows from the Temple (Ezek. 47.12).[37] Hence, with these allusions and quotations Psalm 1.3 describes the righteous person as being much like the righteous in Psalms 52.8(9) and 92.12–15(13–16).

Psalm 1.3 is distinctive, however, in that it says the righteous are secure – as though they dwell on the holy mountain – because they meditate on Torah (v. 2). This seems to mean that Torah has the same life-giving potential as the Temple and gives access to God's presence just as the Temple did.[38] With this rich simile, Psalm 1 invites readers to find a secure place near God by reading and meditating on Torah. All of this meaning – much of it subtle and implied – is packed into the expression 'like trees planted by streams of water'!

---

36 James B. Pritchard, ed., *Ancient Near Eastern Texts Relating to the Old Testament* (3rd edn; Princeton, NJ: Princeton University Press, 1969), p. 422.

37 Jerome F. D. Creach, 'Like a tree planted by the temple stream: portrait of the righteous in Psalm 1:3a', *Catholic Biblical Quarterly*, no. 1 (January 1999), pp. 39–41 (34–46).

38 Susan E. Gillingham, *A Journey of Two Psalms: The reception of Psalms 1 and 2 in Jewish and Christian tradition* (Oxford: Oxford University Press, 2013), p. 275.

3

Did David write the Psalms?

Whatever David says in his book pertains to himself, to all Israel, and to all times.
(*Midrash on Psalms*)

The question 'Did David write the Psalms?' has occupied the attention of scholars and students of the Psalms in one way or another for over two millennia. Throughout the history of the study of the Psalter the issue of authorship, broadly defined, has always been at the heart of the enquiry. Although many modern scholars no longer think that David authored the Psalms, the connection between David and the Psalter remains crucial. To understand why the connection to David is important we must first consider the question of Davidic authorship.

Claims of Davidic authorship

Psalm 3 as a starting point

Psalm 3 is a good place to begin to address the question of authorship since it is the first psalm that presents explicit claims about it. The heading introduces the psalm as 'A Psalm of David, when he fled from his son Absalom'. Taken at face value, the title suggests that Psalm 3 contains the words David spoke during the rebellion narrated in 2 Samuel 15—18. John Calvin takes this as the plain sense of the text when he says concerning Psalm 3: 'How bitter David's sorrow was under the conspiracy of his own household against him, which arose from the treachery of his own son.'[1]

Calvin follows the example of rabbinical interpretation in his reading of the title of Psalm 3. For centuries Jewish interpreters read the psalm as David's words. They did have questions about the claim of the heading, but their queries focused on details of how and when David spoke the words. They

---

1 John Calvin, *Commentary on the Book of Psalms* (Edinburgh: Calvin Translation Society, 1845), vol. 1, p. 27.

wondered if David wrote Psalm 3 at the time Absalom drove him out of the palace (2 Sam. 15.13–31) or after the ordeal was finished (Talmud, *b. Ber.* 7b).[2] They did not entertain the idea, however, that David did not write Psalm 3.

These comments from interpreters of the past highlight the fact that psalm headings are the primary place where we encounter the claim that David wrote the Psalms. The superscriptions that include David's name and identify a psalm 'of David' (*ledawid*) are crucial. Interpreters through the ages read this simple expression, which appears in half the psalms in the Psalter (75 in total), as an ascription of authorship.

David's name alone, however, is not enough to create the link between David and the Psalms. The 'historical' information in the heading of Psalm 3 and in 11 other psalms is most important for the claim of Davidic authorship.[3] The rest of the list of psalms with these headings includes Psalms 18, 34, 51, 52, 54, 56, 57, 59, 60, 63 and 142. Each of these headings has essentially the same sentence structure. After 'of David' the sentence continues with a Hebrew preposition (*be*) that has a temporal meaning ('when'). The sentence then states what David did (e.g. 'when he fled', Pss. 3; 57) or what someone did to him (e.g. 'when the prophet Nathan came to him', Ps. 51; 'when Doeg the Edomite came to Saul', Ps. 52). The implication is that the psalm is 'by David', the words 'of David' on that particular occasion.

Psalm 7 sometimes appears in this list, but the meaning of the heading in Psalm 7 is uncertain ('which he sang to the LORD concerning Cush, a Benjaminite'). We know nothing of anyone named Cush in the David narrative. The form of the historical note is also different from that in other such headings. The syntax of the expression 'concerning Cush' is identical to some of the musical notes in the headings like 'according to The Sheminith' (Ps. 6). Thus some scholars believe the title of Psalm 7 was originally a musical note that scribes misunderstood and eventually 'corrected'. In present form it does say that David 'sang' Psalm 7, but that was probably not the original intention of the heading.

Psalm 18 has a more complex heading, but the structure follows basically the same pattern as the others and it presents the clearest claim of any of these psalms that David spoke the words. Psalm 18 appears also in 2 Samuel 22 as one of the last statements of David before his death. Verse 1 of that chapter

---

2 See Avrohom Chaim Feuer, *Tehillim: A new translation with a commentary anthologized from Talmudic, Midrashic and rabbinic sources* (New York, NY: Mesorah, 1985), p. 74.

3 See Brevard S. Childs, 'Psalm titles and Midrashic exegesis', *Journal of Semitic Studies* 16, no. 2 (Fall 1971), pp. 137–50.

introduces the psalm by saying, 'David spoke to the LORD the words of this song'. In the heading of Psalm 18 the first verb is slightly different in form, but the Hebrew root is the same and the syntax fits the rest of the heading ('of David . . . who addressed the words of this song to the LORD'). The expression 'he addressed' uses the basic verb meaning 'to speak' (*dibber*) and hence states directly that the psalm represents David's words. After the initial statement that David spoke the words to the LORD, the syntax follows the pattern of the other psalms with historical headings ('on the day' includes the same preposition mentioned above). Many scholars have dated Psalm 18 (and 2 Sam. 22) to the time of David. Although dating the Psalms is notoriously difficult to do, this scholarly judgement has enhanced the idea that David authored this particular psalm and adds to the general notion that David is responsible for the book of Psalms.[4]

The 'historical' headings of these 12 psalms typically link the particular psalm to a story that appears in 1 and 2 Samuel and 1 Chronicles. Often the language of the psalm fits with the narrative, thus reinforcing the theory that David spoke the words on that occasion. For example, the setting of Psalm 3 in the events of 2 Samuel 15 makes sense when we consider the details of the prayer in the psalm. Although the psalm has no exact linguistic parallels to 2 Samuel 15, there are significant thematic and conceptual links: in Psalm 3 David complains of a host of enemies rising against him (Ps. 3.1(2); 2 Sam. 15.12); he recognizes that some have abandoned hope for him (Ps. 3.2(3); 2 Sam. 16.8); but David puts his trust in God (Ps. 3.3–4(4–5); 2 Sam. 15.25–28). More specifically, when Psalm 3.5–6(6–7) speaks of lying down and sleeping and waking in the LORD's strength and protection, it parallels neatly the account of David spending the night at the River Jordan and arising the next morning to cross over it in his return to Jerusalem (2 Sam. 16.14; 17.22).[5] Thus, a straightforward reading of the title of Psalm 3, alongside a comparison of the psalm's prayer with the events in 2 Samuel 15—18, seems to affirm the notion that David wrote Psalm 3.

The idea that David wrote Psalm 3, and that he was the author of the other psalms as well, endured throughout the Middle Ages, and most readers assumed it until the Enlightenment. David's life was the backdrop of the Psalms and provided a full explanation for the contents of the Psalter. For

---

4 See the discussion in P. Kyle McCarter, *II Samuel: A new translation with introduction, notes and commentary* (Anchor Bible 9; New York, NY: Doubleday, 1984), pp. 455–75.

5 Childs, 'Psalm titles and Midrashic exegesis', p. 144.

example, it was customary for the rabbis to treat Psalm 3 in the light of all the experiences David had as king, including the judgement of God that came upon him through Nathan the prophet (2 Sam. 12.1–15). They read Psalm 3 not only in the light of Absalom's rebellion but also in the light of the judgement that trouble would arise within David's own household (2 Sam. 12.11). Now, they mused, David's sadness was multiplied as he realized the trouble came from his own son (Talmud, *b. Ber.* 7b). This kind of reading would continue almost unabated for centuries.

Other affirmations of David as author of the Psalms

In some of the earliest interpretations of the Psalms we find affirmation of the idea that David wrote the Psalms. Near the end of a psalms manuscript discovered at Qumran, known as 11QPs[a] (dating to around 50 CE), there is a ten-line description of David that identifies him as a scribe ('literate') and that declares he wrote 3,600 psalms (*tehillim*).[6] The description goes on to say that he wrote songs for nearly every religious occasion. His total compositions, the passage asserts, numbered 4,050.[7] In a similar way the Greek Psalter includes a 151st psalm that purports to be by David. In the song, David attests to playing musical instruments and with them giving glory to the LORD.[8] Although neither of these texts says David wrote the Psalms, it was surely the association of him with the Psalter that led to the larger idea that he wrote liturgical texts and composed songs to praise God.

The New Testament seems to assume that David authored the Psalms. Numerous passages refer to David as the author of a particular psalm or of the book in its entirety. In the Gospels Jesus asks a group of Pharisees for their thoughts about the Messiah: whose son is he? They respond that he is David's son. So, Jesus asks, 'How is it that David by the Spirit calls him Lord?' Jesus is referring to Psalm 110, which begins, 'The LORD said to my lord . . .' The first 'lord' refers to God and the second to the Messiah. Jesus' presumption is that David wrote Psalm 110 and so prophetically spoke in the psalm about the Messiah (Matt. 22.41–45; Mark 12.35–37; Luke 20.41–44). Similarly, in Acts 1.16 Peter declares that David spoke prophetically about the trials of the Messiah. Another example is Hebrews 4.7, which cites Psalm 95 and identifies it with David.

6 James Sanders, ed., *The Dead Sea Psalms Scroll* (Ithaca, NY: Cornell University Press, 1967), p. 6.
7 Sanders, *Psalms Scroll*, pp. 86–7, 134–7.
8 Sanders, *Psalms Scroll*, pp. 94–103.

Questioning David as author of the Psalms

Despite the ancient affirmations that David wrote the Psalms, modern scholars have mounted significant arguments against the idea. They point out that the references to David in psalm headings are not necessarily claims of authorship. In Hebrew the expression is *ledawid*, which simply means 'of David'. Just as the English expression 'of David' can signify any number of things, so also the Hebrew. It can mean the psalm remembers David, honours David or belongs to collections associated with David just as well as it might indicate authorship ('by David').[9] These scholars point out further that the headings of the psalms were not part of the original writing. Scribes added them later as they collected the psalms and gave directions about how to read and perform them (see Chapter 1). This seems obvious given that the headings contain musical directives and other liturgical information. The references to David in the headings likely came from a time when David had grown into a legendary figure and Israelites remembered him as 'the sweet singer of Israel' (2 Sam. 23.1 JPS 1917).

The claims of Davidic authorship become even more difficult to accept when we look at the headings of the psalms in the Greek version of the Hebrew Scriptures. Though the Greek version expands the number of references to David in psalm headings, it also introduces some information that conflicts with the claim that David wrote the Psalms. For example, the heading of Psalm 71 reads, 'Of David, by the sons of Jonadab and the first of those who were taken captive'.[10] Although the Greek version associates the psalm with David, it seems to say that someone else wrote it at the time of the Babylonian captivity (587 BCE), long after David had died. Psalm 96 in the Greek version has the label 'a Psalm of David', but it also identifies the psalm as relating to the time 'when the temple was built after the captivity'. Again, the heading says the psalm is written for a time long after David's life was over. Psalm 137 is about the trauma of exile, and even ancient scribes recognized that David could not have written it. The Greek version labels it a psalm 'of David' but then identifies the prophet Jeremiah as the author. Therefore, the Greek version seems to point to something other than authorship when it says a psalm is 'of David'.

Modern scholars have also found problems with headings that identify a psalm with an event in the life of David. Steven McKenzie points out that

---

9 For this and the following discussion of problems with Davidic authorship, see Steven L. McKenzie, *King David: A biography* (Oxford: Oxford University Press, 2000), pp. 38–43.

10 In the Greek version this is Ps. 70.

these psalms for the most part do not mention any details that would link the psalm with the events mentioned in the headings as the occasions when David spoke them. For example, the heading of Psalm 3 says David prayed the prayer when Absalom revolted against him, but the psalm does not mention Absalom or any specific enemy. It only says 'Many are rising against me' (v. 1(2)) and that tens of thousands have 'set themselves against me' (v. 6(7)). Furthermore, the plural reference ('enemies') seems odd since it was only one enemy who attacked David. In the same way, the heading of Psalm 18 indicates that David spoke it when the LORD delivered him from Saul, but the psalm itself does not mention Saul.[11] These points do not disprove Davidic authorship, but they do call into question the degree to which these psalms fit the setting identified in the heading.

Some of the 12 psalms with historical headings actually contradict the information in the headings or show inaccuracies. The heading of Psalm 34 says David spoke the words when he 'feigned madness before Abimelech'. The story the heading seems to mention is in 1 Samuel 21.10–15, but the king in the story is Achish, not Abimelech (see the reference to Abimelech in Gen. 20; 26.1–16). Psalm 51.18–19(20–21) seems to assume not only a temple in Jerusalem, which David's son built after his death, but the temple the people restored after the Babylonian exile. We could add to this observation that many other psalms 'of David' speak about dwelling in and travelling to the Temple (e.g. Pss. 23.6; 27.4; 52.8(9)).[12] Any reference to the Temple in relation to David is anachronistic.

In addition to these inconsistencies and contradictions, scholars have noted that if we did not have the headings of the psalms we might not associate them with David much at all. Only seven psalms mention David in the body of the psalm itself and only two of these report to be psalms of David (Pss. 18; 144). Psalm 18 ends with a reference to David that suggests he is a figure from the past, the head of a dynasty which God promised to preserve in perpetuity (v. 50(51)). Psalm 144 is largely a reworked version of Psalm 18 that seems to deny the claims about the king's greatness (vv. 3–4). Verse 11 prays for deliverance after declaring that the LORD 'rescues his servant David' (v. 10). This gives the impression that David is not praying the psalm but represents the object of God's compassion, perhaps as a symbol of the monarchy or of the people of Israel as a whole.

---

11 McKenzie, *King David*, p. 40.

12 McKenzie, *King David*, pp. 40–1.

Psalm 72 as turning point in Davidic authorship

Scholars before the modern era also recognized problems with Davidic authorship. They recognized, for example, that David could not have written Psalm 137 unless by prophecy. There are signs within the Psalter itself, however, that the claim of Davidic authorship was not a simple, uncritical proposition. Perhaps the most obvious complication to the idea of Davidic authorship is the colophon at the end of Psalm 72: 'The prayers of David son of Jesse are ended' (v. 20). The note in Psalm 72.20 that David's prayers finish at that point is striking because more prayers of David appear after Psalm 72. One of them, Psalm 86, appears in Book III of the Psalter, the section that follows the declaration that the prayers of David have ended. Modern scholars have typically not considered this point very significant. They have seen the colophon at Psalm 72.20 as simply a marker of the Psalter's development, one of the 'growth rings' of the book.[13] In this way of thinking, when the book continued to grow beyond the two large Davidic collections (Pss. 3—41; 51—72), psalm editors either did not notice or did not care about the apparent contradiction that more prayers of David appear after Psalm 72. Some pre-modern interpreters, however, thought it implausible that those who preserved the Psalms did not notice such a comment. Augustine proposed that a key to understanding this problem is the reference to David as the 'son of Jesse'. He noted that this label appears in no other psalm, and thus in Psalm 72.20 it must refer to the earthly king David, whereas 'David' in other places, especially after Psalm 72, may denote the 'David' of the future, that is, Jesus Christ. Augustine also interpreted the verb in the colophon (*kallu*) to mean 'failed', not simply 'finished'.[14] Thus, Psalm 72 marks the end of any hope the Psalter expresses for God to work through the Davidic kings.

Augustine's specific interpretation works on a David–Christ typology that developed long after the book of Psalms took shape. Nevertheless, the general observation that something changes about 'David' after Psalm 72 is a keen insight. After Psalm 72, references to David never mention any specific circumstances of his life and reign, especially not to his flight from enemies.[15]

---

13 Klaus Seybold, *Introducing the Psalms* (trans. Graeme Dunphy; Edinburgh: T&T Clark, 1990), p. 18.

14 Augustine, *Nicene and Post-Nicene Fathers of the Christian Church*, First Series, vol. 8: *Expositions on the book of Psalms* (ed. Philip Schaff; New York, NY: The Christian Literature Company, 1888), pp. 333–5.

15 Note that the heading of Ps. 142 ('when he was in the cave') is like that of Ps. 57 ('when he fled from Saul, in the cave') but without any specific reference to the enemy.

Thus, Augustine thought specifically that Psalm 72.20 refers to David's prayers failing and thus to the failure of the work of the earthly Davidic kingdom.[16]

Figurative readings of David in the Psalms

When we take a broader view of Davidic authorship we see that many of the earliest interpreters did not really cling closely to 'authorship' in the same way modern readers think of that term. Rather, they often thought references to David were actually pointing to Jesus Christ and that was the real message of the psalm. Concerning Psalm 3, Augustine notes that 'this Psalm is to be understood as in the Person of Christ'.[17] He reasons that the portrait of trouble in Psalm 3 fits better Jesus' Passion than the historical events in the life of David. So, by 'Absalom' we should understand Judas Iscariot. The doubt Augustine expressed about the speaker, however, had little to do with what we would call authorship. Augustine did not seem particularly interested in the question of whether David actually penned Psalm 3.

This kind of reading flourished in the early centuries of the Church. On the title of Psalm 3, the Venerable Bede said, similarly to Augustine, 'By David understand Christ; by Absalom Judas Iscariot.'[18] St Bonaventure interpreted Psalm 3.5(6) (reading it as 'I laid down and slept, and rose up again') as a reference to Jesus' death and resurrection: '*He laid Him down* in the new sepulchre. He *slept* His sleep of three days; He *rose up again*, the third day from the dead.' On Psalm 3.7(8) ('you break the teeth of the wicked'), St Albertus Magnus commented:

> Opposed to these are the teeth of the righteous preachers of the Church, who bring men into the body of Christ, teeth which should not decay through luxury, but be white with innocence, joined in charity, even in justice, firm in constancy, bony in vigour, biting into sin with doctrine and truth.

Although these interpreters spoke without reservation about David in the Psalms, their concern was not David as author, but David as type of Christ, as

---

16 Augustine, *Expositions on the Psalms*, pp. 334–5.

17 Augustine, *Expositions on the Psalms*, p. 4.

18 For this and the following references in this paragraph, see J. M. Neale and R. F. Littledale, *A Commentary on the Psalms: From primitive and mediaeval writers; and from the various office-books and hymns of the Roman, Mozarabic, Ambrosian, Gallican, Greek, Coptic, Armenian, and Syriac rites, vol. 1: Psalms 1–38* (3rd edn; London: Joseph Masters, 1874), pp. 104–8.

symbol of God's work in the Incarnation. Thus, from a modern critical point of view, this loosens further the claim that David actually wrote the Psalms.

If not David, then who?

If David did not write then Psalms, then who did? To answer that question we first need to consider the concept of authorship more carefully. As we will discuss in Chapter 4, most of the psalms contain generic language that is impossible to identify with a single author. The Psalms are not like modern literary works that we can relate to a particular person by style and vocabulary. Rather, most of the language comes from stock expressions that were typical of a particular type of event, not of a certain author. Most of the language in the Psalms arises from common events and does not belong to any one writer.

Another consideration is that writing in the ancient world was largely a professional activity and people like David probably did not write regularly. David would have had scribes whose job it was to write edicts and proclamations, and the records of the events of the kingdom. So, even if we could trace the contents of the Psalms to the person David, we should conclude that scribes wrote the words for him. We should also recognize that writing the Psalms was a complicated matter. Many psalms underwent significant editorial changes (e.g. the addition of vv. 18–19(20–21) to Ps. 51), and scribes copied psalms into collections that perhaps changed over time as well. So, the writing of a psalm and especially of the book as a whole was a complex task that covered a long period. It is inconceivable that one person did all this, another problem for Davidic authorship.

The most likely candidate for authorship of the Psalms is not an individual but the group known as the Levites.[19] Although the Levites appear differently in the various Old Testament traditions, there are some consistent features in descriptions of them that help make the case. The Jewish philosopher Philo refers to the Levites as singers and musicians.[20] The Mishnah cites numerous psalms that the Levites sang at worship services and celebrations in the Jerusalem Temple.[21] There is much we don't know about how the Levites and other priestly groups developed and changed over time. Some early biblical

---

19 For the following discussion see especially Susan E. Gillingham, 'The Levites and the editorial composition of the Psalms', in *The Oxford Handbook of the Psalms* (ed. William P. Brown; Oxford: Oxford University Press, 2014), pp. 201–13.

20 Cited in Mark S. Smith, 'The Levitical compilation of the Psalter', *Zeitschrift für die alttestamentliche Wissenschaft* 103 (1991), p. 262 (258–63).

21 See the list of references in Gillingham, 'The Levites', p. 203.

passages suggest they were a secular tribe originally (Gen. 49.5–7; Deut. 33.8), while others link them to official priestly duties in Israel's sanctuaries (1 Sam. 2—3). Whatever their history and development, however, it seems clear that by the Persian period (after 539 BCE) they were temple servants and musicians. Every mention of them in the passages of this time identifies groups of them in these roles. According to Ezra 2.41 the Asaphites were temple singers (see the genealogy in 1 Chron. 9.33–34 for the Levitical identity). In 1 Chronicles 16.4–5 there is an account of David appointing Levites to take charge of the temple music, with the Asaphites having the lead role. Another group of Levites, the Korahites, are identified in 1 Chronicles 26 as gatekeepers for the Temple.[22] According to Nehemiah 8, the Levites were also responsible for instructing the people in the meaning of Torah.

It is impossible to know how historical these portraits of the Levites are in Chronicles, but the attention the Levites receive and the particular portrait painted of them probably indicates they were leaders in post-exilic temple worship, and their place in the Chronicler's narrative solidified that role by giving them authority rooted in tradition. By appearing in 1 Chronicles 15—16 alongside David, they appear as co-founders of the Jerusalem Temple's worship. The story of them accompanying David as he brought the ark of the covenant to Jerusalem ties them to Moses as well as David, and brings the Jerusalem Temple under the authority of the Sinaitic covenant.

These connections between the Levites and the story of David establishing worship in Jerusalem do not mean that the Levites originally wrote the Psalms. As we observed already, it is impossible to tell who was responsible for the words themselves. The links do raise the strong possibility, however, that the Levites were most influential in selecting, editing and compiling the Psalms, and this may be the closest we can come to determining authorship. Several features of the psalms in the Psalter point to the Levites as those responsible for them.

1. The Psalms rarely use technical, priestly language for sacrifice. Only occasionally do the Psalms mention specific kinds of offerings and sacrifices such as 'freewill-offering' (Ps. 54.6(8)) or 'burnt-offering' (Pss. 20.3(4); 50.8; 51.19(21)). More prominent is a critique of sacrifice as an empty ritual:

Sacrifice and offering you do not desire,
    but you have given me an open ear.

---

22 See again Gillingham, 'The Levites', p. 204, for a more extensive list of passages.

Burnt-offering and sin-offering
   you have not required.
(Ps. 40.6(7))

Psalm 141.2 asks for prayer to count as sacrifice. This focus on piety over ritual fits the identity of the Levites as servants of the Temple who were outside the priestly circles of cult sacrifice.

2. It also makes sense that the Levites would shape a book so thoroughly interested in instructing the faithful in the right path to God's intentions. Psalm 1 begins that emphasis, and numerous psalms with Levitical figures in their headings continue the focus on teaching (Pss. 49, 73 and 78 are prime examples). Again, this fits the portrait of the Levites as those who were involved in teaching the people the meaning and importance of God's instruction.

3. The Psalms' constant concern for the 'poor and needy' might also point to the Levites as those responsible for the book. These terms are common synonyms for the righteous, and describe an identity characterized by humility and dependence on God. In some psalms this language of poverty also appears with questions about the value of sacrifice (Pss. 40.17(18); 69.33(34); 140.12(13)). This identity would fit the description of the Levites as those without land, who live off the offerings made at the Temple.[23]

If this theory of Levitical compilation of the Psalms is right, it might explain two aspects of the portrait of David in the book. First, as king, David was expected to defend the 'poor and needy' above all else. In Books I–III of the Psalter, psalms about the king and his role appear prominently at the end of major sections (Pss. 41 and 72 especially). Second, David's primary identity in the Psalms is as someone who is himself poor and needy, a person who calls on God for help when in trouble. Thus, for the Levites, David represented them in prayer and devotion. He was not only the founder of temple worship and psalmody, but also the prime example of how to pray in times of trouble.

Recovering David in the Psalms

Having discussed the various understandings of David and the Psalms throughout the history of psalms study, it may be obvious now that there is

---

23 Gillingham, 'The Levites', pp. 206–7.

no one simple conception of authorship that has endured. Some pre-critical interpreters thought of David as the author of the book. Others saw some of the references to David as symbolic of a future ruler or perhaps of God's people as a whole. This is particularly true of Augustine's reading of 'David' after Psalm 72.20. For Augustine, 'son of Jesse' is an important historical marker. Other scholars before the modern period were also willing to read any and all references to David as symbolic.

The Protestant Reformation marked a strong move towards reading the Psalms historically again, and that brought something of a recovery of the idea of David as author. Calvin recognized other voices in the Psalms, but the names in psalm headings already made that clear. Any 'psalms of David', however, were considered psalms that David spoke or wrote. For Calvin, David's life provided the backdrop for the psalms that bear his name, and David, in turn, appeared as a model of how to pray. This identity of David as religious example and model pray-er may be the most enduring significance of David in the Psalms. It is certainly possible to read the prayers of the Psalter apart from David, but David's presence there helps define their incarnational character. Some might object to this association of David with the Psalms on grounds that David committed unspeakable crimes. The stories about him suggest he was guilty of adultery and murder, and perhaps rape, not to mention generally being a failure in fatherhood. It is precisely these glaring weaknesses, however, that make David important. The Psalms, like the narratives in 1 and 2 Samuel, do not present him as morally pure or righteous in any objective sense. Rather they remember him as one who throws himself on God's mercy when he comes face to face with mortal weakness. The only redeeming quality he had is that he cried to the LORD when in trouble.

It is because of David's trouble and his prayers while in trouble that Calvin came to identify with him. Calvin found his religious identity in the Psalms as much as, or even more than, any other part of Scripture, and he saw in David one like himself. As a religious refugee from his native France, Calvin identified especially with the suffering of David at the hands of enemies within and without his kingdom. Calvin found in David a ruler who faced persecution and exile and in that persecuted state prayed for deliverance.[24] He found it particularly pertinent that David's greatest opposition came from his own people, even his own son Absalom. So, while Calvin fled from the extermination of Protestants in France, he saw in David's prayers words to pray himself, particularly to lament that those whom he had trusted and with whom he

---

24 Calvin, *Commentary on the Book of Psalms*, vol. 1, pp. xxxix–xlix.

had shared communion had 'lifted the heel' against him (Ps. 41.9(10); cf. Ps. 55.12–14(13–15)).[25]

Throughout the history of the Church many Christians have maintained the link between David and the Psalter, and there is good reason to insist that the connection is important. One of the shortcomings of modern scholarship is the tendency to discount the link between David and the Psalms completely when scholars determine that Davidic authorship as an historical reality is not tenable. The connection is important not so much as an historical point but as a theological one: David appears in the Psalms as our example for how to pray when we are in trouble. He represents our flawed humanity and in turn allows us to see and experience God's grace (Ps. 51.10–12(12–14)). The Psalms, and the Old Testament, remember him not because he is an ideal figure in terms of morality and personal behaviour. Rather, they remember him for his trouble and woe, much of which he brought on himself, and for the simple yet profound way he turned to the LORD for refuge.

---

25 Calvin, *Commentary on the Book of Psalms*, vol. 1, p. xlvi.

4

A psalm for every occasion: types of psalms

The Psalms are an anatomy of all parts of the soul.
(John Calvin)

Psalms study in the twentieth century

One of the standard practices of contemporary psalms study is to classify psalms according to their literary type and to identify the setting in which that type of psalm functioned. This approach is called **form criticism**. In most commentaries on the Psalms this is one way of identifying and classifying the contents of the book.

As we noted in Chapter 1, those who preserved and passed on the Psalms gave us labels for various poems in the Psalter, like 'psalm' (*mizmor*) and 'prayer' and a number of others we do not fully understand (*shiggaion; maskil*). Scholars in the twentieth century created a set of genre labels by comparing the content, vocabulary and literary structure of each psalm as it compares to other psalms in the Psalter.

The classification of psalms into literary types emerged from Old Testament scholarship at the end of the nineteenth century when scholars were riding a wave of historical and literary enquiry. In 1883 Julius Wellhausen published his book *Prolegomena to the History of Israel* in which he outlined what is now called the **Documentary Hypothesis**.[1] Wellhausen's theory was that four primary sources comprise the Pentateuch. Wellhausen proposed that the four 'documents', labelled J, E, D and P, were the work of Israelite scribes from

---

1 Julius Wellhausen, *Prolegomena to the History of Israel* (trans. J. Sutherland Black and Allan Menzies; Cambridge: Cambridge University Press, 2014; German original 1878).

different periods of Israel's history. Editors put the documents together over time, and the authors of the final source, the Priestly document (P), shaped the final product.[2]

Wellhausen's work was so compelling that it suggested for many scholars a fruitful way to study the whole Hebrew Bible. At the time of the publication of *Prolegomena to the History of Israel* scholars were asking questions about authorship, time of composition, and the documents that lay behind the present text of practically every part of the Old Testament, including the Psalms. In the case of the Psalms, however, this type of analysis was far less successful than with the narrative material.

As scholars applied this line of enquiry to the Psalms they asked primarily: who wrote each particular psalm and when? Just as Wellhausen had determined that the link made between Moses and the Pentateuch was an attempt by early editors to assign authority to the work, scholars thought the same was true of David's association with the Psalms.

So, if David didn't write a particular psalm, who did write it? Scholars struggled to answer the question, but that did not hinder them from trying. They assigned some psalms to kings other than David. Hezekiah and Josiah were particular favourites. They assigned others to figures late in Israel's history, such as Ezra and Nehemiah.[3]

Attempts to identify authors for particular psalms seemed to be based on completely circular reasoning. For example, one scholar notes that Psalm 4 'would suit all the conditions' of Ezra 4 when the people of the land opposed the plan of Zerubbabel and Jeshua to rebuild the Temple.[4] Yet, the psalm prays for help with such generalized language that it could fit the circumstances of practically any person in distress ('Answer me when I call', v. 1(2); 'How long, you people, shall my honour suffer shame?', v. 2(3)). The result was that the study of psalms and the Psalter languished, and the Psalms drew much less attention than the Old Testament narrative material, which scholars could mine for literary and historical gems.

---

2 See the summary of Wellhausen's proposal and expansions and critiques in Douglas A. Knight, 'The Pentateuch', in *The Hebrew Bible and Its Modern Interpreters* (ed. Douglas A. Knight and Gene M. Tucker; Chico, CA: Scholars Press, 1985), pp. 263–96.

3 On the attempt to identify authors for the Psalms see Erhard S. Gerstenberger, 'The lyrical literature', in *The Hebrew Bible and Its Modern Interpreters* (ed. Knight and Tucker), pp. 419–21.

4 Charles Augustus and Emily Grace Briggs, *A Critical and Exegetical Commentary on the Book of Psalms* (ICC; Edinburgh: T&T Clark, 1906), vol. 1, p. 30.

Hermann Gunkel and the rise of form criticism

Biblical analysis changed dramatically at the beginning of the twentieth century with the work of German scholar Hermann Gunkel.[5] Gunkel lived in a part of Germany where the Grimm brothers collected their fairy tales, and he recognized something in the Grimms' stories that he also saw in the Psalms. The fairy tales all had a similar structure and language. Readers could recognize them from their first line, 'Once upon a time', and from their similar development and plot. Furthermore, the language of these tales did not point to any particular author. 'Once upon a time' is so generic that the Grimm brothers could not use it to identify an author. Gunkel also recognized that this common language and structure is characteristic of literature that developed orally and grew out of common events in the life of a people. It did not begin with the creative genius of an author. In a similar way, the Psalms contain stereotyped language that does not allow us to identify an author.

Gunkel introduced a revolutionary idea in the study of the Psalms: asking about authorship and the historical setting of individual psalms misses the lifeblood of the material. Gunkel insisted that the written form of the psalms was the last stage in their development. Like a fossil that reveals only something of what a living animal once was, the written form of a psalm shows only hints of what it was when Israelites spoke, chanted or sang the lyrics. The real life of the psalms was in their performance. So, Gunkel argued, studying the written texts and asking about authors and historical settings of writing is like looking for life in a fossil.

To remedy these shortcomings, Gunkel set a new course for enquiry that involved two steps: first, to identify the genre of each psalm from patterns of speech and structural elements; second, to identify the type of situation in which Israelites likely spoke the language of each psalm. Gunkel called this situation the *Sitz im Leben* or 'setting in life'.

By 'setting in life', Gunkel meant a recurring setting in the life of the people, not a fixed time in history. A wedding is one example of a contemporary 'setting in life'. The words a minister speaks during the ceremony are quite distinctive; 'Dearly beloved, we are gathered here today' is a common beginning. A pledge of fidelity that includes the words 'until we are parted by death' is another

---

5   For the following discussion see Hermann Gunkel with Joachim Begrich, *An Introduction to the Psalms: The genres of the religious lyric of Israel* (trans. James D. Nogalski; Macon, GA: Mercer University Press, 1998; German original 1933).

identifying feature. Such words do not identify an author, nor do they identify a particular wedding ceremony. Rather, they are signals to the hearer as to the type of event in which someone speaks the words. Such words might be part of any wedding. These words are meant for a couple to speak as each person pledges his or her life to the other, and only in that context can one really appreciate what they mean. As a literary document the wedding liturgy is rather devoid of life. It has meaning when two people in love commit themselves to each other.

But imagine someone a millennium from now uncovering a copy of the words from a wedding ceremony. Imagine further that expressions like 'wed', 'wedding' and 'bride' have either fallen out of use or completely changed meaning. A major task in understanding the liturgy the person discovered will be to correctly identify the words as the liturgy of a ceremony we call a 'wedding'. If the reader in the future concludes, for example, that the words were part of a corporate merger or political alliance, she or he will completely miss their role in our world. In a similar way, Gunkel concluded that the primary task of interpreting the Psalms is to identify each one as part of a pattern of language that belonged to a type of event in the life of the people of Israel.

One of the clearest examples of a *Sitz im Leben* is the giving of an offering of well-being as an expression of thanks to God (Lev. 3.1–17; 7.11–18). Jeremiah 33.10–11 describes a circumstance in which two people bring such an offering in a time of peace and prosperity and say, 'Give thanks to the LORD of hosts, for the LORD is good, for his steadfast love endures for ever!' The words come directly from Psalm 136.1, but similar words appear in numerous other psalms (Pss. 30.12; 118.1–4, 29; 138.1). Thus, Gunkel noted that 'Give thanks to the LORD' are not the words of a particular author, but words for a type of occasion. The main tasks of interpretation are to identify the type of words (the genre) and the setting from which they came (*Sitz im Leben*). Many of the settings scholars have proposed have been the subject of much debate, since the evidence for them is often scant. The genres Gunkel identified, however, continue to inform the study of the Psalms and help us grasp the variety of material in the book.

Types of psalms

Gunkel's enduring contribution is a list and description of psalms genres that helps readers map the Psalter according to the type of material that appears in individual psalms. Gunkel identified five main types of psalms:

1 prayers for help by an individual;
2 prayers for help by the community;

3 hymns of praise;
4 thanksgiving songs of the individual;
5 royal psalms.

Scholars following Gunkel have refined and expanded these categories. We will begin with Gunkel's main types and present along with them some of the subtypes other scholars have identified. At the outset, however, several limitations are apparent. Gunkel assumed the genres exist as pure types when in reality such pure expressions of a genre are rare. The fact that scholars have nuanced and changed Gunkel's categories is evidence of that fact, and Gunkel himself recognized 'mixed types' and minor types. Gunkel also assumed an exact correspondence between a psalm's genre and its setting in life or *Sitz im Leben*. Scholars now recognize that it's not so simple. As genres are rarely pure forms, so also the match between genre and setting is not so easy to make.

A final word of caution: putting psalms into genre categories can set expectations for what a psalm says and how it moves and develops that discourage a close reading of the psalm. In fact, each psalm is an individual composition and we should pay careful attention to its language and nuances. We should be ready for a psalm to bend and complicate a genre in unique ways. Far from a sign of weakness, this complexity is one sign of the Psalms' great artistic beauty and profundity of expression. We might compare the genre labels and particular psalms' transcendence of them to the music of modern performance artists who defy exact classification. The best artists do not write music and perform according to a formula for hip-hop, country or heavy metal, though those musical genre labels may reflect some basic orientation. So also the Psalms will often defy simple genre categories. The types of psalm we discuss below are therefore only a useful starting point.

1 Prayers for help by an individual

This type of psalm is by far the most numerous in the Psalter. Some scholars prefer to call these psalms 'individual laments' or 'individual complaint songs'.[6] Lament and complaint are but one element of this type, however, so 'prayer for help' reflects more accurately what the psalms actually say. The central feature is a petition for help by someone in serious trouble.

Typical elements of these prayers are:

(a) a petition to God in first-person style in which the psalmist pleads with God to hear, attend to the psalmist's need, or provide rescue from dire circumstances;

---

6 See Gunkel, *Introduction to Psalms*, pp. 121–2.

(b) a description of trouble that presents the reason for the petition;

(c) justification for the petition that lays out reasons why God should act on behalf of the one who prays;

(d) statements of confidence that God will act in response to the prayer;

(e) a pledge of sacrifice or praise that will come after the psalmist emerges from trouble.

Psalm 13 is one of the clearest examples of this type of psalm. The psalm opens with two verses of complaint that also describe the problem:

> How long, O LORD? Will you forget me for ever?
> How long will you hide your face from me?
> How long must I bear pain in my soul,
> and have sorrow in my heart all day long?
> How long shall my enemy be exalted over me?
> (vv. 1–2(3–4))

In the next two verses the psalmist petitions God for help and offers a reason or justification for the prayer:

> Consider and answer me, O LORD my God!
> Give light to my eyes, or I will sleep the sleep of death,
> and my enemy will say, 'I have prevailed';
> my foes will rejoice because I am shaken.
> (vv. 3–4(4–5))

Verse 5(6) turns to an expression of trust:

> But I trusted in your steadfast love;
> my heart shall rejoice in your salvation.

The psalm ends with a promise of praise:

> I will sing to the LORD,
> because he has dealt bountifully with me.
> (v. 6(7))

The setting for these prayers in most cases is not clear, except that they grew out of an individual person's trouble. Psalm 13.2–3(3–4) perhaps suggests the psalmist is sick and needs healing ('Give light to my eyes, or I will sleep the sleep of death', v. 3b(4b)). Another issue the psalm identifies, however, is the presence of an enemy ready to celebrate the psalmist's death (v. 4(5)). Is the enemy a military foe or a personal enemy? Is the enemy someone who merely looks on the psalmist's trouble with glee, or has this person put a curse on the psalmist to try to bring about sickness and death? The slippery language of the psalm's description of the problem and the enemy is typical, and it illustrates again why it has seemed impossible to link a psalm like this to one person. It could have been the prayer of anyone in trouble. See Chapter 5 for more on the setting of this type of psalm.

One nagging question about these prayers for help by an individual is: what caused the sharp turn from complaint to trust and praise (vv. 5–6(6–7))? One explanation is that these psalms developed in two stages. In the first stage, a person prayed for help and deliverance. Then, after receiving God's salvation, the person concluded the prayer with assurance and praise. The standard theory is that some religious professional helped create these prayers and assisted in the two stages of composing and praying them. It is certainly possible that some of these prayers developed along these lines. As they now stand, however, the assurances of hearing and promises of praise are linked to the initial complaints and petitions. The effect of this structure is that the prayers for help are expressions of faith. This may in fact represent the original intention, for many of the psalms begin with petitions that are already grounded in trust: 'Protect me, O God, for in you I take refuge' (Ps. 16.1).

As if to remind us that not everything has a happy ending, however, two of these prayers do not have any resolution (Pss. 39; 88). Psalm 88 is perhaps the starkest psalm in the Psalter and certainly the darkest of the individual prayers for help.

Subcategory: song of trust

As already noted, the sharp turn to confidence in most of the prayers for help by an individual leads some scholars to propose that what comes after the shift was originally a separate psalm. Whether this is true or not, there are some psalms that only express confidence that God will deliver. Such psalms refer to troubled circumstances but highlight the psalmist's confidence in God as a saviour.

Psalm 23 is the most famous psalm of this type. The first three verses express confidence in God's leadership and protecting presence. As shepherd, the LORD guides the psalmist to nourishment and safety. God 'keeps me alive', as CEB translates the psalmist's testimony in verse 3a. Verses 4–5 then acknowledge the danger that exists all around. The 'darkest valley' (v. 3a) and 'the presence of my enemies' (v. 5a) describe the situation in which the psalmist testifies. The tone throughout is confident assurance that God will not let her go and will not abandon her to the forces of evil. Other examples of this type of psalm include Psalms 34; 40.1–10(2–11); and 62.

2 Prayers for help by the community

Prayers for help by the community are similar to the prayers for help in individual style. They are prayers that respond to national or community tragedies with petitions for God to act. The destruction of Jerusalem and its temple seem to be the occasion for Psalms 74 and 79 and perhaps other prayers for help by the community. These prayers typically include the following elements:

(a) petitions for God to hear and attend to the problems of the community;
(b) descriptions of trouble;
(c) appeal to God's honour and faithfulness in the past;
(d) statements of trust in God and God's goodness;
(e) rehearsals of God's past mighty deeds in order to make the community's suffering 'an issue of the LORD's sovereignty in the world';[7]
(f) promises of praise after God delivers the psalmist's community.

Psalms 44 and 74 are excellent examples of this type of psalm.

3 Hymns of praise

The hymn of praise is one of the basic forms we encounter in the Psalms. As we noted in Chapter 1, those who collected the psalms in Hebrew labelled the book 'Praises' (*tehillim*), which may indicate they conceived the hymn as the most fundamental psalm type. Praise appears in bits and pieces throughout many of the psalm types we are discussing, even in psalms that complain to God of trouble. But some psalms lead with praise and have praise as their main feature. These are the psalms we label 'hymns'.

Hymns have the praise of God as their basic function and purpose. Although the exact settings of these psalms remain elusive in most cases, we might well imagine Ancient Israelites singing or reciting the hymns during

7 James Luther Mays, *Psalms* (Interpretation: A Bible commentary for teaching and preaching; Louisville, KY: Westminster John Knox Press, 1994), p. 25.

great festivals like the Feast of Booths (celebrating both the exodus and the harvest), the Feast of Weeks and the Feast of Pentecost. When the people of Israel gathered to celebrate and praise God, the hymns were surely there to give words to their praise. We are using the term 'hymn' here to refer to a communal psalm that praises God. The language of thanksgiving appears in some of the psalms we might classify as hymns (e.g. Ps. 118). We recognize 'give thanks', however, as language that has a special place in psalms with an individual style.

The expression 'hallelujah' (Hebrew *hallelu-yah*) is 'a hymn condensed to one terse Hebrew sentence'.[8] This liturgical cry consists of a plural imperative (*hallelu*) that calls worshippers to 'Praise!' and the short form of the personal name for God (*yah*, the shortened form of 'Yahweh'). Whether a hymn contains this liturgical cry or not, its aim is to praise God.

Language and style of hymns

The hymns in the Psalter vary in length, content and vocabulary, but they typically have one of two elements of style, or a mixture of both. One common feature of the hymns is the imperative call to worship. The word 'hallelujah' that we mentioned above is an example of such an imperative. Some of the hymns contain nothing but these calls to worship and then statements of why worshippers should praise God. The other dominant feature of the hymns is the description of God's mighty deeds. Some hymns contain almost nothing but this element.

Imperative

Psalm 117 is a pristine example of this element of style since it contains nothing but an imperative call to praise God and a statement of the reason for that praise:

Imperative: Praise the LORD, all you nations! Extol him, all you peoples! (v. 1)

Statements of praise: For great is his steadfast love towards us, and the faithfulness of the LORD endures for ever. (v. 2)

---

8 Mays, *Psalms*, p. 26.

Psalm 100 is another example of this hymnic style. It opens with four verses in which imperatives call worshippers to praise or to take on the posture of praise:

> Make a joyful noise to the LORD, all the earth.
>> Worship the LORD with gladness;
>> come into his presence with singing.
> Know that the LORD is God.
>> It is he that made us, and we are his;
>> we are his people, and the sheep of his pasture.
> Enter his gates with thanksgiving,
>> and his courts with praise.
>> Give thanks to him, bless his name.
> (vv. 1–4)

The final verse then states the reason for praise:

> For the LORD is good;
>> his steadfast love endures for ever,
>> and his faithfulness to all generations.
> (v. 5)

Other hymns that feature this style include Psalms 95, 96, 98 and 134.

Description of God's mighty deeds

Another major stylistic feature of the hymns is a description of what God has done or an exaltation of God's character. Some hymns in which this feature dominates use participles to state what God has done or what God is like. English translators typically render these verbs as simple past or present action. Psalm 104 is a good example. The psalm opens with a statement of intention to praise God: 'Bless the LORD, O my soul' (v. 1a). Then, most of the next 23 verses state what God has done that makes God worthy of praise. For example:

> You stretch out the heavens like a tent.
> (v. 2b)

> You set the earth on its foundations.
> (v. 5a)

You make springs gush forth in the valleys.
(v. 10a)

These statements follow upon the initial declaration, 'You are very great' (v. 1a), which has a second-person verb that expresses the idea. The following lines that describe God's mighty deeds, however, just have participles. Translators could render them 'one who stretches out the heavens like a tent' (v. 2b) and similarly, but they supply the 'you' for a smoother rendering and to be consistent with the opening line.

Psalm 8 is a beautiful example of a hymn with this descriptive style. It speaks from start to finish *to* God with declarations of what God has done:

> O LORD, our Sovereign,
>   how majestic is your name in all the earth!
> You have set your glory above the heavens.
>   Out of the mouths of babes and infants
> you have founded a bulwark because of your foes,
>   to silence the enemy and the avenger.
> (vv. 1–2(2–3))

Although some hymns have either imperatives to praise God or descriptions of God's mighty acts as the dominant feature, many have a mix of the two (e.g. Ps. 136). Therefore, another useful way to classify hymns is according to subject matter.

Hymns according to subject matter

Some of the hymns are 'general' expressions of God's goodness. They call for and facilitate celebration of God's mighty deeds and acts of salvation (e.g. Pss. 29; 68; 147).[9] Other hymns, however, have distinct subject matter that leads us to identify them as special types of praise psalms.

Creation hymns

These are psalms that celebrate God's work as creator by presenting elements of the creation itself as evidence of God's greatness. They point to the order and

---

9 See W. H. Bellinger Jr, *Psalms: A guide to studying the Psalter* (2nd edn; Grand Rapids, MI: Baker Academic, 2012), p. 87.

beauty of the cosmos as a primary example of God's handiwork. These psalms share with Israel's neighbours an understanding of the creation like that in Genesis 1.1—2.4a: the heavens above consist of a dome that holds back the waters of a heavenly sea, and God dwells above those waters (Pss. 115.16; 104.3; Gen. 1.6–8); the earth is a flat disc that God set on pillars so that it would be secure (Pss. 104.5; 136.6); God established boundaries for the seas so humans would have a place to live and flourish (Ps. 104.9; Gen. 1.9–13). These hymns focus on the earth's stability and regularity, which are signs of God's power and patience. Psalms 8, 19, 33, 104 and 136 are in whole or part examples of these hymns.

Enthronement psalms

The enthronement psalms celebrate God's kingship and have God's reign over the cosmos as their main subject. While many psalms assume the idea that God is king (see Chapter 7), the enthronement psalms make the point explicit and focus on divine kingship as a primary theological issue. For Ancient Near Eastern people who acknowledged the presence of many gods, the deity who created the world was king and head of them all. To be creator was to be the ruler of the cosmos. The enthronement psalms declare that the LORD is king. Psalm 96.4–5 states this most directly:

> For great is the LORD, and greatly to be praised;
>   he is to be revered above all gods.
> For all the gods of the peoples are idols,
>   but the LORD made the heavens.

Later the psalm declares, 'Say among the nations, "The LORD is king!"' (v. 10a). These psalms celebrate the LORD's reign first and foremost over the elements of the world: the heavens and the earth, sea and mountains (Pss. 93.1b; 97.4–5). The enthronement psalms declare that the LORD 'established' them, which is to say the LORD put them in order and ensured the creation would not crumble into chaos: 'The world is firmly established; it shall never be moved' (Ps. 96.10; see the ordering of the elements in Gen. 1.1–14). By extension, however, the LORD also rules over the nations and calls them to acknowledge the LORD's sovereignty and the idols they worship as worthless images (Ps. 97.6–7). Part of this call to the nations is the special place of Israel in God's reign (Ps. 95.6–7), but the enthronement psalms also insist that God is perfectly just and brings equity to the peoples. Psalms 47, 93, 95, 96, 97, 98 and 99 are primary examples of enthronement psalms.

Zion songs

Zion songs praise God indirectly by celebrating God's dwelling place on Mount Zion and God's governance of the world from that location. The Zion songs recognize that although God created the cosmos and rules over it, God is present in the creation especially in this one place. 'The LORD of hosts is with us' (Ps. 46.11a(12a)) is a claim that only makes sense in the context of worship on the 'holy hill'. The Zion songs speak of and celebrate God's self-revelation as defender of Israel and ruler of the world on this mountain (Ps. 48.3(4)). The title 'LORD of hosts' associates Israel's God with the ark which David brought to Jerusalem when he established it as Israel's central shrine (Ps. 132; 2 Sam. 6). The hymns that celebrate God's presence on Zion depict the city and its temple as a paradise (Ps. 46.4(5)) and place of safety for all who seek God there (Ps. 84.1–4(2–5)). These psalms testify to the incarnational nature of the psalmist's faith as they speak of the walls and ramparts of the city as enduring symbols of God's sheltering care and refuge (Ps. 48.12–14(13–15)). Psalms 46, 48, 76, 84, 87, 125 and 132 are the primary examples of this type of psalm.

Historical hymns

Several hymns trace Israel's history, typically beginning with the exodus and going through the wilderness wandering towards the promised land. These hymns are not merely epics that remember events of the past, but carefully crafted theological remembrances. For example, Psalm 78 recalls God's salvation of Israel particularly to highlight the faithlessness of Israel's ancestors and God's unmatched grace and fidelity. The psalm testifies to God's rescuing the Israelites from Egypt and leading them miraculously through the wilderness (vv. 12–16) only to have them rebel:

> Yet they sinned still more against him,
>   rebelling against the Most High in the desert.
> They tested God in their heart
>   by demanding the food they craved.
> They spoke against God, saying,
>   'Can God spread a table in the wilderness?'
> (vv. 17–19)

The testimony continues with more accounts of God's protection of Israel and Israel's disobedience (vv. 20–37). Perhaps the central verse of the psalm thematically and theologically is verse 39:

He remembered that they were but flesh,
    a wind that passes and does not come again.

The rest of the psalm gives testimony to the recurring salvation and sinfulness of earlier sections and concludes with God's choice of David to lead Israel. The overall message, however, is that God is and has always been faithful.

Psalm 78 also illustrates the challenge of classifying psalms in narrow genre categories. This and other historical psalms teach about God's goodness in a narrative-like style (see Pss. 105; 106; 136). This psalm in particular begins with the language of instruction (vv. 1–4). The dominant feature of the psalm, however, is the recollection of God's deeds in the past, which is one of the staple features of the hymns.[10]

4 Thanksgiving songs of the individual

Thanksgiving songs are prayers by individuals who have experienced God's help during sickness, trauma or other hardship. The songs celebrate deliverance from trouble with promises of praise and sacrifice. In these prayers the psalmist specifically promises to 'give thanks'. The word 'thanks' in Hebrew is *todah*. The word has the general meaning 'give thanks', but it is also the technical name for a sacrifice of well-being (Lev. 7.12). These psalms contain a liturgy of thanksgiving and they provided the context for offering the thanksgiving offering (Jer. 33.10–11). Psalm 116.17 specifically names the thanksgiving sacrifice as a gift the psalmist pledges because of God's deliverance: 'I will offer to you a thanksgiving sacrifice and call on the name of the LORD.'

Although thanksgiving songs grew out of celebrations of well-being, and thus are similar in tone to hymns of praise, they are really the liturgical counterpart to prayers for help by an individual.[11] These songs speak of the same kinds of trouble and distress complained about in the the individual prayers for help, except that the psalmist speaks now after God has delivered him from hardship. Psalm 30 is a prime example. It begins:

I will extol you, O LORD, for you have drawn me up,
    and did not let my foes rejoice over me.
O LORD my God, I cried to you for help,
    and you have healed me.

---

10 See Mays, *Psalms*, pp. 254–5.
11 Mays, *Psalms*, p. 24.

O LORD, you brought up my soul from Sheol,
> restored me to life from among those gone down to the
> > Pit.

(vv. 1–3(2–4))

The remainder of the psalm alternates between words of exhortation for God's goodness (vv. 4–5(5–6)) and further testimony to the turnaround God provided (vv. 6–12a(7–13a)), all leading to the psalmist's expression of thanks which the final line offers: 'O LORD my God, I will give thanks to you for ever' (v. 12b(13b)).

Psalms of this type are few in number when compared with prayers for help. Perhaps the circumstances of the Psalter's collection and editing called for complaint and petition more than thanksgiving. Nevertheless, the thanksgiving songs give witness to God's attention to those who suffer and to the importance of public acts of gratitude.[12] Psalm 40.1–10(2–11) is another example of this type of psalm. Yet, following this thanksgiving portion of Psalm 40 is a prayer for help (vv. 13–17(14–18)), which appears also as Psalm 70. It gives further evidence that the prayer for help is the dominant form in the Psalter.

Thanksgiving songs of Israel

Although thanksgiving songs arose from individual Israelites' experiences with God's salvation, some psalms seem to borrow the individual's voice to represent the nation as a whole.[13] In Psalms 124 and 129 an individual speaks and invites Israel to join in the thanksgiving ('let Israel now say', Pss. 124.1; 129.1). Psalm 103 may also have had this purpose.

5 Royal psalms

Royal psalms are so named because they have the Israelite king or some circumstance of his life as their main subject. Unlike the other genres, we do not recognize this one by style and vocabulary but by subject matter and an assumed setting in life. That is, royal psalms are set in some event in the life of a king. For example, Psalm 2 begins with the problem of the nations opposing the LORD and the LORD's anointed. 'Anointed' is a title for the king in the Old Testament (1 Sam. 24.6, 10; 26.9, 11). In verses 7–9 the king recalls what God had said to him as God installed him in office: 'You are my son; today I have begotten you'

---

12 Mays, *Psalms*, p. 24.
13 Gunkel, *Introduction to Psalms*, p. 22.

(v. 7). From start to finish the psalm focuses on the king, and the language reflects the coronation rituals and language of the Ancient Near East.[14]

The royal psalms reflect a variety of circumstances and events in the life of the king. Psalm 45 is a poem that honours a king at his wedding. It seems to break the Old Testament's caution about not elevating the king above other members of the community (see Deut. 17.14–20) and it also countermands the notion that when choosing a king 'the LORD does not see as mortals see; they look on the outward appearance, but the LORD looks on the heart' (1 Sam. 16.7). Indeed, the psalm begins by praising the king for his good looks (v. 2(3)). As the poem continues, the poet seems to address the king as 'God' (v. 6(7)).[15] This praise for the human king is similar to the court language of surrounding cultures. It reflects the common idea that the king was the ideal human who represented the intentions of God on earth.

It seems helpful to label psalms about the Israelite king 'royal psalms' because they clearly have that figure and the issues of his life as their main concern. As we will explore further in the next chapter, these psalms also remind us of how central the king was in the religious life of the people of Israel. As a special representative of God, the king was a conduit of divine blessings. So, it is not surprising that numerous psalms celebrate and pray for the monarch. Psalms 20, 21 and 72 are examples of prayers for the king.

There are at least two significant problems, however, with the designation 'royal psalms'. One problem is that it is nearly impossible to know where to draw the line in identifying psalms as royal. If a psalm mentions the king explicitly, the identification seems clear enough. Some scholars have expanded the category, however, based on descriptions of circumstances that seem 'royal' even though there may be no explicit mention of the monarch. For example, John Eaton suggests that psalms that pray for military deliverance and that include military imagery are royal psalms. As a result, the label 'royal psalms' becomes like a magnet that attracts practically every prayer by an individual in the Psalter.[16] Thus, it seems best to limit this category to those psalms that explicitly mention the king, pray for the king or in which the king clearly speaks.

The second problem is that the psalms that are directly connected to the king never name a particular monarch. David is the only king whose name appears within the body of any psalm, but when a psalm mentions him he is

---

14 See J. J. M. Roberts, 'The Old Testament's contribution to messianic expectations', in *The Bible and the Ancient Near East: Collected essays* (Winona Lake, IN: Eisenbrauns, 2002), p. 380.

15 The meaning of v. 6(7) is uncertain. It may intend to say 'Your throne is a throne of God', as NRSV proposes as an alternative translation.

16 John H. Eaton, *Kingship and the Psalms* (London: SCM Press, 1976).

a figure of the past. That raises the question of what the royal psalms actually celebrated or prayed for. Since the early period of the life of the Church, Christians have read the royal psalms as messianic prophecies. Modern critical scholars rejected that traditional idea on grounds that it was only later that Christian communities read the royal psalms in the light of Jesus Christ. It was not the original intent of these psalms. But how do we determine what an 'original' intent might have been?

Scott Starbuck notes that in the literature of Israel's neighbours there are two dominant types of royal poems. One type records the voice of a king addressing a deity. Another praises a king for his prowess in war, faithful leadership and just rule. The overwhelming tendency in these royal prayers is to name the king who prays or whom the prayer praises.[17] Such prayers were part of the monarch's public relations efforts. By praying to the deity the king showed himself faithful and pious. He sought the god's help and presented himself as just and upright. Praise for the king highlighted directly the benefits of his rule.[18] Therefore, it is curious that none of the prayers for or by the king in the Psalms name the king in the body of the psalm itself. They are all anonymous and identify a speaker only in the headings that scribes added later. That raises the question of what the present form of these psalms was intended to be. Did scribes pass them on as royal prayers and testimonies, or did they preserve them as prophecies about a future king or as a portrait of ideal kingship? Although those who preserved the royal psalms did not have Jesus in mind, the anonymous character of these poems provided openness for early Christians to see in them descriptions of the life and ministry of Jesus (see further the Conclusion).

This line of questioning reveals one of the weaknesses of the form-critical study of the Psalms. Although it is useful to classify psalms in order to clarify their content, it is more complicated to determine how a particular psalm developed and spoke to audiences after the 'original' version.

Other types of psalms

Psalms that instruct

Another group that is hard to classify are the psalms that instruct their hearers and readers in how to live and how to understand the nature and character of

---

17 Scott R. A. Starbuck, *Court Oracles in the Psalms: The so-called royal psalms in their Ancient Near Eastern context* (SBLDS 172; Atlanta, GA: Society of Biblical Literature, 1996), pp. 68–82.

18 See the sample of Sumero-Akkadian texts that include royal prayers in Starbuck, *Court Oracles in the Psalms*, pp. 70–2.

God. Some scholars apply the label 'wisdom psalms' to these poems. Others oppose that label because it seems to suggest these psalms came from the teachings of sages like the material in the book of Proverbs.[19] Whether 'wisdom' is accurate or not, some psalms express their intention to teach. Psalm 78 begins:

> Give ear, O my people, to my teaching (*torati*);
>> incline your ears to the words of my mouth.
> I will open my mouth in a parable (*mashal*);
>> I will utter dark sayings from of old,
> things that we have heard and known,
>> that our ancestors have told us.
> (vv. 1–3)

The psalm's introduction continues by saying it intends to pass on the story of the past to children and specifically to 'teach' them (v. 5).

In a similar way Psalm 49 begins with a call for the audience to 'hear' (v. 1(2)) and with the declaration:

> My mouth shall speak wisdom;
>> the meditation of my heart shall be understanding.
> I will incline my ear to a proverb;
>> I will solve my riddle to the music of the harp.
> (vv. 3–4(4–5))

Psalm 34 is another psalm that has instruction as a main goal and that includes intentional language about instruction (v. 11(12)). One of the main features of instructional psalms is that they teach alternative ways one can go in life. Often the psalms label these two ways and the people who represent them as 'righteous' and 'wicked' (see Pss. 1; 34; 37).

Liturgies

Liturgies are psalms that contain elements of different styles and subject matter for the purpose of performing the words. One sign of liturgical qualities is the presence of different voices or of questions that then receive a response. Psalms

---

19 Principally, James L. Crenshaw, *Old Testament Wisdom: An introduction* (3rd edn; Louisville, KY: Westminster John Knox Press, 2010), p. 185.

15 and 24 are 'gate liturgies' or 'entrance liturgies' that ask about the requirements of entering the temple precincts:

Who may abide in your tent? Who may dwell on your holy hill?
(Ps. 15.1)

Who shall ascend the hill of the LORD? And who shall stand in his holy place?
(Ps. 24.3)

In both cases a voice answers the questions with descriptions of a person who is spiritually pure and who lives with neighbours justly and compassionately (Pss. 15.2–5; 24.4).

Psalm 121 is a liturgy for pilgrims that seems to envisage either a journey to the Temple from a distance or from the Temple to the home. The pilgrimage leader or a priest sending the people away leads a litany of promises for safe travel and divine protection. The question in verse 1, 'from where will my help come?' receives an answer in verse 2, 'My help comes from the LORD, who made heaven and earth'. The declarations and promises in the rest of the psalm continue to answer the question and may represent yet another voice in the procession.

Conclusion

The genre labels we have sketched here continue to be an important tool that scholars use to classify and describe the psalms in the Psalter. We have observed already, however, that the genre labels have limits and many psalms defy neat classification as they transcend a genre or combine features of more than one genre. Also, some scholars have found other descriptive labels useful. Among them are Walter Brueggemann's categories of psalms of orientation, disorientation and new orientation.[20] The genre labels of Hermann Gunkel, however, intended to connect these psalm types to certain occasions of performance. We now turn to explore some of the theories of the use of psalms.

---

20 See his use of this language in Walter Brueggemann, *The Message of the Psalms: A theological commentary* (Minneapolis, MN: Augsburg, 1984).

5

Settings for performance
of the Psalms

The most valuable thing the Psalms do for me is to express the same
delight in God which made David dance.
(C. S. Lewis)

The Psalms are brimming with activity. They describe and call for shouting,
singing, clapping, dancing, and sounding music with horns, strings and per-
cussion instruments. This seems to confirm the theory that many, perhaps
most, of the psalms grew out of public events in which Israelites performed
their lyrics. It also affirms Gunkel's basic assumption that the Psalms had their
original expression in Israel's worship and only later became written texts.
Gunkel's conclusions have been the broad consensus of Old Testament
scholarship for the past century.[1] When we ask more specifically how Ancient
Israelites performed the Psalms, however, we find a dizzying array of theories that scholars have developed.[2] Despite these uncertainties, the subject is
important because it reminds us that the Psalms grew out of real-life problems and celebrations. The words of the Psalms reflect the prayers and praises
of Ancient Israelites whose lives hung in the balance when they came before
God. For that reason Gunkel thought that recapturing the settings of psalms
in worship revealed the life of the Psalms.

Cultic setting of the Psalms

As we noted in the previous chapter, when Gunkel began his research most
scholars considered psalms artistic pieces that they could interpret in the
light of the life circumstances of their authors. Gunkel shared this view and

---

1 See the summary of this period of research in Erhard S. Gerstenberger, 'Psalms', in *Old Testament Form Criticism* (ed. John H. Hayes; San Antonio, TX: Trinity University Press, 1974), pp. 179–88.
2 See Jerome F. D. Creach, 'The Psalms and the cult', in *Interpreting the Psalms: Issues and approaches* (ed. Philip S. Johnston and David G. Firth; Leicester: Apollos, 2005), pp. 119–37.

specifically thought the Psalter in present form contained the spiritual songs of pious Israelites who lived during the Maccabean period (167–64 BCE). Nevertheless, he did not think the language of the Psalms began with individual authors during that period. Rather, the language of the Psalms grew out of the common life of the people of Israel. The word for those common life events is **cult**.

What is the 'cult'?

Every religion has three dimensions:

1 doctrine – the expression of beliefs, the foundational ideas on which the faith rests;
2 ethics – the system of behaviour that puts basic beliefs into practice;
3 worship – the public celebration and expression of the faith that encourages and practises communion with God.

The term 'cult' refers to the last of these. The Norwegian scholar Sigmund Mowinckel defines it as 'the socially established and regulated holy acts and words in which the encounter and communion of the Deity with the congregation is established, developed, and brought to its ultimate goal'.[3] We must be careful, however, not to divide faith neatly into categories that separate worship completely from doctrine and ethics. In worship, Ancient Israelites expressed their beliefs and also the ideals by which they lived. The Psalms were at the centre of all three of these and had a particular place in worship.

The Jerusalem Temple provided the most high-profile setting for Israel's cult. Worshippers went there to make sacrifices, to celebrate annual festivals, and probably also to participate in national ceremonies such as the coronation of a king, celebrations of victory in battle, or lament after military defeat. Still, there is much we don't know about how all these celebrations took place in the Temple and its precincts. For example, Old Testament texts that describe and prescribe sacrifices do not mention lyrics or music at all. This leads Israel Knohl to conclude that Israel's sacrificial cult was completely silent. He argues that the dancing, singing and clapping that so many psalms describe were part of popular religious expressions outside the Temple.[4] The focus of temple activity was sacrifice, he insists. There are a number of weaknesses to this

---

3 Sigmund Mowinckel, *The Psalms in Israel's Worship* (trans. D. R. Ap-Thomas; Oxford: Blackwell, 1962), vol. 1, p. 15.
4 Israel Knohl, *The Sanctuary of Silence: The Priestly Torah and the Holiness School* (Minneapolis, MN: Fortress Press, 1995), p. 42.

argument, one being that the argument itself is an 'argument from silence'. The fact that prescriptions for how priests should perform sacrifices do not include music or lyrics may only mean the passages' sole interest was in the technical demands and requirements of the sacrificial rituals. A larger problem is that so many passages in the Psalter and outside it speak of the Temple as a place where music, prayer and worship rituals went on in abundance. The words of Psalm 100.4 seem clear on this point:

> Enter his gates with thanksgiving,
>   and his courts with praise.

Psalm 84 speaks explicitly about praising God in the Temple:

> How lovely is your dwelling-place,
>   O Lord of hosts!
> My soul longs, indeed it faints
>   for the courts of the Lord;
> my heart and my flesh sing for joy
>   to the living God.
> Even the sparrow finds a home,
>   and the swallow a nest for herself,
> where she may lay her young,
>   at your altars, O Lord of hosts,
>   my King and my God.
> Happy are those who live in your house,
>   ever singing your praise.
> (vv. 1–4(2–5))

In fairness to Knohl, the Psalms generally downplay sacrifice, and Knohl highlights just how much we do not know about the various worship practices in the Temple and how sacrificial ritual might have been linked, or not linked, to music and lyrical expressions of faith. Much of our opinion depends on how we define 'cult'. If it refers to the narrow world of Zadokite priests and sacrificial rituals, perhaps Knohl is right. The worship of the Temple, however, surely included much more.

As we consider the nature of temple worship, we should also consider that Israel's cult almost certainly involved ceremonies and religious practices that took place outside the Temple. Some 'public' ceremonies such as healing rituals likely took place in family or clan settings. A seriously ill person perhaps could not travel to the Temple, and that person's presence would have rendered the space ritually unclean.[5] Although there is no direct evidence of this type of ceremony in family and clan gatherings, we have stories of Elijah and Elisha healing the children of widows in their homes (1 Kings 17.17–24; 2 Kings 4.18–37). There is also evidence from other cultures of such healing ceremonies, in which a shaman or a recognized healer performed rituals for healing in local gatherings.[6] From our modern perspective we might call such ceremonies 'private', but they involved rituals and religious professionals. For ancient people the line between public and personal was never so exact. Indeed, in ancient society the cult facilitated contact with a reality to which the cult participant ascribed 'life-creating, order-establishing, and meaning-giving power'.[7] Therefore all of life was punctuated by sacral activity of a communal and ritualistic character.

Role of lyrics in the cult

When Gunkel developed the genre categories we considered in Chapter 4, he was working with the theory that the Psalms represented the lyrical component of the cult.[8] There is ample evidence in Old Testament narratives to prove the general point that rituals and lyrics were inextricably bound up in cultic practice.[9] For example, Leviticus 9.22–24 states that Aaron and Moses blessed the Israelites, noting specifically that Aaron 'lifted his hands towards the people' (v. 22). Although we do not know the contents of the blessing Aaron gave, this type of setting and action likely form the backdrop to the great priestly blessing in Numbers 6.22–26. Another example appears in Numbers 21. When the Israelites came to Beer (meaning 'well') to seek water, they sang:

> Spring up, O well! – Sing to it! –
>   the well that the leaders sank,
> that the nobles of the people dug,
>   with the sceptre, with the staff.
> (Num. 21.17–18)

---

5 Erhard S. Gerstenberger, 'Non-temple psalms: the cultic setting revisited', in *The Oxford Handbook of the Psalms* (ed. William P. Brown; Oxford: Oxford University Press, 2014), pp. 339–41 (338–49).

6 Gerstenberger, 'Non-temple psalms', pp. 341–2.

7 Franz Stolz, *Psalmen im nachkultischen Raum* (Theologische Studien 129; Zurich: Theologischer Verlag, 1983), p. 7.

8 Hermann Gunkel with Joachim Begrich, *An Introduction to the Psalms: The genres of the religious lyric of Israel* (trans. James D. Nogalski; Macon, GA: Mercer University Press, 1998; German original 1933), p. 11.

9 Note the fuller list of examples in Gunkel, *Introduction to Psalms*, pp. 7–13.

Here the people included in their search for water a ritual that included a song. Perhaps the best general example, however, is the account of Israel's celebration after the defeat of Pharaoh and his army at the Red Sea in Exodus 15.1–21. The text reports that Miriam and the women of the camp danced, played tambourines (v. 20) and praised God saying:

> Sing to the Lord, for he has triumphed gloriously;
>> horse and rider he has thrown into the sea.
> (v. 21b)

Other passages portray similar victory celebrations with women dancing, playing instruments and singing (Judg. 11.34; 1 Sam. 18.6–9).

Hints of cultic settings

Outside the Psalter

In addition to these general illustrations of lyrics bound to cultic acts, there are passages outside the Psalms that provide direct evidence that some psalms specifically, or elements of language used in some psalms, were part of cultic events and celebrations. Numbers 10.35–36 reports that when the ark moved from its place Moses would say, 'Arise, O Lord, let your enemies be scattered, and your foes flee before you' (v. 35), and likewise when the ark came back to its place he would say, 'Return, O Lord of the ten thousand thousands of Israel' (v. 36). This narrative uses language that appears in numerous psalms that refer to the Lord 'on the move'. For example, Psalm 68.1(2) calls on God to 'rise up' and scatter the enemies. Later in the psalm there is record of God 'going out' before the people and 'marching' through the wilderness (v. 7(8)). The Israelites likely experienced God arising and moving as the ark of the covenant symbolized God's presence in battle. Psalm 132.8 calls on God to 'rise up' and 'go to your resting-place'. This psalm recalls directly how David brought the ark to Jerusalem and there established a 'dwelling-place' for the Lord (v. 5). The narrative in Numbers 10 thus gives us a picture of how a procession involving the ark might have taken place and how the language of the Psalms might have played a part in it. See also Psalm 24.7–10.

As we noted in Chapter 4, Jeremiah 33.10–11 associates a particular psalm with a cultic act. The passage reports Jeremiah's prophecy that when the Lord restores good fortune to Judah there will once again be occasion to bring thank-offerings to the Temple (see Lev. 7.11–18). Jeremiah declares that Israelites will bring such offerings and will recite the words of Psalm 136.1:

Give thanks to the LORD of hosts,
  for the LORD is good,
for his steadfast love endures for ever!
(Jer. 33.11)

Likewise, Job 33 gives a scenario of a person who experiences healing and then comes into God's 'presence with joy' (v. 26) and 'sings' a testimony to what God has done (vv. 27–30). Both of these passages indicate the act of giving thanks in worship through song and, in the case of Jeremiah 33, also with an offering.

In the Psalms

Psalm headings

As we noted in Chapter 1, psalm headings contain a variety of comments that appear to direct those who performed the psalms in worship. Some seem to give directions for instruments to accompany the lyrics ('with stringed instruments', Pss. 4; 6; 54; 55; 61; 67; 76; and perhaps 'for the flutes', Ps. 5). Others give information on a tune or mode of performance. This is perhaps the meaning of the term 'according to', which was attached to expressions like 'The Deer of the Dawn' (Ps. 22), 'Lilies' (Pss. 45; 69) and 'The Dove on Far-off Terebinths' (Ps. 56). The mention of harps and lyres in 1 Chronicles 15.20–21 suggests that these expressions indeed relate to a way of performing music. That passage reports that David established the music and worship of the Temple and that certain musicians specialized in particular types of performance: 'Zechariah, Aziel, Shemiramoth, Jehiel, Unni, Eliab, Maaseiah, and Benaiah were to play harps *according to Alamoth*; but Mattithiah, Eliphelehu, Mikneiah, Obed-edom, Jeiel, and Azaziah were to lead with lyres *according to The Sheminith*'.[10] 'According to The Sheminith' and 'according to Alamoth' also appear in psalm headings (Pss. 6; 12; 46).

Some of the headings also include notes about an occasion for the use of that particular psalm:

Psalm 30: 'a Song at the dedication of the temple';
Psalm 38: 'for the memorial offering';
Psalm 92: 'a Song for the Sabbath Day'.

---

10 Emphasis added.

The headings of Psalms 120—134 may also indicate how Israelites used them in worship. The common words 'A Song of Ascents' connect them to the practice of pilgrimage to Jerusalem.[11] Jewish tradition holds that these psalms were the songs of exiles as they returned from Babylon.[12] The heading does not necessarily mean Israelites recited them while on their way to Jerusalem. It is possible this little collection promoted the practice and that Israelite communities used it to teach such devotion and piety. It is easy to imagine, however, how the words of these psalms supplied liturgy for pilgrimage. Psalm 121 in particular has a liturgical character that claims promises of God's protection for those who are travelling:

> The LORD will keep you from all evil;
>> he will keep your life.
> The LORD will keep your going out and your coming in
>> from this time on and for evermore.

Instructions and invitations within the Psalms

The psalms themselves frequently reference ritual acts and give directions to worshippers. On the most basic level, many of the hymns include imperatives that call worshippers to praise God (47.1(2); 95.1–2; 96.1–3; 98.1; 100.1; 105.1–2; 113.1; 134.1–2). Many psalms also invite worshippers to sing (81.1–2(2–3); 144.9; 147.7) and play instruments (81.2–3(3–4); 144.9; 147.7; 149.3; 150.3–5). They direct the audience to clap and shout (47.1(2)), dance (149.3), process (132.7) and make sacrifices (118.27). All of this suggests these songs are part of an active, public performance, not originally for private reading and reflection.

In addition to these direct statements about cultic performance, many psalms have antiphonal qualities (as Ps. 121 above) that suggest worshippers read or recited them in parts. Psalm 118 opens with an invitation to praise, 'O give thanks to the LORD, for he is good' (v. 1a), followed by a statement of why God is worthy of praise, 'his steadfast love endures for ever' (v. 1b; see also v. 29). The response in verse 1b then recurs throughout the next three verses, showing that various groups uttered the words of the psalm (Israel, v. 2; house of Aaron, v. 3; those who fear the LORD, v. 4): 'His steadfast love endures for ever' (see also Pss. 115.9–11; 135.19–20; 136).

---

11 See the history of interpretation summarized in Loren D. Crow, *The Songs of Ascents (Psalms 120–134): Their place in Israelite history and religion* (SBLDS 148; Atlanta, GA: Scholars Press, 1996), pp. 1–27.

12 *The Midrash on Psalms* (trans. William G. Braude; Yale Judaica Series 13; New Haven, CT: Yale University Press, 1959), vol. 2, p. 289.

In some psalms a simple shift in voices seems to indicate a performance that involved more than one person. For example, Psalm 75 begins with a declaration of praise spoken by a worshipper (v. 1(2)). Then the LORD himself speaks for the rest of the psalm (vv. 2–10(3–11)). Similarly Psalm 81.1–5a(2–6a) expresses a call to worship and a congregation's response, but verse 5b(6b) introduces 'a voice I had not known'. The voice is the voice of God, who speaks to the end of the psalm (vv. 6–16(7–17)). This gives the psalm a dramatic character and suggests a community recited it.

Imagining the Psalms in worship

All of these features of the Psalms we have highlighted suggest they grew out of performances of psalms. Exactly what that performance looked and sounded like, however, is a great mystery. Many scholars have attempted to 'read between the lines' of references to gestures and activities in order to sketch out how and when various psalms might have played a role in cultic practice.

Parades and processions

At least one passage outside the Psalter gives us a picture of a worship event that involves the Psalms directly. The picture is of a grand parade that led to the site in Jerusalem on which the Israelites would build their temple. According to 1 Chronicles 15.1—16.36, David led a procession of the ark to Jerusalem, accompanied by Levites appointed to play and sing. They brought up the ark 'with shouting, to the sound of the horn, trumpets, and cymbals, and made loud music on harps and lyres' (1 Chron. 15.28). When the ark was in place David 'appointed the singing of praises to the LORD by Asaph and his kindred' (1 Chron. 16.7). The passage records the content of their praise to be segments of Psalms 105, 95 and 106 (1 Chron. 16.8–34). The original version of this event in 2 Samuel 6 is less elaborate and does not include these details related to the Psalms, but both versions of the event show us a picture of worship as a parade, a grand procession to the site of the Temple. That is enough to fuel the imagination as to how worshippers might have performed some of the Psalms.

As we have already noted, quite a number of psalms speak of the LORD on the move (e.g. Ps. 68.7–18(8–19)). Psalm 68.24–27(25–28) speaks specifically of this in connection with procession into the sanctuary:

Your solemn processions are seen, O God,
the processions of my God, my King, into the sanctuary –

the singers in front, the musicians last,
    between them girls playing tambourines:
'Bless God in the great congregation,
    the Lord, O you who are of Israel's fountain!'
There is Benjamin, the least of them, in the lead,
    the princes of Judah in a body,
    the princes of Zebulun, the princes of Naphtali.

While this psalm describes the procession, other psalms seem to include liturgy for such a parade. The language of Psalm 24.7–10 suggests the psalm was a liturgy accompanied by a grand procession, perhaps featuring the ark of the covenant entering the Temple and taking its place in the holy of holies. The psalm's labels for God – 'King of glory' and 'Lord of hosts' – identify God as one who moved to the sanctuary and sat enthroned above the cherubim. The psalm as a whole seems to imagine and dramatize that procession.

Psalm 118 begins with liturgy (vv. 1–4) and verses 26–27 speak of movement that seems to indicate a processional of some kind:

Blessed is the one who comes in the name of the Lord.
    We bless you from the house of the Lord.
The Lord is God,
    and he has given us light.
Bind the festal procession with branches,
    up to the horns of the altar.

The New Testament testifies to how Israelites at a later time recited the words of this psalm during the Passover festival and how some participants saw Jesus dramatically taking on the identity of 'one who comes in the name of the Lord' (Matt. 21.6–11; Mark 11.7–11; Luke 19.35–38; John 12.12–13).

Israel's festivals

A more specific setting for some psalms involves Israel's great festivals. According to Leviticus 23, Israel had three 'appointed festivals' each year that all adult males were to attend:

1 Festival of Unleavened Bread and Passover (Lev. 23.4–8);
2 Festival of Harvest or 'First Fruits' (see Lev. 23.9–14);
3 Festival of Ingathering, which occurred seven weeks after the reception of first fruits (Lev. 23.16).

Each of these festivals had connections to agricultural celebrations and later incorporated celebrations of the exodus, wilderness wandering and giving of the law.

Although we don't know exactly how Ancient Israelites celebrated these festivals, many scholars imagine how certain psalms might have fitted within them. Given the connection of the autumn festivals to the harvest, words like those in Psalm 65.9–13(10–14) seem pertinent:[13]

> You visit the earth and water it;
>   you greatly enrich it;
> the river of God is full of water;
>   you provide the people with grain,
>   for so you have prepared it.
> You water its furrows abundantly,
>   settling its ridges,
> softening it with showers,
>   and blessing its growth.
> You crown the year with your bounty;
>   your wagon tracks overflow with richness.
> The pastures of the wilderness overflow,
>   the hills gird themselves with joy,
> the meadows clothe themselves with flocks,
>   the valleys deck themselves with grain,
>   they shout and sing together for joy.

Since Israel's festivals also highlighted the story of its salvation, psalms that rehearse that story would also seem to have had a place in the celebration. For example, we might imagine the liturgy in Psalm 136.10–15 as part of the Passover celebration:[14]

> who struck Egypt through their firstborn,
>   for his steadfast love endures for ever;
> and brought Israel out from among them,
>   for his steadfast love endures for ever;
> with a strong hand and an outstretched arm,

---

13 See Marvin E. Tate, *Psalms 51–100* (Word Biblical Commentary 20; Waco, TX: Word Books, 1990), p. 143.

14 See Frank-Lothar Hossfeld and Erich Zenger, *Psalms 3: A commentary on Psalms 101–150* (trans. Linda M. Maloney; Hermeneia; Minneapolis, MN: Fortress Press, 2011), p. 504.

for his steadfast love endures for ever;
who divided the Red Sea in two,
    for his steadfast love endures for ever;
and made Israel pass through the midst of it,
    for his steadfast love endures for ever;
but overthrew Pharaoh and his army in the Red Sea,
    for his steadfast love endures for ever.

Although these connections between the language of the psalm and the festival celebrations highlight the possible ways Israelites used such psalms in worship, they also illustrate how much we do not know about Israelite worship. We also note that Israelites reread and reinterpreted psalms like these as they passed them on. Psalm 136 now stands alongside Psalm 135 as its 'twin' in the Psalter. These two psalms together give a grand testimony to God's salvation of Israel. They also appear immediately before the great complaint in Psalm 137, which leads us to wonder what theological role these psalms played beyond the celebrations of Israel's festivals.

The prophets speak?

Psalms 50, 81 and 95 share one prominent feature: they contain God's word to worshippers. For example, in Psalm 50 God speaks against the people for offering sacrifices without true faith:

Hear, O my people, and I will speak,
    O Israel, I will testify against you.
    I am God, your God.
Not for your sacrifices do I rebuke you;
    your burnt-offerings are continually before me.
I will not accept a bull from your house,
    or goats from your folds.
For every wild animal of the forest is mine,
    the cattle on a thousand hills.
I know all the birds of the air,
    and all that moves in the field is mine.
(vv. 7–11)

In Psalm 81.5(6) the psalmist declares, 'I hear a voice I had not known'. Then the 'voice' enters. It is God speaking in first person to remind the Israelites of their salvation from slavery in Egypt (vv. 6–16(7–17)):

I relieved your shoulder of the burden;
  your hands were freed from the basket.
In distress you called, and I rescued you;
  I answered you in the secret place of thunder;
  I tested you at the waters of Meribah.
(vv. 6–7(7–8))

In a similar way Psalm 95.8–11 recalls how the Israelites did not listen to God's voice and tested God at Meribah. The one who pronounces the judgement by this memory of the past is the LORD, who led them through the wilderness.

In each of these psalms we have the words of God that come in the midst of other speech by worship leaders. The best theory about how the Israelites performed these psalms in worship is that a prophet voiced the words of God, just as the prophets spoke directly for God in their oracles.[15] Once again, however, the exact nature of ceremonies in which prophets spoke these words is shrouded in mystery.

Educational settings

Quite a number of psalms have didactic elements that lead some scholars to give them genre labels like 'wisdom' or 'instruction' (Pss. 9–10; 25; 33; 34; 37; 39; 49; 73; 78; 112). Prominent here are psalms that teach the difference between the righteous and the wicked (Ps. 1) and assure hearers that the wicked will perish in the end (Ps. 73). The psalms that highlight and promote the benefits of Torah belong to this group (Pss. 1; 19; 119). Scholars have debated furiously their origin and purpose. Some think these psalms came from scribal schools or 'wisdom' circles like those that produced the books of Proverbs and Ecclesiastes.[16] Although their origins are far from clear, their intention to teach is. Some psalms in this group call hearers to pay attention and to receive instruction. Psalm 78 opens:

Give ear, O my people, to my teaching;
  incline your ears to the words of my mouth.
I will open my mouth in a parable;
  I will utter dark sayings from of old,

---

15 See Tate, *Psalms 51–100*, pp. 321–3.

16 Contra this view see James L. Crenshaw, *Old Testament Wisdom: An introduction* (3rd edn; Louisville, KY: Westminster John Knox Press, 2010), pp. 180–5.

things that we have heard and known,
    that our ancestors have told us.
We will not hide them from their children;
    we will tell to the coming generation
the glorious deeds of the LORD, and his might,
    and the wonders that he has done.
(vv. 1–4)

Although we have no exact information about how Israelites recited or sang psalms like this one, we have a possible model in the story of Torah instruction in Nehemiah 8. The story says the people gathered around Ezra, who read from a Torah scroll. After Ezra read from the scroll, the Levites instructed people in what it meant (vv. 5–8).[17]

Specific theories of cultic settings

New Year festival and the enthronement psalms

Just as Gunkel introduced genre categories that help us see the variety of material in the Psalms, his student, Sigmund Mowinckel, presented theories about how Israelites performed various psalms. Mowinckel's theories still command attention today.

Mowinckel drew extensively from evidence outside the Bible, particularly documents that detail the great New Year festival in Babylon, the Akitu festival. The Akitu festival culminated when the Babylonians declared their chief god, Marduk, to be king of the pantheon of gods. Mowinckel thought the Akitu festival represented a general pattern of religious belief and practice that would have influenced the Israelites. So, he proposed that the Israelites too celebrated a New Year festival in the autumn, at the time later texts identify with the harvest festival (Exod. 23.16; 34.22; Lev. 23.33–43). He thought the centre of this celebration was a claim of the LORD's kingship just as the Babylonians declared Marduk king. The primary evidence within the Psalms was the so-called enthronement psalms, which focus on the theme of God as king (Pss. 47; 93; 95—99). Mowinckel believed the final day of the festival was a grand enactment of the LORD's enthronement, marked by a procession of the ark to the Temple. Central to the celebration were the words 'The LORD is king'

---

17 See Gerstenberger, 'Non-temple psalms', pp. 345–6.

(Pss. 93.1; 97.1; 99.1), which he proposed the Israelites shouted as they concluded their parade to the holy place.[18]

Mowinckel thought further that the Israelite king led this celebration of God's kingship and the procession to the Temple, and the Israelites also reaffirmed and celebrated his reign, just as the Babylonians did for their monarchs in the Akitu festival. Thus, Mowinckel thought the royal psalms were at the centre of the Israelite New Year festival along with the enthronement psalms. They provided words to declare and celebrate the earthly king as chief representative of the heavenly rule of God (Pss. 2; 89.1–37(2–38); 110). Furthermore, Mowinckel proposed that the 'I' in the prayers for help in most cases represented the voice of the king. The king was not expressing personal complaints for the most part; rather, he was representing Israel's 'corporate personality'. So he thought the Israelites ritually enacted the king's reign in the festival – his struggle with enemies, his victories and defeats.

There have been three prominent opinions on Mowinckel's theory.

1. Some scholars reject Mowinckel's notion of a central New Year festival. They note that the Old Testament contains no direct evidence of such a celebration. Moreover, some critics have pointed out that Mowinckel relies too heavily on later rabbinical material that describes Israel's festivals. They point out that such material is too far removed from the time of Israel's kings to provide useful information for reconstructing a festival in the monarchical period.[19]

2. Other scholars accept Mowinckel's view that a Babylonian-like event occurred in Israel and they go even further to propose that Israel's cult fitted a general pattern in Ancient Near Eastern religious expression. Among the more radical proposals was that put forward by scholars in the so-called Myth and Ritual School. They held that the Israelite king stood in the place of God in the cult and was himself understood as a semi-divine character. The Myth and Ritual adherents hence pressed Mowinckel's ideas in ways he did not intend.[20]

3. Perhaps most scholars have agreed with Mowinckel's proposal in general, but they have modified it modestly. For example, Gunkel agreed with

---

18 Mowinckel, *Psalms*, vol. 1, pp. 106–92.

19 Mowinckel, *Psalms*, vol. 1, pp. 121–5. See the summary of critiques in J. J. Stamm, 'Ein Vierteljahrhundert Psalmenforschung', *Theologische Rundschau* 23 (1955), pp. 48–9; for an excellent evaluation in English, see John Eaton, 'The Psalms and Israelite worship', in G. W. Anderson, ed., *Tradition and Interpretation: Essays by members of the Society for Old Testament Study* (Oxford: Clarendon Press, 1979), pp. 241–72.

20 Gerstenberger, 'Psalms', p. 186.

Mowinckel that the Israelites likely had a New Year festival that focused on the LORD's kingship. He disagreed with him, however, on the cultic nature of the enthronement psalms as they now appear in the Psalter. Gunkel's objection was based on the fact that the enthronement poems occur in bits and pieces also in Isaiah 40—66, a portion of the book of Isaiah that dates to the Babylonian exile (587–539 BCE) or afterwards.[21] For the great prophet of the exile, these poetic lines are eschatological pieces that look forward to God's reign, which would become clear when Judah returned to its homeland. Gunkel thought it logical that the prophet had reinterpreted the enthronement material for his own historical situation. Since the enthronement psalms in the Psalter are identical in form and content to what we have in the latter part of Isaiah, it also seemed to follow that these psalms are not the cultic originals, but later eschatological poems influenced by Isaiah 40—66.[22] Therefore, for Gunkel the psalms at the heart of Mowinckel's proposal were not from the First Temple period, but later poems that were not cultic at all.

Cultic rituals and psalms of the individual

Just as there are competing theories regarding how Israelites used the Psalms in national cultic events, there are also many views on how particular poems functioned in ceremonies centring on individuals. As we have already seen, some scholars understand the 'I' of these psalms to be the king. There are several interrelated theories, however, that attempt to explain how ordinary Israelites used psalms in ceremonies related to sickness and healing.

Concerning the individual prayers for help Mowinckel also had a theory. He believed some of these psalms came from times of sickness caused by curses or spells the psalmist's enemies had cast on him. He identified the people whom the psalms call 'evildoers' with these cursing enemies (Ps. 10.15). Mowinckel imagined that healing from such maladies took place in the Temple, in rituals designed and carried out by priests.[23]

Since the time of Mowinckel a number of other scholars have developed theories that explain the setting for the prayers for help differently. Hans Schmidt proposed that some of these psalms grew out of a judicial process in which an accused person sought vindication through a trial in the Temple.[24] Numerous passages describe such a trial (1 Kings 8.31–32; Deut. 17.8–13;

21 Isa. 40.10; 44.23; 49.13; 55.12; 59.19; 60.1; 62.11.

22 Gunkel, *Introduction to Psalms*, pp. 80–1.

23 Mowinckel, *Psalms*, vol. 2, pp. 1–8.

24 Hans Schmidt, *Das Gebet der Angeklagten im Alten Testament* (Giessen: Alfred Töpelmann, 1928).

21.1–8). Deuteronomy 17.8–13 most clearly identifies the Temple and the Levites on duty as the locus of judgement. Psalm 17 is an example of a psalm that we might read against this backdrop. It begins with a call for hearing in verses 1–2 ('Hear a just cause, O LORD'), and the rest of the psalm presents images of adversaries who falsely accuse the psalmist. The fact that the psalmist asks for God's favourable judgement and for the LORD to confront the accusers (v. 13) lends credence to Schmidt's proposal.

His thesis has continued to gain adherents through the years and other scholars have expanded it with more imaginative details. L. Delekat proposes a setting similar to that of Schmidt, but he emphasizes that the accused stayed overnight in the Temple, which many of these psalms imply. He describes in amazing detail what took place during the night, how the accused received oracles, had dreams and underwent ordeals. He proposes that the accused inscribed the psalms that express this experience on temple or sanctuary walls.[25] Karel van der Toorn revised these theories of a judicial process by focusing on the ordeal that the accused underwent during the night in the Temple. He imagines that the psalmist submitted to a drinking ordeal, like that described in Numbers 5.11–31. For him, this theory explains the presence of a cup in some of these psalms (Pss. 11.6; 16.5; 23.5).[26]

This final expression of the thesis in a general way illustrates both the strengths and weaknesses of them all. Van der Toorn is right to emphasize the temple setting of the psalms in question, for there are frequent references to seeing God's face (Ps. 11.7) or dwelling in the holy place (Ps. 23.6). To make the psalms fit the details of his thesis, however, he must apply some of the data in ways that seem contrary to their intention. For example, it is unlikely that the references to a cup in these psalms indicate ordeals. Cups usually relate to celebration (Ps. 23.5), they symbolize God's protection (Ps. 16.5) or they indicate God's judgement upon the psalmist's enemies (Ps. 11.6).

Erhard Gerstenberger offers a promising explanation for some psalms that is different from the theories we have just described. He focuses on psalms he believes arose from healing ceremonies. Gerstenberger proposes that many of these psalms grew out of family ceremonies of healing in which a local cult figure officiated. To support the notion of such a ceremony in the home, he notes that Hezekiah sought out a ritual expert (the prophet Isaiah) when he was sick (Isa. 38). Likewise 2 Samuel 12 depicts David practising penitence

25 L. Delekat, *Asylie und Schutzorakel an Zionheiligtum* (Leiden: Brill, 1967).

26 Karel van der Toorn, 'Ordeal', in *Anchor Bible Dictionary* (ed. David Noel Freedman; Garden City, NY: Doubleday, 1992), vol. 5, pp. 40–2.

at home. According to Gerstenberger, these examples raise the possibility, indeed the likelihood, that many psalms had their setting in the Second Temple period and apart from the official worship of the Temple itself.[27] He proposes that many psalms of sickness reflect an ancient version of 'group therapy' in which the priest from the clan or tribe restored the infirm to full communion with the family group.[28]

Re-use of cultic psalms

When we survey the theories about how Israelites performed the Psalms it becomes apparent that the evidence for specific proposals is scant, and yet the language of the Psalms is pliable enough that it can bend to the efforts of scholars like those we have discussed. The Psalms were primary liturgical material in the Second Temple period (and beyond), as psalm superscriptions and some Old Testament narratives (1 Chron. 15—16) clearly indicate. Some of the psalms may also reflect the worship of the period of Israel's kings. Nevertheless, the precise number of psalms that are cultic and the exact manner in which the Israelites performed them eludes us, with the possible exception of the song of thanksgiving (see Jer. 33.10–11). Furthermore, even psalms that show clear connections to Israel's worship underwent changes as the Israelites reread and re-used them. Psalm 30 bears classic signs of the song of thanksgiving: a description of being rescued (vv. 1–3, 11(2–4, 12)) and the inclusion of terminology for giving thanks (v. 12(13)). Yet, its superscription assigns it another purpose: 'A Song at the dedication of the temple'. Similarly, the language of individual thanksgiving dominates Psalm 129 (vv. 1a, 2–3), but the worshipping community came to use the psalm as its prayer, as the phrase 'let Israel now say' (v. 1b) indicates.

As Israelites used the Psalms in new contexts, they obscured the previous ones. Therefore, the scholarly effort to recover how Israelites performed the Psalms amounts to peeling back layers of reading and interpreting these passages. In the past several decades many scholars have decided it is fruitful to go in the other direction. Instead of trying to get behind the present form of the Psalms, they are looking at the present form and asking how it fits within the immediate literary context.

---

27 Erhard S. Gerstenberger, *Der bittende Mensch* (Neukirchen-Vluyn: Neukirchener Verlag, 1980), pp. 167–9.

28 Gerstenberger, *Der bittende Mensch*, p. 165.

The current interest in the Psalter as a literary product has also made an impact on the discussion of the psalms' relationship to the cult. There is now an increased awareness that some psalms in their present form bear signs of editorial manipulation, which raise anew questions about what elements in the psalms are cultic. Psalm 2.10–12 is a good example. J. J. M. Roberts proposes that the address to the 'kings of the earth' had in mind rulers of Israel's subservient territories who were present for an Israelite king's coronation. He finds support for this view in records of similar Egyptian ceremonies in which the Egyptians instructed their vassals to pay homage to Pharaoh.[29] Roberts' discussion is quite helpful for understanding the possible origins of these poetic lines. Nevertheless, the fact that Psalm 2.12a warns the foreign kings with language so similar to that of Psalm 1.6b raises the possibility that the end of Psalm 2 came into its present form in the Psalter to enhance its connection to Psalm 1 as a dual introduction to the book. Regardless of the original setting for the psalms, their present place in the Psalter is the most certain setting. The next chapter will consider this literary setting for the psalms, their setting in the book.

---

29 J. J. M. Roberts, 'The religio-political setting of Psalm 47', *Bulletin of the American Schools of Oriental Research* 221 (1976), p. 132.

Part 2
READING THE PSALMS TOGETHER

6
Going by the book: the Psalter as a guide to reading the psalms

As Moses gave five books of laws to Israel, so David gave five books of psalms to Israel.
(*Midrash on Psalms*)

The arrangement of the Psalms, which seems to me to contain the secret of a mighty mystery, hath not yet been revealed unto me.
(St Augustine)

One must therefore begin from the outset by using the order found in the actual book of Psalms, not the order of the events themselves; the psalms do not occur in order, instead each occurring as it was found.
(Diodore of Tarsus)

As we discussed in the previous chapter, most psalms had their original setting in the worship of Ancient Israel. As scribes preserved them and passed them on to us, however, they became part of a book of Scripture. For most of two millennia the psalms' place in the book has been the primary key to their interpretation.

Before the modern era, Christians read the Psalms as a book that had coherence and unity like any other book in the Bible. Despite Augustine's qualification, that the mystery of the order of the Psalms 'hath not yet been revealed unto me', he assumed it had an order and that we have to work to discover it.[1] Pre-critical interpreters assumed the Psalter was coherent theologically in large part because they conceived it as the product of the person David and the context of his role as God's anointed.

When modern scholars rejected the notion that David wrote the Psalms, the Psalter as a book fell on hard times. This was especially true during the

---

1 Augustine, *Nicene and Post-Nicene Fathers of the Christian Church*, First Series, vol. 8: *Expositions on the book of Psalms* (ed. Philip Schaff; New York, NY: The Christian Literature Company, 1888), p. 681.

period when form criticism dominated the study of the Psalter. Proponents of that method concluded that the Psalter is a collection of disparate pieces with limited purposeful organization. They could not see any ordering principle in the Psalter since the psalms of any given genre were not together but scattered throughout the book.[2] Apart from the fact that many psalms were part of small collections (e.g. Davidic (Pss. 3—41), Korahite (Pss. 42—49)) prior to becoming part of the Psalter, there was little organization to the book at all.

The nature of the Psalms as collection literature supported the view of form critics. At first glance the book may seem like a 'book' only in a loose sense. A hymnal is a book, but not in the same way as books of narrative, which have a plot that holds them together.[3]

Despite these challenges to reading the Psalms as a book, many scholars late in the twentieth century began to question the notion that the Psalter is a collection of disparate pieces and sought to recover the age-old idea that the Psalms are a distinct unit within Scripture.[4] Now many of them argue that the editors of the book of Psalms gave it a theologically significant 'shape' that provides a context in which to read and interpret individual psalms.[5]

This way of approaching the Psalms is part of a broad movement in biblical studies in which readers appreciate books as more than the sum of their parts. To interpret them requires more than consideration of the origins of the material. In the case of the Psalms, scholars recognize that those who preserved them and transmitted them also revised and reread them. As the various psalms came together to form the present book, they took on a different context from their original context in Israel's cult. In other words, the Psalter is not just a collection of ancient songs and liturgies, the 'hymnbook of the Second Temple', but a unique literary product with its own theological message. Therefore, the present literary context invites readers to study the collection as a whole in order to determine the meaning of individual pieces within

---

2 Hermann Gunkel with Joachim Begrich, *An Introduction to the Psalms: The genres of the religious lyric of Israel* (trans. James D. Nogalski; Macon, GA: Mercer University Press, 1998; German original 1933), pp. 334–5.

3 See Patrick D. Miller, 'The Psalter as a book of theology', in *Psalms in Community: Jewish and Christian textual, liturgical, and artistic traditions* (SBL Symposium Series 25; ed. Harold W. Attridge and Margot E. Fassler; Atlanta, GA: Society of Biblical Literature, 2004), p. 87 (87–98).

4 The most important and groundbreaking work was Gerald H. Wilson, *The Editing of the Hebrew Psalter* (SBLDS 76; Chico, CA: Scholars Press, 1985); see also the essays in J. Clinton McCann Jr, ed., *The Shape and Shaping of the Psalter* (JSOTSup 159; Sheffield: Sheffield Academic Press, 1993); and the detailed work of Frank-Lothar Hossfeld and Erich Zenger, *Psalms 2: A commentary on Psalms 51–100* (trans. Linda M. Maloney; Hermeneia; Minneapolis, MN: Fortress Press, 2005) and *Psalms 3: A commentary on Psalms 101–150* (trans. Linda M. Maloney; Hermeneia; Minneapolis, MN: Fortress Press, 2011).

5 See Brevard S. Childs, *Introduction to the Old Testament as Scripture* (Philadelphia, PA: Fortress Press, 1979), p. 513; and Miller, 'The Psalter as a book of theology'.

it.[6] This emphasis on the book is important for the Church because it represents a way of reading that is closer to those who preserved it and to the New Testament authors and early Christians who read it as testimony to God's work in Christ (Luke 24.44).

Signs of coherence

To read the Psalms as a book is to see in it literary features that organize the collection of psalms around specific topics and theological interests. What are those literary features and topics in the Psalter?

To begin to answer that question, recall the basic structural elements of the Psalter we listed in Chapter 1 and what they tell us further about the coherence of the book.

1. Psalms 1 and 2 are an introduction to the Psalter. The first two psalms present two possible ways to go in life. Psalm 1 says the way God prefers and rewards is revealed in Torah, or God's instruction, on which the faithful person should meditate constantly (v. 2). That declaration gives the sense that what follows in the book is 'instruction about the Lord and the Lord's way'.[7] Thus, the Psalter is a 'Torah of David' that stands alongside the 'Torah of Moses'.[8]

2. Psalms 146—150 serve as a conclusion to the Psalter. The last five psalms hold together with the expression 'Praise the Lord' (*hallelu-yah*), which occurs at the beginning and end of four of them (Pss. 146.1, 10; 147.1, 20; 148.1, 14; 149.1, 9), and Psalm 150 has this or a similar expression in all six of its verses. This final crescendo of praise is important for the coherence of the Psalter at the most basic level. These psalms cap off a movement in the Psalter from laments (complaints and petitions to God) that appear in greater numbers at the beginning, to psalms of praise that occur in greater numbers at the end.[9]

---

6   James Luther Mays, *The Lord Reigns: A theological handbook to the Psalms* (Louisville, KY: Westminster John Knox Press, 1994), pp. 119–20.

7   Miller, 'The Psalter as a book of theology', p. 88.

8   Bernd Janowski, 'Die "Kleine Biblia": zur Bedeutung der Psalmen für eine Theologie des Alten Testaments', in *Der Psalter in Judentum und Christentum* (ed. Erich Zenger; Herder's Biblical Studies 18; Freiburg: Herder, 1998), p. 403 (381–420).

9   On the movement from plea to praise, see Claus Westermann, *Praise and Lament in the Psalms* (Atlanta, GA: John Knox Press, 1981) and *The Psalms: Structure, content and message* (Minneapolis, MN: Augsburg, 1980); see also the application of Westermann's ideas by Walter Brueggemann, 'The costly loss of lament', *Journal for the Study of the Old Testament* 36 (1986), pp. 57–71.

The pain in psalms early in the Psalter finds resolution in the praise that dominates in the final psalms.

3. The Psalter has five divisions or 'books':

Psalms 1—41;
Psalms 42—72;
Psalms 73—89;
Psalms 90—106;
Psalms 107—150.

Four doxologies that conclude the last psalm in each of the first four books create these divisions (Pss. 41.13(14); 72.18–19; 89.52(53); 106.48). The *Midrash on Psalms* gives us the traditional explanation for this fivefold division, namely that the book of Psalms contains David's *torah* or instruction that mimics the five books of Torah Moses gave.[10]

In recent years, scholars have detected a larger message in the Psalter's book divisions. The first three books have royal psalms (psalms about Israel's king) at the 'seams' between them.[11] Psalms 2, 72 and 89 certainly fit that label, and Psalm 41 may as well. Moreover, there is a certain progression in these psalms about the king:

- Psalm 2 speaks of God establishing the king on Zion to express God's will on earth.
- If Psalm 41 is a royal psalm, it expresses the ideal of monarchy, to ensure justice for the poor (vv. 1–3(2–4)). Ancient readers perhaps heard its words as a royal testimony to just rule.
- Psalm 72 suggests the passing of kingship from one ruler to another and offers prayer for the king to rule according to the ideals Psalm 41 expressed.
- Psalm 89 laments the downfall of the monarch and questions the covenant loyalty the Lord had promised to David.

This structure around the king and promises to the kingdom of David reflects one of the main themes the Church has always seen in the Psalms, namely the key role of the LORD's anointed that found fulfilment in Jesus Christ. The

---

10 *The Midrash on Psalms* (trans. William G. Braude; Yale Judaica Series 13; New Haven, CT: Yale University Press, 1959), vol. 1, p. 5.

11 On the editorial features that divide the Psalter into these two sections see Gerald H. Wilson, 'The use of royal psalms at the "seams" of the Hebrew Psalter', *Journal for the Study of the Old Testament* 35 (1986), pp. 85–94.

royal structure in the Psalter itself, however, raises the question of the efficacy of the human king. Though the Church would find resolution to this problem in Jesus, the Psalter reflects the painful struggle of the people of Judah in the wake of the Babylonian captivity which ended the monarchy (587 BCE). The question of what God is doing with the promises to David are front and centre in the book.

Going further: the theological shape of the Psalter

Psalms 1 and 2: The two ways

If Psalms 1 and 2 introduce the Psalter, what ideas or subjects do they put before us as central to the Psalms? The first word in Psalm 1, and thus the first word in the Psalter, is an important clue. In NRSV the word is 'happy', and in other translations 'blessed' (e.g. NIV). The term *'ashre* is the Hebrew equivalent of the Greek word that introduces the beatitudes of Jesus (Matt. 5.3–11). Beatitudes pronounce a state of fortune or favour. Thus, Psalm 1 opens by identifying a way of life and a type of person God approves and rewards. At the same time, the first psalm presents a way God does not approve, and it sets the two alongside each other for us to consider which way we will choose.

Psalm 1 labels those who live according to God's ways 'righteous' and those who go the other way 'wicked'. To many contemporary readers these words may seem archaic and also 'self-righteous'. Those the Psalter calls righteous, however, never claim that identity for themselves. 'Righteous' is essentially God's judgement about those who bear the label. Furthermore, their main character trait is humility before God (Ps. 34.13–18(14–19)). The main thing they claim for themselves is that they are helpless on their own so they depend on God completely (Ps. 37.39–40). Psalm 1.2 declares that the righteous show their reliance on God and their desire to bend their will to the LORD's will by meditating constantly on the LORD's instruction (*torah*). The psalm does not say more about what constitutes this instruction, but it is clear that a God-approved life involves seeking and following the LORD's way and not yielding to one's own insight and understanding (Prov. 3.5).

The wicked, on the other hand, are arrogant and self-assured. They act as though God is not really sovereign (Ps. 14.1), and they manifest their arrogance in violence against those who are weak and vulnerable (Pss. 10.2–11; 73.8–9).

After Psalm 1 establishes these contrasting profiles of the righteous and the wicked, it then makes a final declaration:

The LORD watches over the way of the righteous,
  but the way of the wicked will perish.
(v. 6)

When we read further in the Psalter, however, we notice two things about this declaration.

1 Psalm 1's emphasis on the righteous and the wicked properly anticipates the ubiquitous references to these two groups in the rest of the book. The two groups appear at every turn in the Psalter.
2 Despite Psalm 1's confident assertion about God's reward for the righteous and judgement on the wicked, present circumstances seem to defy the claim. The psalmist repeatedly protests that the ways of the wicked 'prosper at all times' (Ps. 10.5) and complains that 'many are the afflictions of the righteous' (Ps. 34.19(20)). Therefore, the promises of Psalm 1.6 point to the future of God's work and to the establishment of God's kingdom.

Psalm 2 puts this focus on the two ways an individual may go in life in relation to God's reign. Those who go the right way acknowledge God's sovereign rule. Those who take the wrong path oppose the LORD's intentions. The most tangible sign of this opposition is their rejection of the authority of 'the LORD's anointed', the king whom God installed on Mount Zion (Ps. 2.1–6). This focus on the nations and the LORD's Messiah adds another dimension to the identity of the righteous and the wicked. The wicked are not only those individuals who oppress the poor and helpless; they are also the nations who oppose and oppress God's people (see Pss. 9.5(6), 17(18); 10.15–16).

Psalm 2 ends with a beatitude that ties the two introductory psalms together: 'Happy are all who take refuge in him' (v. 12). This final line of the Psalter's introduction both repeats the pronouncement of divine favour that opened Psalm 1 and introduces a vocabulary that the righteous will use to express their dependence on God. They will declare over and again that they 'seek refuge' in the LORD (e.g. Pss. 16.1; 18.1–2(3–4); 31.1(2); 43.2; 57.1(2)). To 'seek refuge' in God is to choose the LORD over other sources of power and protection. It is to trust in God's provisions above all else and to wait for God to act.[12] This notion of seeking refuge in God becomes in the Psalter the main distinction between the righteous, who seek refuge in the Lord, and the wicked who do not (e.g. Ps. 52.7(9)).

Psalms 3—72: The prayers of David

The heading of Psalm 3 and the colophon at the end of Psalm 72 cast the psalms in Books I and II as the prayers of David. Through the voice of David in prayer, these psalms continue and deepen the concerns and convictions of Psalms 1 and 2. In large measure the psalms in this section of the Psalter illustrate what it means to 'seek refuge' in God (see Ps. 2.12) as David cries out to God for help and expresses trust that God will deliver him. David here represents those whom Psalm 1 calls righteous, and his opponents illustrate the cruelty and arrogance of the wicked. This dual focus on trouble and dependence begins in Psalm 3.

Psalm 3 is set 'when he [David] fled from his son Absalom'. This historical note points to the story in 2 Samuel 15. Absalom vied for his father's throne and forced David out of Jerusalem. Thus, the prayers of David begin with this prayer that shows David at the mercy of an enemy. As some of the other prayers will complain, it is an enemy that should be an ally, a situation that makes it all the more painful (see Ps. 55.12–14(13–15)). This first glimpse of David in the Psalter also gives us a particular view of him. Though he is king of Israel, the Lord's anointed, he appears here as one who is helpless in the face of his enemies, and he confesses as much to God.

The psalm opens with David recognizing that his adversaries have overwhelmed him: 'O Lord, how many are my foes!' (v. 1(2)). He also reports the enemy's taunt that God cannot or will not come to his aid: 'There is no help for you in God' (v. 2(3)). The word 'many' appears three times in the first two verses to denote the dire circumstances ('how many are my foes', v. 1a(2a); 'many are rising against me', v. 1b(2b); 'many are saying', v. 2(3)). Those who oppose David speak as the wicked do, denying that God reigns and judges the earth, and saying essentially, 'You will not call us to account' (Ps. 10.13). Yet David confesses, contrary to his foe's claim that God cannot help him, that 'you, O Lord, are a shield around me' (v. 3(4)).

---

12 For a discussion of this and related language and how it appears in the Psalms see Jerome F. D. Creach, *Yahweh as Refuge and the Editing of the Hebrew Psalter* (JSOTSup 217; Sheffield: Sheffield Academic Press, 1996), pp. 22–48.

In the face of enemies rising against him (v. 1b(2b)), David calls on God to 'rise up' and deliver him (v. 7a(8a)). Matching the threefold reference to the 'many' foes, Psalm 3 uses the word 'deliverance', 'salvation' or 'help' three times to confess that God alone can deliver (the Hebrew word is the same in each case; see vv. 2(3), 7a(8a), 8(9)). The three appearances of the term have a sequence that drives home this point. The adversaries taunt that there is no 'help' in God (v. 2(3)); David cries for God to 'help' or 'deliver' (v. 7a(8a)); then at the close of the psalm he confesses that 'deliverance' belongs to God (v. 8(9)). There is no sense here of self-sufficiency. Only the LORD can rescue and save. Speaking as one of the righteous, David relies on God and calls on God in his distress.

This type of prayer and the circumstances that prompted it dominate the first two books of the Psalter. Although there are psalms that celebrate God's salvation (e.g. Pss. 46; 48) and the place of God's servants in the world (e.g. Ps. 8), the primary mode of expression is lament. The confession that 'I am poor and needy' is typical (Ps. 40.17(18)). Throughout these psalms David identifies with the lowly and models the faith of one who 'seeks refuge' in God (see Ps. 2.12).

A second point of focus in these psalms, however, is the belief that the LORD's anointed is an instrument through whom God works to make things right in the world. Scattered throughout Books I and II are prayers for the king that assume God can and will work through the monarch (Pss. 20; 21; 45; 72). The last of these is the most extensive in its praise for the king and expansive in its expectations for his reign:

> May he be like rain that falls on the mown grass,
>   like showers that water the earth.
> In his days may righteousness flourish
>   and peace abound, until the moon is no more.
> (vv. 6–7)

The king will be the best friend and defender of those who are vulnerable:

> For he delivers the needy when they call,
>   the poor and those who have no helper.
> He has pity on the weak and the needy,
>   and saves the lives of the needy.
> From oppression and violence he redeems their life;
>   and precious is their blood in his sight.
> (vv. 12–14)

With this confident prayer for the king Book II concludes and 'the prayers of David son of Jesse are ended' (Ps. 72.20).

There are hints already in this first major division of the Psalter, however, that the human king is limited in his ability to protect God's people and secure them for the future. We noted in Chapter 1 that Psalms 15—24 form a chiastic structure that seems to bring questions about the king into focus. An outline of this section of psalms is as follows:

Psalm 15 Entrance liturgy: Who may abide in the LORD's tent?
    Psalm 16 Trust in God's salvation
        Psalm 17 Plea for deliverance
            Psalm 18 Royal psalm
                Psalm 19 The law of the LORD is perfect!
            Psalms 20—21 Royal psalms
        Psalm 22 Plea for deliverance
    Psalm 23 Trust in God's salvation
Psalm 24 Entrance liturgy: Who may ascend God's holy hill?[13]

The grouping as a whole then seems to suggest the following message that transcends the individual psalms: God's instruction is the key to life (Ps. 19) and the primary guiding force for those who would enter the Temple (Pss. 15; 24); the king is the primary example of one who abides by Torah. Much like Deuteronomy 17.14–20, this grouping of psalms suggests that the king stands under the authority of Torah and leads rightly only as Torah guides him.

There are also two other foci in this section of psalms that become crucially important in the rest of the book. First, the section ends with a declaration that the LORD is king (Ps. 24.10). Although this does not deny the role of the human ruler in God's reign, it reminds us who the sovereign of the universe is: the LORD and not a human being. Second, the presence of prayers for deliverance from trouble (Pss. 17; 22) alongside royal psalms reminds us of the primary identity of the anointed, namely as one who suffers and, in turn, depends on God (as in Ps. 3).[14] In other words, this arrangement of psalms suggests that Israel should not rely on a human ruler as its deliverer. That role belongs to God alone.

---

13 See William P. Brown, *Seeing the Psalms: A theology of metaphor* (Louisville, KY: Westminster John Knox Press, 2002), p. 97.

14 See Miller, 'The Psalter as a book of theology', pp. 91–2.

Psalms 73—89: After David's prayers failed

With Book III comes a marked change in the role of the king. As we discussed in Chapter 3, the note in Psalm 72.20 marks the end of David's prayers. One possible interpretation of this note is that Psalm 72 signifies the end of any hope the Psalter expresses for God to work through the Davidic kings. Whether psalm editors intended this or not, the psalms in Book III clearly bring the downfall of the monarchy into view, and psalms later in the Psalter warn against putting trust in human rulers. At the same time, they raise questions about the central claims of the two introductory psalms, namely, that 'the LORD watches over the way of the righteous, but the way of the wicked will perish' (Ps. 1.6).

Psalm 73 begins with a basic affirmation that echoes Psalm 1.6: 'Surely God is good to Israel, to those who are pure in heart' (v. 1 NIV). Some modern translators have thought the term 'Israel' here is a mistake. They have proposed that the correct reading is 'to the upright' (as NRSV). This would seem to make more sense for the first verse of a psalm that is the reflection of an individual who struggles with the fact that the wicked are prospering. And yet, the identification of Israel in the first verse is part of all the ancient translations. The identification indicates that the Psalter in its present form presents the righteous sufferer as a representative of Israel in its suffering.

After stating the central tenet of faith that opens the psalm ('God is good to Israel'), the next two verses call it into question:

> But as for me, my feet had almost stumbled;
>   my steps had nearly slipped.
> For I was envious of the arrogant;
>   I saw the prosperity of the wicked.
> (vv. 2–3)

The psalmist recognizes the suffering of the righteous as a great problem, especially in the light of the 'prosperity' of the wicked (v. 3). Psalm 73 ends with a confident assertion that eventually the wicked will get what they deserve, a truth the psalmist has gained in the sanctuary (v. 17), but the question of God's justice to the 'upright', to Israel, sets the tone for the rest of Book III.

Book III contains more prayers for help by the community than any other section of the Psalter. Psalm 74 is the first of those, and it expresses the struggle of Israel with some key language and themes it shares with Psalm 73. The sanctuary in which the psalmist in Psalm 73.17 envisages the downfall of the wicked lies in ruins in Psalm 74.3. Though Psalm 73.18 sees a future in which the wicked 'fall to ruin', Psalm 74.3 declares the sanctuary has suffered that fate instead. The rest of Book III alternates between hymns that praise God for deliverance and prosperity (Pss. 75; 76; 78; 81; 82; 84; 87) and complaints that God's people suffer and stand in need of deliverance (Pss. 77; 79; 80; 83; 85; 86; 88; 89). It ends, however, on a decidedly stark note.

Psalm 89 concludes Book III with a prayer that pleads for answers concerning God's covenant faithfulness to David. The problem is that God had promised unconditionally 'I will not remove from him [David] my steadfast love' (v. 33(34)) and 'I will not violate my covenant' (v. 34(35)) regardless of how David's descendants violate God's statutes (vv. 30–32(31–33)). But now it seems that God has indeed broken the covenant. Therefore, the psalmist asks, 'Lord, where is your steadfast love of old, which by your faithfulness you swore to David?' (v. 49(50)). Is God being unfaithful to the covenant? Is God unable to uphold it in the face of enemy threats? The psalm suggests, however, that the complaint does not come from the monarch himself, but from the people who now grope in darkness without the king's leadership and protection. Verse 50(51) in the Masoretic Text may be the original reading of the complaint. It reads, 'Remember, O LORD, how your *servants are* taunted'. Many translators change the plural reference to a singular, 'your servant is taunted', reasoning that the verse intended to speak of the king. It may well be, however, that the psalm is a complaint by God's servants, people in the community who now feel taunted and insulted in their devastation. The answer they seek from God is not specifically about the return of the monarchy but about their place among the nations and in God's plans for them.

Psalms 90—106: 'The LORD reigns!'

If the psalms of Book III heighten the problems for the righteous and for Israel, the psalms of Book IV begin to present a resolution to the problem. Gerald Wilson calls Book IV the 'editorial centre' of the Psalter. Most of the psalms in this section do not have a heading, or if they do, they are not part of a collection like those we see in Books I–III. Together these psalms seem to address the problems and questions raised in Book III and to give a definitive answer to the complaint that God has broken the covenant with David.[15]

Two features of Book IV provide a response to the questions about God's faithfulness. First, the psalms in Book IV hark back to the time of Moses with a reminder that before Israel had a king, God had led Israel as a flock through the wilderness. The LORD who leads the people of Israel in this new reality is

---

15 Wilson, *Editing of the Hebrew Psalter*, pp. 214–15.

the same as the One who led them out of Egypt and through the wilderness. Second, these psalms present a claim about God's kingship, over Israel and over the nations. The recurrent declaration that 'the LORD reigns' (also translated, 'the LORD is king') dominates this portion of the Psalter (Pss. 93.1; 96.10; 97.1; 99.1; see further Chapter 7). Along with the frequent mention of Moses, this claim of God's sovereignty reminds Israel that the LORD is still in control of the cosmos even if the Davidic monarch is absent. David does appear in the superscriptions of Psalms 101 and 103, which may indicate that hope for the monarchy remains alive, but the focus clearly shifts to Moses and to the time when the LORD was Israel's only king.

Psalm 90: Moses' prayer for God's people

The psalms in Book IV show a marked interest in Moses and the Mosaic era through the simple fact that Moses' name appears seven times in these psalms (Pss. 90 (superscription); 99.6; 103.7; 105.26; 106.16, 23, 32), compared to only one occurrence of his name in the rest of the Psalter (Ps. 77.20(21)). A more detailed and nuanced focus on Moses appears, however, in the content of Psalm 90.

Psalm 90 is the only psalm in the Psalter with 'Moses' in its heading. The superscription identifies it as 'A Prayer of Moses, the man of God'. The prayer, presumably *by* Moses, is a prayer *for* Israel. Thus, in this psalm Moses plays a role for Israel in exile like the role he played for Israel in the exodus and period of wilderness wandering. Namely, he stands before God and pleads to God on behalf of the people.

Psalm 90 opens with a statement about the place of God's people in God's presence:

> Lord, you have been our dwelling-place
>   in all generations.
> Before the mountains were brought forth,
>   or ever you had formed the earth and the world,
>   from everlasting to everlasting you are God.
> (vv. 1–2)

The word translated 'dwelling-place' (*ma'on*) is closely related to other terms such as 'refuge', 'fortress', 'hiding place' and 'shade', all of which are frequent labels for God used by the faithful when they offer their prayers in the Psalter.[16]

---

16 Creach, *Yahweh as Refuge*, p. 94.

Hence, this psalm declares that 'in all generations', including the present generation that has suffered exile, God's presence is available in unmediated form. The king, the Temple and the land could all be lost, but God would remain a dwelling place, a refuge for God's people wherever they are and in whatever condition.

Moses' petition for Israel in Psalm 90 harks back to Exodus 32 and to Moses' prayer for the people when God threatened to destroy them because they had worshipped the golden calf: 'Turn, O LORD! How long? Have compassion on your servants!' (Ps. 90.13; cf. Exod. 32.12).

In both Psalm 90 and Exodus 32 Moses cries to God because of the anger and wrath God displays towards Israel (Exod. 32.10, 11, 12; Ps. 90.7, 9, 11). The emphasis of the psalm, and the subject of Moses' prayer, is the connection between divine wrath and the brevity of life. He speaks of mortality as a sign of God's judgement (vv. 3–6, 7–8). It also seems, however, that the failure to confess one's mortal limitations is the gravest of sins, the primary sin from which one must repent. So, verse 12 declares, in the light of God's wrath, 'teach us to count our days that we may gain a wise heart'. Moses seeks God's compassion (v. 13) then because of Israel's mortal weakness. The hope Moses puts forward for the people of Israel is for their limited days to be useful and filled with joy and purpose:

> Satisfy us in the morning with your steadfast love,
>> so that we may rejoice and be glad all our days.
> Make us glad for as many days as you have afflicted us,
>> and for as many years as we have seen evil.
> Let your work be manifest to your servants,
>> and your glorious power to their children.
> Let the favour of the Lord our God be upon us,
>> and prosper for us the work of our hands –
>> O prosper the work of our hands!
> (vv. 14–17)

The extended reflection in Psalm 90 echoes elements of the king's complaint in Psalm 89.47–48(48–49). The complaint focuses on mortality:

> Remember how short my time is –
>> for what vanity you have created all mortals!
> Who can live and never see death?
>> Who can escape the power of Sheol?

The brevity of life is here a metaphor for the failure of the king's leadership. Hence, the king casts himself as sharing the plight of all mortals just as Moses highlights in his prayer that all humans have lives that are fleeting (Ps. 90.5–6).

Earlier in the Psalter Psalm 78 proclaims that God has taken note of human limits in the past and has extended mercy precisely on that basis. This psalm indicts Israel's ancestors for their unfaithfulness in the wilderness, and then it declares that God was merciful because he knew the limits of the people: 'He remembered that they were but flesh, a wind that passes and does not come again' (v. 39).

The hope for Israel is to trust in God's refuge (Ps. 90.1–2) and to look for God's steadfast love (Ps. 90.14).

Psalms 105—106: 'Gather your people'

At the other end of Book IV Moses appears again with a message similar to that in Psalm 90. Moses' intercessory work brackets Psalms 90—106 by the presence of Mosaic references and themes in Psalms 105 and 106 (see Ps. 106.6–33, esp. 16, 23, 32). What is more, the psalms that frame Book IV focus on the same set of events in Israel's history, namely the wilderness period that followed the exodus and Moses' intercessory role on Israel's behalf. As noted above, Psalm 90 is cast as a prayer of Moses for Israel in exile that harks back to his intervention for Israel during the golden calf episode in Exodus 32. Psalms 105—106 form a unit at the other end of Book IV that highlights the same work of Moses. Psalm 105.26–45 notes that God sent Moses and Aaron to perform signs in Egypt that would precipitate Israel's release from captivity. Psalm 106 then picks up the story of Israel's salvation where Psalm 105 left off. When this final psalm of Book IV begins its rehearsal of Israel's history, however, it focuses from the beginning on Israel's rebellion. The ancestors 'did not consider your wonderful works' in Egypt, but 'rebelled against the Most High at the Red Sea' (v. 7); 'they were jealous of Moses in the camp, and of Aaron, the holy one of the Lord' (v. 16). The golden calf incident gets particular attention: 'they made a calf at Horeb and worshipped a cast image' (v. 19; cf. vv. 20–23). This sets the stage for Moses' intercession:

> Therefore he said he would destroy them –
>   had not Moses, his chosen one,
> stood in the breach before him,
>   to turn away his wrath from destroying them.
> (v. 23)

This text recalls the same occasion of Moses' prayer for Israel as Psalm 90, and it uses the same language as well. In both passages Moses acts to turn God's wrath away from his people (Ps. 90.7, 9, 11, 13).

With these parallels, Psalms 90 and 105—106 begin and end Book IV and provide a hermeneutical guide for reading the intervening psalms. The psalms in this segment of the Psalter are cast under the authority of Moses and are to be understood in the light of Moses' intercessory work for Israel in the wilderness. The closing lines of Psalm 106 reveal the circumstances of God's people:

Save us, O LORD our God,
    and gather us from among the nations,
that we may give thanks to your holy name
    and glory in your praise.
(v. 47)

These psalms also offer some hint of a solution to the problem of the broken Davidic covenant and the absence of a king. These two final psalms in Book IV do not mention David or God's promises to David. They do, however, insist that the earlier and larger promise to Abraham will never be revoked or neglected:

He is mindful of his covenant for ever,
    of the word that he commanded, for a thousand generations,
the covenant that he made with Abraham,
    his sworn promise to Isaac,
which he confirmed to Jacob as a statute,
    to Israel as an everlasting covenant . . .
(Ps. 105.8–10)

Just before and just after this promise, the psalm speaks of the people as a whole with language that other psalms applied to the king. The 'children of Jacob' are God's 'chosen ones' (v. 6; see Ps. 89.3(4)) and the LORD's 'anointed ones' (v. 15; see Ps. 89.51(52)). This may suggest that the editors of the Psalter are conceiving afresh what the covenant with David means and the form it will take in the future. It may not appear in the form of a single political figure reigning as king in Jerusalem. Rather, the people as a whole may take on the role of 'David' as God fulfils the promises of old. The covenant with Abraham and the covenant with David now seem to merge as God continues the promises to Israel. In this way Book IV of the Psalter is very similar in its theological orientation to Isaiah 40—55, which addresses essentially the same issues of defeat and humiliation.[17] The key to this covenant faithfulness is the continuing reign of God in Israel and among the nations.[18]

Psalms 93—100: 'The LORD reigns!'

Psalms 93—100 stand in the centre of Book IV and offer the repeated claim, 'The LORD reigns!' Psalm 100 serves as a conclusion to this grouping by summing up and repeating many of the emphases of Psalms 93—99, repeating particularly the vocabulary of Psalm 95.[19] Psalms 93—99 themselves hold together thematically perhaps more than any other grouping of psalms in the Psalter. They have in common the claim that 'the LORD reigns' or, as some translations have it, 'the LORD is king' and the celebration of that claim. Even Psalm 94, which does not contain this statement, highlights God's kingship by its portrayal of the LORD as judge of the earth (vv. 2, 12–15, 23).

These psalms also highlight God's sovereignty in language that harks back to Moses. Psalm 93 introduces Torah, which Moses gave, as another sign of God's sovereignty:

Your decrees are very sure;
  holiness befits your house,
  O LORD, for evermore.
(v. 5)

Psalm 99 combines the themes of the LORD's kingship ('Mighty King, lover of justice', v. 4) and Moses' intercessory role:

Moses and Aaron were among his priests,
  Samuel also was among those who called on his name.
They cried to the LORD, and he answered them.
(v. 6)

---

17 See Jerome F. D. Creach, 'The shape of Book Four of the Psalter and the shape of Second Isaiah', *Journal for the Study of the Old Testament* 80 (1998), pp. 63–76.

18 Adam Hensley argues that, earlier in the Psalter, Davidic covenant promises borrow from language about the covenant with Abraham to suggest that 'David' is the covenant partner who fulfils the promises in earlier covenants. See Adam D. Hensley, *Covenant Relationships and the Editing of the Hebrew Psalter* (Library of Hebrew Bible/Old Testament Studies 666; London: T&T Clark, 2018), pp. 185–208.

19 For a detailed treatment of the unifying features of Psalms 93–100 see David M. Howard Jr, *The Structure of Psalms 93–100* (Biblical and Judaic Studies 5; Winona Lake, IN: Eisenbrauns, 1997), pp. 166–83; and 'Psalm 94 among the kingship-of-Yhwh psalms', *Catholic Biblical Quarterly* 61, no. 4 (1999), pp. 667–85.

The psalm then describes the faithfulness of Moses, Aaron and Samuel in terms of Torah obedience:

> He spoke to them in the pillar of cloud;
>> they kept his decrees,
>> and the statutes that he gave them.
> (v. 7)

Hence, Psalms 93—99 bracket the sections of psalms that declare 'the LORD reigns' with reminders that the LORD formed Israel and directed its people in the time of Moses. Torah was Israel's authority and guide, a primary sign of God's reign.

These combined references to Moses and to the LORD's kingship do not deny hopes for a revival of the Davidic monarchy, nor do they undo the promises to David on which the monarchy rested. They do, however, put the promises to David in the larger context of God's choice of Israel and the promises to Israel's ancestors with a reminder that the LORD's kingship has been the constant in Israel's history. As long as the LORD reigns, Israel can be sure of its future. As Mays says, 'The reign of the LORD is at stake in the destiny of David.'[20] That is the problem behind the complaint in Psalm 89. The message of Book IV seems to be, however, that the LORD's reign will take on different forms in the future and that the identity of David and his role will bend to the larger purpose of God's kingship.

Psalms 107—150: 'Gather your people, O LORD'

The first verse in Book V (Ps. 107.1) is identical to Psalm 106.1:

> O give thanks to the LORD, for he is good;
>> for his steadfast love endures for ever.

This leads Erich Zenger to conclude that Book V is a kind of commentary on Books I–IV.[21] Whether that was the intention of psalm editors or not, Book V does continue the themes already observed in Books I–IV: the central truth of the LORD's reign (Ps. 118.27–28); the crucial place of Torah in God's

---

20 Mays, *The Lord Reigns*, p. 124.

21 Erich Zenger, 'The composition and theology of the fifth book of Psalms, Psalms 107–145', *Journal for the Study of the Old Testament* 80 (1998), p. 88.

governance of the world (Ps. 119); assurance that the LORD watches over those who depend on God (Ps. 145.20).

Book V focuses attention on God's faithfulness and God's care for the poor and needy by centring on promises of the LORD's steadfast love (Hebrew *hesed*) to Israel. These references bracket the final portion of the Psalter. The term appears six times in Psalm 107 (vv. 1, 8, 15, 21, 31, 43); it appears in the first and last verses of the psalm and in a fourfold refrain that structures the poem (vv. 8, 15, 21, 31). It also appears in Psalm 145.8 in a declaration that 'The LORD is gracious and merciful, slow to anger and abounding in steadfast love'. Psalms 107 and 145 likewise declare God's care for the righteous and his certain provision for a secure future. Psalm 107 emphasizes throughout that God cares for those in distress (e.g. v. 9 declares that he 'satisfies the thirsty' and fills the hungry), but verses 41–42 put this in familiar language:

> but he raises up the needy out of distress,
>   and makes their families like flocks.
> The upright see it and are glad;
>   and all wickedness stops its mouth.

In a similar way Psalm 145.18–20 concludes Book V proper with the voice of David, who echoes the promise of Psalm 1.6 that the righteous will flourish and the wicked will perish (Ps. 1.6):

> The LORD is near to all who call on him,
>   to all who call on him in truth.
> He fulfils the desire of all who fear him;
>   he also hears their cry, and saves them.
> The LORD watches over all who love him,
>   but all the wicked he will destroy.

As the Psalter comes to a close, David appears as he did earlier in the Psalter, as one who calls on the LORD when enemies oppress him.

Psalms 146—150 conclude the Psalter with a crescendo of praise. The words 'Praise the LORD' tie these five psalms together. Psalm 150 includes these or similar words in each verse. Before these concluding psalms give way to the pure praise in the final psalm, however, they state again what is perhaps the central message of the Psalter:

The LORD watches over the strangers;
    he upholds the orphan and the widow,
    but the way of the wicked he brings to ruin.
(Ps. 146.9)

Do not put your trust in princes,
    in mortals, in whom there is no help.
When their breath departs, they return to the earth;
    on that very day their plans perish.
(Ps. 146.3–4)

These promises and directions come through David's own voice. David, the LORD's anointed, gives instructions about God's goodness and protection, including a warning not to rely on human rulers!

As David offers these final words, he also leads us into the Psalter's final concatenation of praise that rests on the assurance that God will right the wrongs done to the righteous. Praise in this case is not triumphal assurance that all is well now, but hope-full claims that God is still in control of the world, that the LORD reigns! That faith provides the strength to live in the midst of suffering. The Psalter as a whole, therefore, leads its readers on a spiritual pilgrimage through the promise that 'happy are all who take refuge' in the LORD (Ps. 2.12). By the dominating presence of complaints and prayers for help, it makes clear that those who trust in God will likely suffer in this life, but suffering is not the last word. Indeed, the final word is the promise that the LORD has not abandoned the promises made to Israel and to the righteous. The final word is 'the LORD reigns!' So, 'Praise the LORD!'

Conclusion

The Psalter is a complex book that developed over a long period of time, and we cannot explain the placement of every psalm within it. Nevertheless, some aspects of the shape of the book seem clear: the book as a whole reflects the trauma of Judah's exile in Babylon, and especially the loss of the monarchy. The book answers the complaints over the disruption exile has caused with a clear promise that God is reliable, even if human rulers are not. The literary structure of the Psalter communicates a message we may express in three positive declarations: 'The LORD reigns!' 'Happy are all who take refuge in the LORD.' 'Praise the LORD!'

7
The theology of the Psalms, Part I: 'The LORD reigns!'

As we read the Psalms in all their variety, aware of the many ways Ancient Israelites perhaps read and recited them in worship, the question naturally arises: 'Is there anything that holds the Psalms together?' To put it more specifically, 'Are there ideas about who God is and what God does that are consistent enough in the book that we may say those claims hold the book together?' Can we speak of a 'theology of the Psalms'?

In one sense we may say the Psalter has many 'theologies', for it presents various claims about, and portraits of, God and God's activity.[1] Some scholars insist it is impossible to find neat harmony among the divergent themes and genres in the Psalms. Some Jewish scholars in particular have argued that 'polydoxy' – the presence of competing truth claims – characterizes this book and the Old Testament as a whole.[2] Although there is a growing interest in something like a theology of the Psalms among Jewish scholars, this remains largely a question Christian scholars and theologians have asked.[3] It has been common for Christian scholars to search for a theological dimension that comes consistently through the variety of different statements about God. For them, this quest is an attempt to discern the Psalms' witness to the character and activity of God that enhances and informs a larger Christian theology that has Jesus Christ at its centre.[4] However we conceive the nature and purpose of the theology of the Psalms, the key question is: are there claims

---

1 For an example of this argument see Erhard S. Gerstenberger, 'Theologies in the book of Psalms', in *The Book of Psalms: Composition and reception* (ed. Peter W. Flint; Vetus Testamentum Supplements 99; Leiden: Brill, 2005), pp. 603–25.

2 See Marc Zvi Brettler, 'Psalms and Jewish biblical theology', in *Jewish Bible Theology: Perspectives and case studies* (ed. Isaac Kalimi; Winona Lake, IN: Eisenbrauns, 2012), pp. 188–90 (187–97).

3 See again Brettler's discussion in 'Psalms and Jewish biblical theology'; and in his essay, 'Jewish theology of the Psalms', in *The Oxford Handbook of the Psalms* (ed. William P. Brown; New York, NY: Oxford University Press, 2014), pp. 485–98.

4 Rolf A. Jacobson, 'Christian theology of the Psalms', in *The Oxford Handbook of the Psalms* (ed. Brown), p. 498 (498–512).

about God in the Psalter that allow us to speak of a theological 'centre' of the Psalms?

God's kingship as the centre of the Psalms

The LORD reigns!

James Luther Mays argues that the theological centrepiece of the Psalms is the sentence 'The LORD reigns!' This statement expresses the main point of the so-called enthronement psalms (Pss. 47; 93; 95—99), but it is much more than a feature of this one psalm type. The sentence is a root metaphor in the Psalter that is a key to practically everything the Psalms say about who God is and what God does. (On the nature of metaphors in the Psalms see Chapter 2.)[5]

The sentence in Hebrew consists of two words. The first is the divine name, translated 'LORD'. The name seems to be a form of the Hebrew verb meaning 'to be' and perhaps originally referred to God's creative and life-giving activity.[6] The original writing of it was perhaps 'Yahweh'. As Ancient Israelites invoked the name, over time they came to believe the name itself was sacred. To acknowledge that belief, they ceased saying or reading the name and instead said or read the common word for 'lord' (Hebrew 'adonai). By writing the word 'lord' mostly in small capital letters, namely 'LORD', translators into English acknowledge the presence of the name 'Yahweh' in a passage and honour the ancient scribes who signalled readers to say 'adonai, 'lord'. Regardless of its origins and the history of its use, it is the personal name of Israel's God and in the Old Testament identifies the God who brought Israel out of Egypt and established Israel as a people (Exod. 3.13–15). The name refers to Israel's Lord, the one whom Israel worships. As Patrick Miller observes, that God whom Israel knew as the LORD is the subject of the Psalms.[7] The Psalms sometimes use the general term for God (Hebrew 'elohim), but that and every other reference to the deity in the Psalms is to the LORD.

The second word in the sentence is a verb, *malak*, 'to rule' or 'to act in a position of authority'. Two translations are equally plausible: 'The LORD reigns!' (RSV) or 'The LORD is king!' (NRSV). The verbal sentence, however,

---

5 James Luther Mays, *The Lord Reigns: A theological handbook to the Psalms* (Louisville, KY: Westminster John Knox Press, 1994), pp. 12–13.

6 Frank Moore Cross Jr, *Canaanite Myth and Hebrew Epic* (Cambridge, MA: Harvard University Press, 1973), pp. 65–9.

7 Patrick D. Miller, *The Lord of the Psalms* (Louisville, KY: Westminster John Knox Press, 2013), p. xi.

captures the dynamic sense of the claim best.[8] 'To be king' suggests the LORD has an office and occupies a place in a system of authority. While this is true to what the Psalms say about God, the reign of the LORD is more an activity than an office. 'The LORD reigns!' has more to do with what God does and will do than a status or position of power. According to this sentence then, the LORD who is Israel's God acts as *the* authority in the world.

According to the Psalms, the LORD's reign extends to two realms that constitute the whole of reality. First, the LORD is responsible for the order and purposefulness of the world. To say the LORD reigns is to say the LORD creates. The act of creating is first an act of ordering what was previously disordered and chaotic. This is the sense of the verb *bara'* ('create') in Genesis 1.1 ('God created the heavens and the earth'), and it captures what many psalms say about God putting the elements in place. Psalm 136.5–9 rehearses parts of the first creation story as it tells of God establishing the heavens (v. 5), the earth (v. 6), and the two great lights (v. 7) that rule the day (v. 8) and the night (v. 9). The issue is not so much the existence of these parts of the cosmos as their meaningful order. The Psalms show an awareness, however, that everything depends on God for its life and existence. So Psalm 104.30 speaks of God as the source of life itself: 'When you send forth your spirit, they are created'.

Most of the claims about God reigning over the creation derive from a fear that the order of the cosmos will come undone, that the order God established in the beginning might end. The story of the Flood in Genesis 6—9 testifies to the belief that the creation is fragile and can come apart. The LORD alone is able to hold it together, and the declaration that the LORD reigns over the elements of creation is an expression of confidence in God's ability and willingness to do that. These psalms assume, however, that the elements are not naturally cooperative (see further below). The waters of the cosmos 'roar' in opposition (Ps. 93.3), but the LORD rules over them. The world is secure because the LORD is 'mightier than the noise of many waters' (Ps. 93.4 KJV). The LORD 'set the earth on its foundations, so that it shall never be shaken' (Ps. 104.5).

Inherent in the Psalter's claim concerning God's control in the first realm (ordering the cosmos) is the belief that the LORD is the chief of all the gods.

---

8   James Luther Mays, 'The God who reigns', in *The Forgotten God: Perspectives in biblical theology. Essays in honor of Paul J. Achtemeier on the occasion of his seventy-fifth birthday* (ed. A. Andrew Das and Frank J. Matera; Louisville, KY: Westminster John Knox Press, 2002), p. 31 (29–38).

Although the Old Testament at points comes close to a belief in pure monotheism, it mostly speaks of monotheism functionally. Other gods may exist,
but the LORD is the undisputed head of them all:

> For the LORD is a great God,
>> and a great King above all gods.
> (Ps. 95.3)

The Psalms then speak of the LORD as creator as part of the larger claim that
the LORD is the chief of all deities and thus alone has authority and power to
create:

> In his hand are the depths of the earth;
>> the heights of the mountains are his also.
> The sea is his, for he made it,
>> and the dry land, which his hands have formed.
> (Ps. 95.4–5)

The second realm of the LORD's reign is the activity of the creatures of the
earth, the historical movement of those God created. The enthronement
psalms combine claims that the non-human elements bow to the LORD's
authority and that the people of the earth also live under the LORD's rule (Ps.
97.5–7). The foundational idea that the LORD creates and maintains the world
forms the basis on which the nations learn to obey. The One who creates also
directs the peoples of earth in the way they should go:

> Say among the nations, 'The LORD is king!
>> The world is firmly established; it shall never be moved.
>> He will judge the peoples with equity …'
> (Ps. 96.10)

The Psalms' definitive statements about the LORD's reign speak also about
forces that oppose divine sovereignty. Psalms 47 and 93 present the two
primary opponents most clearly. Psalm 93.3–4 names the 'floods' and 'waters'
as one opponent:

> The floods have lifted up, O LORD,
>> the floods have lifted up their voice;
>> the floods lift up their roaring.

More majestic than the thunders of mighty waters,
    more majestic than the waves of the sea,
    majestic on high is the LORD!

The pairing of 'floods' (*neharoth*) and 'waters' (*mayim*) echoes the Canaanite account of the god Baal doing battle with the forces of chaos, which it names 'River' and 'Sea'.[9] These terms in the Psalms do not denote deities and they are not a threat to the LORD's work. They serve as a foil for the LORD's might. Nevertheless, their appearance highlights the fact that the cosmos would be vulnerable to chaos if the divine king were not at work.

The other opponent of the divine king is the nations. Psalm 2 opens with a statement of the problem:

Why do the nations conspire,
    and the peoples plot in vain?
The kings of the earth set themselves,
    and the rulers take counsel together,
    against the LORD and his anointed . . .
(vv. 1–2)

This problem assumes Israel has a special place in the LORD's reign. The secure place of Israel is a central concern. So, Psalm 47.3–4(4–5) declares how Israel and the nations fit within the LORD's administration:

He subdued peoples under us,
    and nations under our feet.
He chose our heritage for us,
    the pride of Jacob whom he loves.

Despite the exalted place of Israel, however, the LORD does not reject the nations, but gathers them into the divine reign and purpose:

God is king over the nations;
    God sits on his holy throne.
The princes of the peoples gather
    as the people of the God of Abraham.

---

9 Frank-Lothar Hossfeld and Erich Zenger, *Psalms 2: A commentary on Psalms 51–100* (trans. Linda M. Maloney; Hermeneia; Minneapolis, MN: Fortress Press, 2005), p. 449.

For the shields of the earth belong to God;
    he is highly exalted.
(Ps. 47.8–9(9–10))

The LORD's reign and the practice of justice

One of the most important features of the LORD's reign is the LORD judging the nations and ensuring justice for the peoples. Thus, one way the Psalms extend the metaphor of God as king is to portray God as judge. The psalmist calls on God to 'rise up' as judge of the earth (Ps. 94.1–2). Just as the verb *malak* has a dynamic sense of 'to reign', so also the verb for judging (*shaphat*) suggests active and constant work. In the Old Testament God's judgement denotes God restoring harmony to communities that are broken.[10] So, the Psalms' statements about God 'judging' the nations refers to God's work to restore the harmony and goodness God intended in creation.

The vocabulary of judgement and justice refers to practices that maintain communities and encourage human flourishing. In relation to the LORD's reign, justice is central to the way the LORD governs. So, Psalm 97.2b declares, 'righteousness and justice are the foundation of his throne', and Psalm 98.9 proclaims, 'He is coming to judge the earth. He will judge the world with righteousness, and the peoples with equity.' These psalms suggest that 'righteousness and justice' are foundational principles that are part of the fabric of creation itself. A crucial part of the LORD's reign, therefore, is to maintain righteousness and justice. The terms apply especially to God's work of protecting those who are vulnerable. We cannot reduce 'justice' to legal decisions that seem fair based on evidence, though such decisions may be evidence of justice. The Psalms present claims that inform and support the notion that God has a preference for the poor. They are God's special concern and the subject of God's work for justice precisely because the presence of those who cannot maintain and defend themselves is a sign of a broken human community and of a creation that has devolved from God's intentions for *shalom*, that is, well-being or wholeness.

Psalm 82

When we consider the LORD's central role as judge and protector of the weak and powerless, Psalm 82 takes centre stage. This psalm is central to understanding what it means that the LORD reigns. In fact, noted Jesus scholar

---

10 G. Liedke, 'שׁפט špṭ to judge', in *TLOT*, vol. 3, pp. 1393–4 (1392–9).

John Dominic Crossan argues that this psalm is 'the single most important text in the entire Christian Bible'.[11] It may be impossible to pick one text as most important above all others, but Crossan correctly identifies the treatment of the poor and vulnerable as a central concern in the Bible. Thus, he rightly sees the identity of God with the cause of the poor as crucial as well.

Psalm 82 is a unique psalm in form and content. It presents a scene in the heavens in which God presides over a council of gods and pronounces judgement on them. The problem is that the gods are favouring the wicked instead of protecting the poor (vv. 2–4). As a result, the stability of the earth itself is at risk (v. 5). To address the problem, God 'demotes' the gods so they will die like mortals (v. 7).

The psalm has three parts. Verse 1 sets the stage: God enters the divine council and passes judgement on the gods. The gods in this psalm seem to represent the deities of Israel's neighbours. The psalm's underlying presumption is that the gods of the nations exist, but they are inferior to Israel's God. Their role is to oversee the well-being of humans under the LORD's direction. A similar picture appears in Deuteronomy 32.8–9. There the 'Most High' gave the nations their inheritance and apportioned territories for them by assigning a patron deity to each.

Verses 2–6 report God's pronouncement concerning the gods. The question in verse 2 ('How long will you judge unjustly?') sums up the charge against them. They are to care for the weak, orphaned, lowly, destitute and needy (see Pss. 9.7–9, 18(8–10, 18); 10.17–18). Instead, these gods are judging unjustly and showing 'partiality to the wicked' (v. 2). The pronouncements in verses 3–4 essentially declare what they are not doing that they should do. Verse 5 is probably also part of the judgement against the gods (as NIV indicates with quotation marks), but it also notes the outcome of the gods' failure to do justice ('the foundations of the earth are shaken'). Then in verse 6 God gives the sentence: the gods will die like mortals.

As verses 6–7 pronounce a sentence on the gods ('you shall die like mortals, and fall like any prince') they reveal a single criterion for divinity. As McCann says: 'what it means to be God – what characterizes divinity – is to protect and provide for the lives of the most threatened and the most vulnerable.'[12]

---

11 John Dominic Crossan, *The Birth of Christianity: Discovering what happened in the years after the execution of Jesus* (San Francisco, CA: HarperSanFrancisco, 1998), p. 575.

12 J. Clinton McCann Jr, 'The single most important text in the entire Bible: toward a theology of the Psalms', in *Soundings in the Theology of the Psalms: Perspectives and methods in contemporary scholarship* (ed. Rolf A. Jacobson; Minneapolis, MN: Fortress Press, 2011), p. 66 (63–75).

The psalm ends with a plea for God to 'rise up', to take God's rightful place as judge. This prayer assumes the unjust gods are now dethroned and it asks God to deal with the inequities they failed to correct.

Psalm 82 makes two fundamental claims about God's reign and work as king. First, it identifies the primary work of God to ensure justice on earth. As McCann says, that is the very definition of divinity.

Second, the psalm conceives justice to be like the glue that holds the world together. To say that 'all the foundations of the earth are shaken' (v. 5b) is to say that the fabric of creation itself is in danger.[13] Martin Luther thought that the 'gods' (v. 1b) to whom God speaks in the psalm are earthly princes, government officials with the capacity to defend the poor.[14] The psalm more naturally suggests that the gods are members of the divine court and represent the gods of the nations. Nevertheless, the immediate perpetrators of injustice are powerful human beings. Psalm 82 puts such persons and their practices in divine perspective: God stands decidedly against them, as God stands against anyone who does not defend the weak and lowly (Deut. 27.17–19). The Psalms insist this is the heart of God's rule over the world.

King as root metaphor

When we recognize the connection between the images of God as king and God as judge, we begin to see signs that 'the Lord is king' is a root metaphor. It gives rise to practically every image for God in the Psalter. In the Ancient Near East kings exercised extensive authority as they provided protection and support in every area of life. As the Psalms speak of God as a monarch, they extend the metaphor of divine rule into multiple dimensions of God's work:

- *As king, the Lord is also warrior.* God is the one who defends creation from chaos and defends Israel from its enemies (e.g. Ps. 29).

- *As king, the Lord is shepherd.* The benefits of divine rule included God guiding Israel in right paths, keeping them safe in the presence of enemies, and providing for their needs (e.g. Pss. 23; 80).

- *As king, the Lord is a refuge.* The Lord's care and provision includes God sheltering the people from the storms and conflicts of life. As one could

13 Hossfeld and Zenger, *Psalms 2*, pp. 330–1.
14 *Luther's Works, vol. 11: First Lectures on the Psalms II, Psalms 76–126* (ed. Hilton C. Oswald; St Louis, MO: Concordia, 1976), p. 111.

escape to a fortress or a mountain hideaway during an enemy attack, so also the psalmist declares he can flee to God's 'shelter' (e.g. Pss. 57.1(2); 62.2(3)).

Administration of the Lord's reign

Like any strong metaphor, the image of God as king in the Psalms expands and extends beyond the simple equation of the Lord to a ruler. The Psalms speak of the Lord 'enthroned' and administering divine rule. The administration of the Lord's reign has three primary dimensions. It proceeds from a particular place, Mount Zion. The divine rule makes use of a human representative, called 'the anointed'. Finally, divine decrees go forth under the label *torah* or 'instruction'. Each of these dimensions of God's reign affirms that God's governance of the world is incarnational. It appears in tangible expressions of God's work on earth and is accessible to the human community through the various manifestations of the Lord's sovereignty.

Zion: city of the great king

The hymns we call 'Zion songs' testify to the presence and work of God from Jerusalem and its temple (Pss. 46; 48; 76; 84; 87; 122; 126; 132). Psalm 48 is a good example of a psalm that speaks of the city as the seat of the Lord's administration. The psalm celebrates Mount Zion as the place God chose to dwell. It follows appropriately on Psalm 47, which depicts God's enthronement (v. 5(6)) and declares God's universal sovereignty (vv. 2–7(3–8)). We may read the opening line of Psalm 48 ('Great is the Lord and greatly to be praised', v. 1(2)) as a liturgical response to the call for praise of God and the description of God's majesty in the preceding psalm.[15]

The psalm emphasizes that God is to be praised '*in* the city of our God' (v. 1(2)).[16] But more importantly, the city serves as a symbolic representation of God's strength and protection. Thus, the praise in the psalm comes by observing and reflecting on the features of Zion.

'Zion' in geographical and historical terms refers to the settlement David captured from the Jebusites and made his capital (2 Sam. 5.6–10). The description of the city in the psalm, however, is from the perspective of those who experience God's presence in the Temple on Zion and therefore see the city with eyes of faith (v. 9(10)). This is most evident in the accolades in verses

---

15 J. Clinton McCann Jr, 'The book of Psalms', in *The New Interpreter's Bible* (ed. Leander E. Keck; Nashville, TN: Abingdon Press, 1996), vol. 4, p. 871 (641–1280).

16 Emphasis added.

1b–2(2b–3). Zion is God's 'holy mountain' (v. 1b(2b)). Verse 2a(3a) declares it 'beautiful in elevation' and 'the joy of all the earth'. Both descriptions come from an admiring poetic imagination that understands Zion as the centre of the earth. 'In the far north' (v. 2b(3b)) is inaccurate if we take it as a geographical detail of the city. Jerusalem is located in the southern kingdom of Judah and it is not even that kingdom's northernmost city. The key to this reference may be the fact that the word translated 'north' is 'Zaphon', the name of the mountain the Canaanites thought to be the dwelling place of the gods and the place they identified as the abode of their god, Baal. Thus NIV translates this line 'like the heights of Zaphon is Mount Zion'. The implication is that the LORD is the rightful ruler over the world and is greater than the Canaanite deity. Another way to state the meaning of the reference to the far north is: Zion is the real dwelling place of the gods, and there is only one true God, the one who chose Zion and dwells there and rules the world.

Verses 4–8(5–9) describe Zion as an impregnable city that turns away would-be attackers in fear. Some scholars believe this picture of Zion grew out of the events in 701 BCE when the Assyrian king Sennacherib surrounded Jerusalem but then abandoned the siege and returned home, only to be assassinated (2 Kings 18.13—19.37).[17] The influence of this event on the psalm is not certain. What does seem clear, however, is that Psalm 48 presents God with God's kingdom of justice and righteousness overcoming the powerful rulers of this world and their kingdoms. The reference to the 'east wind' that destroys the 'ships of Tarshish' contributes to this message (v. 7(8)). 'East wind' recalls Exodus 14.21 in which an east wind drove back the sea for the Israelites. Ancient people knew Tarshish as a seaport from which ships carried precious metals, the kind of ships wealthy kings would build and employ to enhance the wealth of their kingdoms (1 Kings 22.49; Isa. 23.1, 14; Ezek. 27.25). Thus, the sight of Mount Zion was like the powerful wind that could destroy these vessels at sea to remind humans that only God is in control.

The memory of God's defeat of Israel's enemies takes place in the Temple on Mount Zion. God's power and protection of God's people is an expression of 'steadfast love' (hesed), the faithful, unending love that God shows in covenant with God's people (v. 9(10)). The psalm ends with an invitation to walk about Zion, counting its defensive structures as a way of recounting God's goodness. In other words, the physical features of God's city act like the stations on a prayer labyrinth to signal thanksgiving and praise.

---

17 J. J. M. Roberts, 'The Davidic origin of the Zion tradition', *The Bible and the Ancient Near East: Collected essays* (Winona Lake, IN: Eisenbrauns, 2002), p. 329.

Other Zion songs advance various aspects of these images of the city and its temple. Psalms 46 and 84 emphasize the beauty of the place and the blessings of being there. Because of the beauty that God's presence creates, pilgrims long to enter its gates and 'dwell' there (see Ps. 84.3–4(4–5)). Zion is the ultimate refuge, a symbol of the sheltering protection of the LORD (Ps. 46.1(2)). All of these claims begin, however, with the sure belief that Zion is the place from which God reigns and from which God will eventually make peace among the nations and bring about the final purpose of the creation (Pss. 46.8–11; 76.1–2(2–3); Isa. 2.1–4//Mic. 4.1–4).

The anointed

The Psalms also declare that God administers divine rule through a person, the anointed. 'Anointed' is the English term that describes one installed by having oil poured over the head as Samuel did to Saul (1 Sam. 10.1–8) and David (1 Sam. 16.1–13). Although the Old Testament expresses some reservations about Israel having a king and the potential abuses of a monarchy (1 Sam. 8), the narratives in 1 Samuel eventually give way to the idea that the one whom God anoints has a unique role in carrying out the LORD's will on earth. In the story of David's rise to power, David twice refuses to kill Saul and take the throne because Saul is 'the LORD's anointed', one to whom God gave the special role of king in God's reign (1 Sam. 24; 26). The Psalms speak of the office of the king in God's kingdom without debate, reservation or explanation. This idea appears prominently in the so-called royal psalms that focus on the life and events of the king (see Chapter 4). Psalm 2 first presents the idea in the Psalter as it raises the problem that the nations and their kings rebel against the LORD's authority by opposing the anointed:

> Why do the nations conspire,
>   and the peoples plot in vain?
> The kings of the earth set themselves,
>   and the rulers take counsel together,
>   against the LORD and his anointed, saying,
> 'Let us burst their bonds asunder,
>   and cast their cords from us.'
> (vv. 1–3)

In the Ancient Near East a king was responsible for every aspect of the welfare of his people. He was a military leader and protected them from external enemies with his army; he sponsored a court system and thus ensured fair judgements when citizens had disputes; and the king especially protected those who were vulnerable. The Psalms testify to all of these roles for the LORD's anointed: military leadership (Ps. 20.6) and justice for the weak and powerless (Ps. 72.1–4) are quite prominent. The defence of the poor, however, stands out. Psalm 72 is a prayer for the king to defend the cause of the poor:

> May he defend the cause of the poor of the people,
>> give deliverance to the needy,
>> and crush the oppressor.
> (v. 4)

In this effort the anointed mirrors on earth what God does from heaven (Ps. 37.39–40).

Based on this crucial role to oversee justice for the weak and powerless, the Psalms pray for the welfare of the anointed (Ps. 72.5). He does not live to advance himself, but to bless the people through his reign (Ps. 72.6). The rule of the anointed was to make manifest the justice and righteousness of God.

It is easy to see how the kings of Israel and Judah imperfectly fulfilled these hopes, and their reign came to an end altogether in 587 BCE. These failures naturally gave way to expectations for a future king who would rule perfectly. The early Church saw Jesus as the ultimate fulfilment of expectations for the anointed. Nevertheless, the Psalms never give up on the idea that God's reign finds tangible expression in a human person through whom God works to bring about the divine purpose on earth.

Torah

Just as a human monarch administers rule through decrees and declarations, so also the Psalms say the LORD administers divine rule through Torah. Although the term 'law' sometimes translates it, that word is very misleading and limits the understanding of Torah in the Psalter. Torah can indeed refer to a legal injunction (Exod. 12.49) or to a collection of laws (Deut. 4.8), but the word in the Psalter usually refers to something much more dynamic. The word *torah* derives from a verb (*yarah*) that means 'to teach'.[18] In Job 6.24, for instance, this verb appears in parallel with another word that means 'understand' (*bin*): 'Teach me, and I will be silent; make me understand how I have gone wrong.' Hence, *torah* essentially means 'instruction'.

---

18 See the full discussion in G. Liedke and C. Petersen, 'תּוֹרָה *tôrâ* instruction', in *TLOT*, vol. 3, pp. 1415–22.

Torah sometimes refers to instruction in the form of written texts, that is, Scripture. Deuteronomy reports that Moses delivered speeches to Israel on the plains of Moab that would be instructive for Israel's life in the land. After promulgating the law to Israel, Moses commanded the people to erect stones after entering Canaan, and 'write on them all the words of this law' (Deut. 27.3). Hence, this passage identifies Torah as the written deposit of Moses' speeches.[19] Eventually 'Torah' became a term for all of the Pentateuch (Genesis to Deuteronomy), the five 'books of Moses'. It is *the* Torah, the first and most authoritative portion of the Jewish canon.[20]

But in the Psalms Torah does not seem to refer to written texts exclusively, perhaps not even in a majority of cases. Psalm 119, which highlights the benefits of Torah, is a primary example. It does not mention Moses, Sinai or even the term 'book'. Given the alphabetic arrangement of the work, it would have been easy to work such references into sections that begin with the letters mem (the first letter in the name Moses) or samekh (the first letter in *sepher*, 'book'). The absence of such terms does not mean that the psalmist here does not associate Torah with the Mosaic legislation at all, but it seems that such an association does not exhaust the meaning of the term. That Torah implies more than an authoritative text in Psalm 119 is clear from what the psalm does say directly. The psalmist throughout the poem prays for illumination in order to understand and observe the will of God:

> Teach me, O LORD, the way of your statutes,
> and I will observe it to the end.
> Give me understanding, that I may keep your law
> and observe it with my whole heart.
> Lead me in the path of your commandments,
> for I delight in it.
> (vv. 33–35)

Torah here seems to include something that is already known and something that continues to be revealed as well. As Jon Levenson says of the psalmist's commitment to Torah in these verses: 'On the one hand, he knows the Torah and has spent his life learning it. On the other, he prays to have it disclosed

---

19 For the implications of these references, see S. Dean McBride Jr, 'Polity of the covenant people', *Interpretation: A journal of Bible and theology* 41 (1987), pp. 229–44.

20 See Jon D. Levenson, 'The sources of Torah: Psalm 119 and the modes of revelation in Second Temple Judaism', in *Ancient Israelite Religion: Essays in honor of Frank Moore Cross* (ed. Patrick D. Miller, Paul D. Hanson and S. Dean McBride Jr; Philadelphia, PA: Fortress Press, 1987), p. 559 (559–74).

to him as if it is new.'[21] Indeed, Torah includes 'received traditions', which is identified with wisdom handed down by teachers (vv. 99–100), but probably also with texts we now know as part of the Old Testament. It also includes, however, truth about God revealed by nature (vv. 89–91) and 'unmediated divine teaching' (vv. 26–29).[22]

In sum, the word *torah* in Psalm 119 and wherever it appears in the Psalter refers to something dynamic. The term assumes normative written texts, but it is not limited to them. Torah also includes other expressions of the divine will and the divine vision for reality that illuminate the truth known already in texts considered Scripture. Therefore, the term *torah* probably also includes the Psalms themselves.

Torah, in whatever form it takes, is for the psalmist a source of protection and an expression of divinely supplied security, just as Mount Zion and the anointed are in certain psalms. According to Psalm 1, meditation on Torah (v. 2) has a direct bearing on the righteous person being secure, 'like [a tree] planted by streams of water' (v. 3). Psalm 19.11b(12b) declares that 'in keeping them [the divine precepts] there is great reward'.

The central importance of Torah in the Psalms comes through most clearly in Psalm 119, if we have the patience to read it all the way through! Many readers and many commentators summarize this massive psalm, in part because it seems impractical to pay attention to each line. Its repetition and constant reference to Torah lends itself to such a cursory reading. Nevertheless, these features of the psalm tell us something important about Torah. The psalm's regular octads and the repetition of synonyms for Torah create a meditative experience for the reader, an experience that is itself revelatory in some sense. Levenson suggests that the structure of the psalm functions like a mantra.[23] We cannot get the message of the psalm in a summary statement or in propositions. Rather, we must experience the message through the constant reading of and reflecting on its 176 verses. Upon reading the whole psalm, one is overwhelmed by Torah! It applies to everything.

One of the main ideas that emerges from reading Psalm 119 is that meditation on Torah brings security to the reader. The psalm frequently includes the language of trust and dependence to speak of the benefits and protective potential of Torah, and it petitions God for help based on the fact that the psalmist meditates on Torah:

---

21 Levenson, 'Sources of Torah', p. 565.

22 Levenson, 'Sources of Torah', p. 570.

23 Levenson, 'Sources of Torah', p. 566.

Let your mercy come to me, that I may live; for your law is my delight.
(v. 77)

May my heart be blameless in your statutes, so that I may not be put to shame.
(v. 80)

I am yours; save me, for I have sought your precepts.
(v. 94)

Seeking, hoping and trusting in Torah in this psalm is the mark of devotion to God and the basis on which the psalmist prays for deliverance. Torah has become a surrogate for the LORD, indeed an instrument God uses to direct and reign over the world. Torah is all-encompassing and ultimately takes on roles of protection and blessing that some psalms link to Mount Zion and the anointed. Historically this makes sense since Israel experienced the loss of Zion and the king in the Babylonian exile. The claim that 'the LORD reigns' in the light of the exile makes the role of Torah crucial. It is the one aspect of the administration of divine rule that does not fall victim to the rebellion of the nations.[24]

---

24 See Jerome F. D. Creach, 'Like a tree planted by the temple stream: portrait of the righteous in Psalm 1:3a', *Catholic Biblical Quarterly* 61, no. 1 (January 1999), pp. 34–46.

8

The theology of the Psalms, Part 2: What is the human being?

'What is the human being?' is the natural counterpart to 'Who is God?' It is another essential question of theology, and the Psalms show particular interest in the subject. Psalm 8 explores the question directly, though with the language of prayer that acknowledges first the sovereign rule of God. The psalm asks not simply 'What are human beings?', but 'What are human beings *that you are mindful of them*; mortals *that you care for them*?' (v. 4(5)).[1]

Psalm 8 answers the question by pointing to the unique place of humans before God and in relationship to the rest of creation. Like Genesis 1 and 2, this psalm presents human beings as God's representatives on earth. Humans exercise authority and care for the rest of creation within God's overarching sovereignty. They have a royal office within God's kingdom, as Psalm 8.5(6) indicates:

Yet you have made them a little lower than God,
  and crowned them with glory and honour.[2]

The answer is not what we might expect. The question in verse 4(5) highlights the weakness of humans by using terms that carry an association with the dust from which God made humans. The Hebrew term *'enosh* ('human being') comes from a root that means 'to be weak' (*'anash*; e.g. Job 34.6 NRSV translates 'is incurable') and *ben-'adam* ('son of a human' or 'mortal') comes from the same root as the Hebrew word for 'soil' (*'adamah*; see Gen. 2.7). Therefore, it may seem surprising that the testimony to humankind's exalted position within God's reign places humans within the divine administration. Humans are the primary instruments of God's purpose.

---

1 Emphasis added.
2 See James Luther Mays, *Psalms* (Interpretation: A Bible commentary for teaching and preaching; Louisville, KY: Westminster John Knox Press, 1994), pp. 65–70.

Later in the Psalter, Psalm 144.3 will ask the question of the identity of the human again and will answer by stating the fact of human weakness (v. 4; see also Job 7.17–18). Psalm 144 balances Psalm 8's testimony about the high place of human beings with the sober judgement that human life is fleeting and humans are nothing in the presence of God. The ephemeral existence of human beings is also part of the reflections related to Israel's failures and their loss of the monarchy (Pss. 89.47–48(48–49); 90.5–10; 103.15–16). As a result, it is tempting to look here at the interplay between these psalms to answer the question of how the Psalms deal with the question 'What is the human being?'

Nevertheless, these reflections, as important as they are in the Psalter, are occasional occurrences. By far the most dominant way of addressing the nature of humankind is not the question of how God made humankind or the place God intended humans to have within God's administration, but how each human being responds to the reality of God's reign. In fact the main question for the Psalms seems to be, 'Does a person depend on God, and look to God as lord of the universe, or does that person rely on his or her own resources to get through life?' In the Psalms these are the two primary choices and they point to two categories of humanity. As the Psalter classifies humankind into these two groups, the main labels it gives are 'righteous' (*tsadiq*) and 'wicked' (*rasha'*). In the Psalms these are the most basic types of people, and the interest in the two groups is so pervasive that it constitutes one of the main subjects of the book.

As we recognize this language in the Psalms we also recognize that it is not common in most contemporary faith communities. The word 'righteous' and the related word 'wicked' have all but fallen out of the vocabulary of religious speech today. Perhaps for that reason the problem of the righteous and their future has been generally overlooked in discussions of the theology of the Psalter. Nevertheless, this theme is pervasive in the book of Psalms and is the main issue in the identity and nature of humans before God.

We may illustrate the central importance of this language in the Psalms by the sheer frequency of its occurrence. The Psalter begins with a psalm that sets forth the life of the righteous over against the wicked (Ps. 1.1–3) and then declares what the end will be like for the two groups: the wicked will be swept away in judgement while the righteous are kept in God's care (vv. 4–6). In the psalms that follow, these labels appear constantly. The term 'righteous' occurs 52 times in the Psalms. Only Proverbs uses the term more often (66 times). A host of related words are also prevalent. The word 'upright' appears 25 times, more often in the Psalms than in any other book. Other related words include 'poor' (*'ebyon*), 'needy' (*dal*) and 'afflicted' (*'ani*). In all, these terms that describe the righteous appear 125 times in the Psalter. Furthermore, the word 'wicked' appears 82 times in the Psalter, far more frequently than in any other book of the Old Testament.

The impressive number of occurrences of this terminology alone makes it hard to escape the crucial role the righteous and wicked play in the Psalter. Yet, the interest is even more pervasive than this vocabulary indicates. The righteous appear again and again in the Psalter in the voices of those who pray. Put another way, the prayers in the Psalter that call out to God for help are the prayers of those the Psalms call 'righteous'. When we account for this fact, it is clear that 'righteous' is the primary designation for those who seek God in the Psalms.[3] So, the Psalter treats the question of 'What is the human being?' by presenting prayers of the righteous as models of what it means to be in relationship with God and by describing the ideal person with language of dependence and trust. One way of distinguishing this interest in humankind is to say that it is an interest in human experience, especially human struggle and how the human responds to it.[4]

One who trusts

The term 'righteous' in the Psalms primarily designates those who depend on God for protection (Ps. 34.6(7)). This portrait, in turn, has several dimensions. The righteous depend on God when they are in trouble, and they are often in trouble because they have strong enemies who pursue them (Ps. 143); they depend on God because they recognize they are sinful (Ps. 38.18(19)); because they recognize their dependence, they worship God in humility (Ps. 17.15). In the language of God's reign, the righteous are those who identify themselves as servants of the divine king (see further Chapter 9).[5]

Prayer: the activity of the righteous

The act of prayer is characteristic of the righteous because it indicates their dependence on God. In prayer the righteous recognize that they are 'poor and needy', and seek God's protection and care. Indeed, prayer distinguishes the

---

3 As Patrick D. Miller notes concerning the righteous and the wicked, 'how these two groups act, the way they go – whether one means their path of life or their ultimate fate – is very much the subject matter of the psalms'; see 'The beginning of the Psalter', in *The Shape and Shaping of the Psalter* (ed. J. Clinton McCann Jr; JSOTSup 159; Sheffield: JSOT Press, 1993), p. 85 (83–92).

4 Patrick D. Miller, *The Way of the Lord: Essays in Old Testament theology* (Grand Rapids, MI: Eerdmans, 2007), pp. 243–9.

5 James Luther Mays, *The Lord Reigns: A theological handbook to the Psalms* (Louisville, KY: Westminster John Knox Press, 1994), p. 27.

righteous, who know they need God's salvation, from the wicked, who think
they are self-sufficient.

The prayer in Psalm 131 is one of the most powerful expressions of dependence on God in the Psalter. In its three brief verses this psalm captures the humility that is at the heart of the righteous person's relationship with God. The
psalm consists of two sections. Verses 1–2 contain the prayer itself. In these
verses the psalmist expresses complete trust in God. Verse 3 then urges this
dependence on God upon all Israel.

Verses 1–2 express a childlike faith that summarizes what it means to depend on God:

> O LORD, my heart is not lifted up,
>   my eyes are not raised too high;
> I do not occupy myself with things
>   too great and too marvellous for me.
> But I have calmed and quieted my soul,
>   like a weaned child with its mother;
>   my soul is like the weaned child that is with me.
> (vv. 1–2)

Narrative and prophetic traditions in the Old Testament characterize those
with a 'heart lifted up' and 'eyes raised' as presumptive towards God (2 Chron.
32.25). Ezekiel 28 goes so far as to suggest that one who lives in this way is
pretending to be God (vv. 2, 5, 17).[6] The one who speaks Psalm 131, however,
knows well that only God is God and that she needs God's protective presence
more than anything else.

The psalmist here speaks with Job who, in his final speech, confesses that his
charge against God was uttered in ignorance: 'Therefore I have uttered what
I did not understand, things too wonderful for me, which I did not know' (Job
42.3).[7] Job has struggled with and protested at his circumstances. He trusts in
God and confesses that God's ways are ultimately a mystery to humans. So
also the speaker of Psalm 131 is not occupied 'with things too great and too
marvellous for me'. As the psalmist attests in verse 2, the limitations of the
dependent child become a way of existing before God. The one who prays in

---

6 Mays, *Psalms*, p. 408.

7 See Patrick D. Miller, *They Cried to the Lord: The form and theology of biblical prayer* (Minneapolis, MN:
Fortress Press, 1994), pp. 240–1.

Psalm 131 has become like a child before God (Matt. 18.1–5; Mark 9.33–37; Luke 9.46–48).

Prayer functions for the righteous as an avenue into God's presence, which is what they seek more than anything else. Mays puts the relationship between prayer and the presence of God this way: 'To "call on the name of God" is to place oneself in his presence. The prayer describes the self, presents the self to God in all its weakness and need.'[8]

The righteous do not live rightly in order to be rewarded in the future; rather, the way they live is their future because they live in and for the presence of God. Prayer is a key to being in that presence.

Praise and worship

The Psalter also speaks of praise as something the righteous do, implying that this too sets them apart from the wicked. The righteous are those who understand that their 'chief end' is to praise God.[9]

Psalms 32 and 33 make this connection explicit. Psalm 32 is one of the so-called 'penitential' psalms. The psalm alternates between proclamation of the benefits of the LORD's gracious forgiveness (vv. 1–2, 10), instruction in the ways of penitence and faith (vv. 8–9, 11), and testimony by one who has approached God in confession of sin and now knows the LORD's mercy (vv. 3–7). The psalm ends with two verses that give assurance to the righteous of God's protective care and of the certain end of the wicked:

> Many are the torments of the wicked,
>> but steadfast love surrounds those who trust in the LORD.
> Be glad in the LORD and rejoice, O righteous,
>> and shout for joy, all you upright in heart.
> (vv. 10–11)

Psalm 33 begins the same way Psalm 32 ended, with a call for the righteous to praise God:

> Rejoice in the LORD, O you righteous.
>> Praise befits the upright.
> (v. 1)

---

8 Mays, *The Lord Reigns*, p. 41.

9 According to one creed of the Reformed tradition, praise is the 'chief and highest end of humanity'. *The Constitution of the Presbyterian Church (U.S.A.), Part I: Book of Confessions* (Louisville, KY: Geneva Press, 1999), 7.001 and 7.111.

What Psalm 32.10–11 says of praise continues and advances in Psalm 33. Psalm 33.2–3 goes even further than Psalm 32.11 in describing praise. It implies that praise is not something one can do by rote; rather, it requires skill, effort and imagination. Verse 2 includes two statements about praising God with musical instruments:

> Praise the LORD with the lyre;
>> make melody to him with the harp of ten strings.

Then verse 3 continues this call to praise with two statements that indicate praise is an activity that the relationship with God forever renews and refreshes:

> Sing to him a new song;
>> play skilfully on the strings, with loud shouts.

Verses 4–5 (and the rest of the psalm) give reasons why the righteous should offer praise. The content of praise in these verses presents a marvellous view of God and the world as the righteous envisage them:

> [4] For the word of the LORD is upright,
>> and all his work is done in faithfulness.
> [5] He loves righteousness and justice;
>> the earth is full of the steadfast love of the LORD.

Verse 4 has a structure in Hebrew that enhances its message. It begins and ends with words that describe the reliability of God: 'upright' and 'faithfulness'. At the centre of the verse are two phrases that express what it is about God that is upright and faithful. Namely, the righteous can count on the 'word of the LORD' and 'all his work'. It is hard to imagine a broader or bolder statement of God's character. All God says (in Scripture, through prophets, priests and sages) and all God does is evidence of God's consistent benevolence.

The next verse continues this portrait of God, but it includes the world as well. The LORD loves righteousness and justice. This statement is perhaps not surprising since other texts declare that 'righteousness and justice are the foundation of his throne' (Ps. 97.2). The words that follow, however, show that the righteous see the world in a way that may seem counter to reality. They declare that 'the earth is full of the steadfast love of the LORD'. The Hebrew of verse 5b actually favours an active verb in the translation that may make the point more emphatic: 'the steadfast love of the LORD fills the earth.' In other words, God's *hesed* rules the world! This claim, of course, is a way of saying that 'the LORD reigns'. The LORD and the LORD's vision for the world are ultimately in charge and will prevail. That is the claim of the righteous and the content of their praise. Praise, and prayer, set them apart from the wicked because these activities require the one who engages in them to acknowledge that God is sovereign and, in turn, to confess dependence and trust.

Right behaviour: Psalms 15 and 24

As we observed at the beginning of this chapter, the righteous do not bear that label because they are morally pure. They are righteous because they depend on God and not on their own resources, including their own perceptions of goodness. Nevertheless, the Psalter testifies that those who depend on God naturally bear out that dependence in the way they live. Humility breeds compassion and empathy; praising God raises awareness of the needs of others. Therefore, the righteous do bear some characteristics of behaviour that set them apart from the wicked.

Psalms 15 and 24 both address the issue of right living as it relates to the righteousness and holiness of God. Psalm 24.3 asks, 'Who shall ascend the hill of the LORD?' Psalm 15.1 asks similarly, 'Who may dwell on your holy hill?' Thus, these two psalms associate right living with being among worshippers who praise God in the Temple.

Psalm 24 begins with an affirmation of the LORD's kingship: 'The earth is the LORD's and all that is in it' (v. 1). God is in control of the world. The LORD reigns. The subsequent question about who may ascend the 'hill of the LORD' is really a question of who acknowledges God's reign, who lives as a servant of the divine king.

The answer that follows describes certain behaviour. On close examination, however, it is clear that the characteristics of those permitted to enter the holy place are not so much requirements to participate in worship as characteristics of those who do worship 'in spirit and in truth' (cf. John 4.24). Indeed, the psalm describes the holiness of those who ascend the holy mountain in comprehensive terms that resist a narrow legalistic understanding of human righteousness. Psalm 24.4 answers the question of who is worthy to be in God's presence with two sweeping statements. The first half of the verse says the righteous have 'clean hands and pure hearts' (v. 4a). 'Hand' and 'heart' refer alternatively to exterior acts and inner motivation.[10] The verse may

---

10 Hans-Joachim Kraus, *Psalms 1–59: A continental commentary* (trans. Hilton C. Oswald; Minneapolis, MN: Fortress Press, 1993), p. 314.

suggest compliance with laws ('clean hands'), but such obedience grows from proper attention to the spirit of the law ('pure hearts'). In the pairing of these two aspects of righteousness the psalm is like the teachings of Jesus in the Sermon on the Mount, which pushes the notion of obedience and faithfulness to the most extreme limits (Matt. 5.21–48).

The second half of Psalm 24.4 fills out the profile of righteous activity with descriptions of deeds that are similar to Old Testament commands, but verse 4b also gives a comprehensive cast to the righteous obedience, obedience that comes from relationship with God. This portion of the verse makes two statements about the righteous: they do not 'lift up their souls to what is false' and they do not 'swear deceitfully'. Swearing deceitfully refers to lack of faithfulness in dealing with one's neighbour. The same language of 'deceit' appears in Hosea 12.7 and Micah 6.11 to refer to false weights used by dishonest merchants to cheat their customers. Hence, to 'swear deceitfully' implies taking advantage of a neighbour by dishonest means. The language is thus sweeping, referring to the overall obligation to act rightly – to be fair and just – towards others. The phrase 'lift up their souls to what is false' is more oblique. Nevertheless, it seems to point to comprehensive right action towards God. The same terms translated 'lift up' and 'false' appear in the third commandment: 'You shall not swear falsely by the name of the LORD your God' (Exod. 20.7 JPS 1985). The word 'false' in some other texts refers to idols (Ps. 31.6; Jer. 18.5). Therefore, this portion of Psalm 24.4 could mean that the righteous do not 'lift up their souls' (that is, bow down in worship) to other gods. Regardless of the exact intention, it seems clear that the description of the righteous as those who do not 'lift up their souls to what is false' is of people who are faithful in all ways to God.[11]

Like the Decalogue, this psalm presents right relationships in two categories: one must be right with God and with one's neighbour. Also like the Ten Commandments, Psalm 24 portrays the right actions of the righteous as actions that arise from a 'pure heart'. Indeed, just as the commandments conclude with a requirement of the heart ('Do not covet'; see Exod. 20.17; Deut. 5.21), so Psalm 24.4 introduces the requirements for righteousness as a matter of internal purity.[12] In other words, Psalm 24 and the Decalogue suggest that ethics begins with dependence on God, not on adherence to a legal code. The order of these two dimensions of righteousness is essential for understanding

---

11 See Mays, *Psalms*, p. 121.

12 On the significance of the first commandment for internal purity see Patrick D. Miller, *The God You Have: Politics, religion, and the first commandment* (Facets; Minneapolis, MN: Fortress Press, 2004), pp. 45–60.

the activity of the righteous. Their right action is always based on and grows out of relationship, and therefore righteousness can never be obtained in the abstract. The characterization of the righteous in relationships to God and neighbour also shows that the righteous are those who do not focus primarily on themselves and their own desires. Rather, they are open to God and God's reign on the one hand and they are open to the needs of others, to the well-being of the community, on the other hand. This openness to instruction (from God) and need (that they see in others) separates them from the wicked, who are most concerned about their own possessions and power.

Psalm 15 presents a more extensive description of the activity of the righteous, but the description in this psalm, like that in Psalm 24, 'is a picture, not a prescription'.[13] The specific points of conduct illustrate the righteous person's orientation to God that produces right actions towards a neighbour. Also like Psalm 24, Psalm 15 presents the activity of the righteous in terms of outward acts coupled with inward motivation. Verse 2 introduces those able to 'dwell on your holy hill' (v. 1b) as those who 'walk blamelessly', 'do what is right' and 'speak the truth from their heart'. The first two statements describe exterior acts in general terms. The word 'blameless' translates a Hebrew term that we might also render 'with integrity'. The same term describes the character of Job, for example (Job 1.1; cf. Prov. 2.7). Hence, 'blameless' refers to a type of life that is consistent and complete, in every way in line with God's intentions. The second statement, referring to those who 'do what is right', is similar to the first and qualifies it further. Righteous people maintain the order of the world God established by means of actions that uphold that order.[14] The final description in verse 2 makes clear that the right actions the psalmist has in mind do not amount to rote adherence to a legal standard. Rather, they grow out of the meditations of the heart.[15] In other words, the people Psalm 15 describes are like the people portrayed in the first psalm, those whose 'delight is in the law of the LORD' and who 'meditate' on the law day and night (Ps. 1.2). Hence, obedience follows devotion and submission to God's direction.

The specific behaviours of the righteous that appear in Psalm 15, though illustrative and not comprehensive, nevertheless give insight into the orientation of the Psalms towards right action. The actions all have in common a

---

13 Mays, *Psalms*, p. 84.

14 On the concept of righteousness as world order see Hans Heinrich Schmid, 'Creation, righteousness, and salvation: "creation theology" as the broad horizon of biblical theology', in *Creation in the Old Testament* (ed. Bernhard W. Anderson and Dan G. Johnson; Issues in Religion and Theology 6; Philadelphia, PA: Fortress Press, 1984), pp. 102–17.

15 Kraus, *Psalms 1–59*, p. 229.

concern for the well-being of the community on various levels. It makes clear that the activity of the righteous shows they align themselves with God's desire to create community well-being *and* their activity is *part of* God's creative, justice-establishing efforts.

David as righteous

Given his many failures to act rightly towards others, David would not seem to fit the description of 'righteous' that we have just seen in Psalms 15 and 24. Nevertheless, he fits the profile in many ways, mainly in his suffering at the hands of enemies and, in fact, David's main identity in the Psalms is that of one who prays to God and puts himself humbly into God's hands. When in trouble, David 'seeks refuge' in the LORD (see Ps. 2.12).

As we have already observed, David appears in 12 psalms that present events in his life as the contexts in which he prayed the words of those psalms (Pss. 3; 18; 34; 51; 52; 54; 56; 57; 59; 60; 62; 142; see Chapters 1 and 3).[16] In each case, David speaks as one who suffers, who pleads to God for mercy and who expresses confidence that God will deliver him. David's name also appears in the simple ascription ('of David') in 61 other psalm titles. Although these references probably did not signify authorship originally, readers in time understood them in the light of the longer headings. As Mays says concerning David's appearance in these psalms, David's name here and elsewhere 'does not so much claim the psalms as the voice of a king as it identifies him, in the psalms that are claimed for David, with the lowly'.[17] In other words, David in the Psalms represents the righteous who suffer at the hands of the wicked.

The identity of David as one of the righteous does not negate his role as king; rather it makes use of that role to portray Israel's suffering. In numerous psalms the righteous and the wicked take on a corporate identity. For example, Psalm 9.17(18) makes the connection directly: 'The wicked shall depart to Sheol, all the nations that forget God' (see also Ps. 10.15–16). The wicked are enemies of the people of God by virtue of the fact that they are God's enemies, those who plot against the LORD's anointed (Ps. 2.1–2). David's appearance as king has a dual purpose: he represents the suffering righteous, and he also defends the righteous (Pss. 41.1(2); 72).

---

16 On the form and hermeneutical significance of the titles of these psalms see Brevard S. Childs, 'Psalm titles and Midrashic exegesis', *Journal of Semitic Studies* 16, no. 2 (Fall 1971), pp. 137–50.

17 Mays, *The Lord Reigns*, p. 123.

Although confession of sin is not the primary subject of the prayers in the Psalter, it is an important aspect of David's prayers (see further Chapter 9). Given his egregious sins, he could not appear as one of the righteous if he did not recognize them and plead for forgiveness. This is the subject of Psalm 51, which the heading introduces as 'A Psalm of David, when the prophet Nathan came to him, after he had gone in to Bathsheba'. This and other prayers that confess sinfulness show an important aspect of the righteous: they struggle within their own souls for what is right; they recognize their own brokenness; and in their imperfect and needy state, they find refuge in God.

An important aspect of this relationship between the king and the righteous for the Church is the fact that David is the only king identified in the Psalms. David appears in the text of five psalms that identify him as the ruler of Israel (Pss. 18.50(51); 78.70; 89.3, 20, 35, 49(4, 21, 36, 50); 132.1, 10, 11–12, 17; 144.10; see also the reference to the 'house of David' in Ps. 122.5). This is a relatively short list. It is important, however, because the reader learns by these references who the David of the psalms' titles is. In these psalms David is identified as the king, the servant of the LORD, the chosen one, the anointed one, the one with whom God covenanted to establish his dynasty for ever. The identification of David in these ways, and the absence of any other figure in the Psalter so identified, encourages an exclusive association of David with the royal labels, even when the psalms do not make such a connection explicit. As Mays astutely observes:

> These few texts furnish the inner textual code for reading other psalms in which David is not mentioned. When these titles appear in psalms which do not name David, they furnish the identification for the speaker or subject of the psalm. The 'messiah' or 'the king' or God's 'servant' are textual directions to think of David.[18]

The nearly exclusive identification of David with kingship in the Psalter gives a cast to the Psalter's view of kingship that must guide conclusions on the Psalter's theology with regard to human rule and the nature of humankind as well. In the final form of the book of Psalms David is *the* king. Hence, David is an authoritative voice from the past that instructs and provides hope for Israel in exile and beyond. Because of the exclusive association of the king with David, the Psalter creates the expectation of a new David who will stand with the lowly as their defender. This double identity of David – as one

---

18 Mays, *The Lord Reigns*, p. 96.

of the righteous who suffers and as their defender – prepares the way for the Church to understand the ministry of Jesus. He is the 'son of David', the 'king of the Jews', but he is also the righteous sufferer who cries out to God for deliverance (Mark 15.34; Ps. 22.1).[19]

---

19 Though as W. D. Davies and Dale C. Allison point out, the identification of Jesus as a 'son of David' could be intended to associate Jesus with Solomon since Solomon was remembered in Jewish tradition as a healer; see *A Critical and Exegetical Commentary on the Gospel According to Saint Matthew* (ICC; Edinburgh: T&T Clark, 1988–1997), vol. 1, pp. 156–7.

Part 3

THE PSALMS AS PRAYERS

9

The tradition of psalmic prayer, Part I: Opening fully to God

What utterances I used to send up to Thee in those Psalms, and how was
I inflamed toward Thee by them!
(St Augustine)

The more deeply we grow into the psalms and the more often we pray
them as our own, the more simple and rich will our prayer become.
(Dietrich Bonhoeffer)

The belief that human beings can have a relationship with God, and that communication is possible between the two, is perhaps the most basic element of
religious faith. Prayer is the primary mode of acting on that belief. As Eugene
Peterson says, prayers are 'tools' for 'being and becoming'. They are 'tools that
God uses to work his will in our bodies and souls. Prayers are tools that we use
to collaborate in his work with us.'[1] And, Peterson insists, the Psalms are our
primary tools for prayer.

The Psalms are and always have been an important guiding force in
Christian prayer and piety. From Augustine to Bonhoeffer, the Psalms have
been models for Christian prayer. Before that, however, Jesus prayed the
Psalms, especially in his darkest hour (Matt. 27.46; Mark 15.34; Luke 23.46;
John 19.28; see further the Conclusion). As we noted in Chapter 1, those who
collected the Davidic psalms likely conceived them as collections of exemplary
prayers (Pss. 3—41; 51—72). Thus, the Church's appropriation of the psalms as
examples of how to pray continues a tradition that was well established before
Christian prayer as such even existed.

---

1 Eugene H. Peterson, *Answering God: The Psalms as tools for prayer* (San Francisco, CA:
HarperSanFrancisco, 1989), p. 2.

Neglect of the Psalms in Christian prayer

Despite the ancient tradition of praying the Psalms and shaping prayer around language and themes in them, Christian prayer in the modern period often proceeds without accounting for the Psalms in any serious way.[2] The disconnection between typical Christian attitudes towards prayer and the Psalms likely stems from a basic misunderstanding of the nature of prayer and genuine faith. As Ellen Davis says, we should think of Christian prayer as communication with God that involves 'full disclosure' of ourselves to God and, in turn, opens us to God's transforming presence.[3] A common practice of prayer, however, is the opposite. Prayer often proceeds with careful, guarded language that keeps us closed both to our own pain and to the potential for God's Spirit to work on us. The dominant form of prayer in the Psalter is the prayer for help (see further Chapter 4). These are prayers that arise out of trouble of various kinds and in them the psalmist pleads with God for relief, healing and deliverance. They may be the best example of prayer that gives 'full disclosure' of the one who prays to God.

The reasons Christian prayer often shies away from this type of prayer, which we often call 'lament', may be legion. Walter Brueggemann identifies one general reason when he says, 'I think that serious religious use of the lament psalms has been minimal because we have believed that faith does not mean to acknowledge negativity.'[4] As Brueggemann points out, the problem with this attitude when it comes to our prayers is that so much of human experience is steeped in suffering.[5] So, to ignore the prayers that complain to God is to ignore the human condition.

Perhaps this denial of lament is also the result of a particular conception of God. Indeed, much prayer seems to grow out of the idea that we need to be extremely careful with what we say when we believe God is listening. We need to curb anger towards other people or our circumstances, and, above all, restrain any notion of anger towards God. Davis declares, however, that the Psalms expose this as 'hollow sentimentality that often masquerades as prayer'.[6] Since prayer is the means of communication in an intimate relationship, it must be

---

2 Ellen F. Davis, *Getting Involved with God: Rediscovering the Old Testament* (Lanham, MD: Cowley, 2001), pp. 5, 7–13.

3 Davis, *Getting Involved with God*, p. 5.

4 Walter Brueggemann, *The Message of the Psalms: A theological commentary* (Minneapolis, MN: Augsburg, 1984), p. 52; see also 'The costly loss of lament', *Journal for the Study of the Old Testament* 36 (1986), pp. 61–5 (57–71).

5 Brueggemann thus treats the lament psalms under the heading of 'psalms of disorientation'; see *Message of the Psalms*, pp. 15–23, 51–122.

6 Davis, *Getting Involved with God*, p. 8.

honest, and the Psalms model honesty to God better than any other resource for prayer. The Church has always recognized that the Psalms are 'God's gift to train us in prayer that is comprehensive' and 'honest'.[7]

Another problem many Christians face when praying the Psalms is that, at least at first blush, many of the prayers we encounter in the Psalms seem counter to Jesus' model prayer: 'Our Father in heaven, hallowed be your name. Your kingdom come. Your will be done, on earth as it is in heaven' (Matt. 6.9–10). The words of Jesus' prayer seem measured and reserved. The idea that this is the character of Christian prayer, however, overlooks two basic truths. First, from the examples we have in the Gospels, Jesus' own practice of prayer was anything but reserved or measured: 'Let this cup pass from me' (Matt. 26.39; Mark 14.36; Luke 22.42); 'My God, my God, why have you forsaken me?' (Matt. 27.46; Mark 15.34). Jesus definitely gives 'full disclosure' of himself to the Father. Second, the idea that the Lord's Prayer is measured and reserved relies on a reading of it as a series of narrow formulae that does not take account of the radical nature of each line. Instead of reading that way, we should read each line of the prayer as a doorway into a whole mode of speaking to God and about God.[8] There is an ancient tradition that the Psalms fill out the brief model prayer that Jesus gave. Jesus' instruction to 'pray this way' offered an outline that psalmic prayer then expanded and completed.[9]

To illustrate the connection between the Lord's Prayer and the prayers in the Psalms, consider the first and broadest petition in the Lord's Prayer: 'Your kingdom come. Your will be done, on earth as it in heaven' (Matt. 6.10). It is easy to say these words by rote and fail to take account of what a radical petition it is. The line assumes that the imperial powers on earth exercise their authority and create a sense of normalcy that is at odds with what God desires (God's 'will'). As John Dominic Crossan says, this line in the prayer

> imagines how the world would be if the biblical God actually sat on an imperial throne down here below. It dreams of an earth where the Holy One of justice and righteousness actually gets to establish – as we might say – the annual budget for the global economy.[10]

---

7 Peterson, *Answering God*, p. 3.

8 See Patrick D. Miller, *They Cried to the Lord: The form and theology of biblical prayer* (Minneapolis, MN: Fortress Press, 1994), pp. 304–35.

9 James Luther Mays, *The Lord Reigns: A theological handbook to the Psalms* (Louisville, KY: Westminster John Knox Press, 1994), p. 41.

10 John Dominic Crossan, *The Greatest Prayer: Rediscovering the revolutionary message of the Lord's Prayer* (New York, NY: HarperOne, 2010), p. 78.

The petition in Matthew 6.10 implies a complaint that the world's present con-figuration is unfair, unjust and cruel. The prayer for God's kingdom to come is sweeping – it covers the whole earth! It captures and calls out the accu-mulation of all that is wrong with the present world. The psalms specialize in expressing the awareness of such wrong, often on a local level. Again, the language of lament, which dominates the Psalter, features complaints about present circumstances. It is most accurate to say that lament is one prominent element in prayers for help. Nevertheless, 'lament' captures this movement in psalmic prayers quite well, for the word suggests prayerful protest against what brings pain and diminishes life. The prayer for God's kingdom to come emerges from a keen awareness of the sources of pain. The most frequently occurring type of prayer in the Psalter comes from personal experiences of them. The one who prays often testifies to being 'harassed, persecuted, ill, or dying' and seeks to overcome these tragic conditions by means of prayer that features lament most prominently.[11] The prayers of the Psalms point us beyond personal trouble, however, as they call on God to right the wrongs of the whole creation.

The nature of psalmic prayer: out of the depths

What is the nature of prayer that gives full disclosure of ourselves, this prayer that so often has lament at its centre? It is helpful to think of the first verse in Psalm 130 as a model and starting point for such prayer: 'Out of the depths I cry to you, O LORD' (v. 1). This line points to the fact that humans always approach God in need – of salvation, forgiveness, healing, or something. We do not come into God's presence immediately reconciled and prospering. Our praise and thanksgiving come naturally and necessarily *after* we express our need to God. The structure of the Psalter as a whole suggests this start-ing point. As we noted in Chapter 6, the Psalter begins overwhelmingly with prayers for help, complaints and protests, and moves towards the end to praise. We see this movement in other parts of the canon as well. The culmination of the story of Israel's exodus from Egypt is the great hymn of praise in Exodus 15. This praise only comes, however, after Israel had cried to God in earlier chapters (Exod. 3.7, 9).

---

11 Bernd Janowski, *Arguing with God: Theological anthropology of the Psalms* (trans. Armin Siedlecki; Louisville, KY: Westminster John Knox Press, 2013), p. 4.

When we read through the prayers in the Psalter it becomes apparent that complaint over troubled circumstances is their centrepiece. This is especially true for the prayers in Books I–III and in the two large Davidic collections (Pss. 3—41; 51—72). Prayers for help outnumber other types of psalms, and the prayers almost always begin with complaints about the circumstances that drive the person to pray. Other important elements of prayer accompany the complaints. Nevertheless, the complaints are striking because of the sheer number of them and because of the extreme language in which the psalmist complains and describes her circumstances.

For example, Psalm 6.2(3) complains that 'my bones are shaking with terror'. Then in verse 6(7) the psalmist declares:

I am weary with my moaning;
    every night I flood my bed with tears;
    I drench my couch with my weeping.

Davis translates the final verb with the imagery the verb normally offers, and thus renders the line worthy of its expressed emotion: 'With my tears I melt my mattress.'[12] She comments that such language intends to get God's attention, and if God is a blues fan it surely does![13]

Such language is ubiquitous in the prayers of the Psalter. It can be disconcerting if the reader's prayers follow patterns of calm and courteous address. The language makes sense, however, if we consider what is at stake in the prayers. The psalmist obviously faces trouble and is desperate for help. Yet, that alone cannot explain the language he chooses for his prayers. The prayers in the Psalter rather assume there is something wrong in the cosmic order, that the foundations of the universe are in danger of crumbling, and the psalmist takes her present circumstances as an ominous sign that the world is going in that direction. As Brueggemann says, the Psalms often speak of 'a new reality of disorientation, when everything in heaven and on earth seems skewed'.[14] We see the connection of these ideas in the famous prayer in Psalm 22 that begins with the so-called 'cry of dereliction': 'My God, my God, why have you forsaken me?' (v. 1(2)). As the prayer turns to confidence in verse 22(23), the psalmist links her own salvation with God's reign over the cosmos:

---

12 The verb *masah* refers to melting in other texts such as Ps. 147.18.
13 Davis, *Getting Involved with God*, p. 19.
14 Brueggemann, *Message of the Psalms*, p. 123.

All the ends of the earth shall remember
    and turn to the Lord;
and all the families of the nations
    shall worship before him.
For dominion belongs to the Lord,
    and he rules over the nations.
(vv. 27–28(28–29))

The logic of this expressive move in the psalm is that the psalmist depends on the Lord and counts herself as one of the lowly. That dependence on God is the primary prerequisite for God's favour (Ps. 2.12). Thus, if the one who depends on the Lord is suffering persecution and shame, the world must be teetering out of control.

This observation brings us back to our original point: the prayers for help in the Psalter are cries to God that arise from the same world-view and set of concerns that produced the prayer for 'your kingdom come'. The prayers in the Psalter assume God is the creator and ruler of the world who actively governs it. As E. M. Cioran says, 'A cry means something only in a created universe. If there is no creator, what is the good of calling attention to yourself?'[15] The psalmist believes in a created universe. The problem is that it seems at present to be running out of control, at least in the psalmist's neighbourhood.

As we have already said, the reason this element of prayer is so crucial is that it ties directly to a stance before God that the first petition of the Lord's Prayer expresses: 'Your kingdom come. Your will be done, on earth as it is in heaven' (Matt. 6.10). We may sum up the motivation for such prayer as concern for and awareness of human brokenness. We see it in other parts of Scripture as well. The indictment of Amos 6.1–6 expresses the same idea:

Alas for those who are at ease in Zion, and for those who feel secure on Mount Samaria, the notables of the first of the nations . . . who drink wine from bowls, and anoint themselves with the finest oils, but are not grieved over the ruin of Joseph!

The prayers in the Psalms protest against living life at ease and not acknowledging that the world is moving in many ways against the intentions of the Creator. This is in part what it means to pray 'out of the depths'.

---

15 Cited in Mays, *The Lord Reigns*, p. 55.

At the same time, the Psalms will simply not allow anyone who prays them – who has knowledge of the whole Psalter – to do so while glibly waiting for the world to return to normal. Those who pray these psalms must sit with the pain that they express. The Psalter resists such easy expectation for the world to turn to the good in at least two ways. First, it includes two prayers for help that do not have any turn to thanksgiving and praise (Pss. 39; 88). Psalm 88 is the starkest psalm in the Psalter in this regard. Brueggemann thus says, 'Psalm 88 is an embarrassment to conventional faith.'[16] If by 'conventional' he means the kind of easy prayer for help that expects and receives immediate help, he is certainly right.

The Psalter also hedges against the 'easy solution' prayers by including some psalms that turn from thanksgiving back to complaint. For example, Psalm 40 opens by thanking God for deliverance from trouble. Then verses 11–17(12–18) return to a troubled state with petitions and pleas for help: 'For evils have encompassed me without number' (v. 12(13)). The final portion of the psalm, verses 13–17(14–18), is identical to Psalm 70 and it seems likely that psalm editors borrowed Psalm 70 to create the ending to Psalm 40. This complaint, which comes in both cases after thanksgiving near the end of Books I and II, conveys the message that the way to God's kingdom is a way of suffering.

The identity of those who pray the Psalms

The confidence often shown by the psalmist concerning the Creator, however, also highlights something about the identity of the ones who pray these prayers in the Psalter. Mays captures this identity well when he says of the prayers' language, 'They are all the language of servants ('ebed) of a king to the king who is their lord ('adon).'[17] This identity of the one who prays has two dimensions. First, the prayer believes God is a cosmic sovereign who has power over life's circumstances as over the cosmos in its entirety. In other words, those who pray such prayers acknowledge that 'the LORD reigns!' (see Chapters 6 and 7).

Second, the one who prays understands the King of the universe also to be her personal God to whom she devotes herself completely. The psalmist ex-presses the personal nature of God with labels that include the first-person pronoun: 'my God' (Ps. 22.1(2)); 'my king and my God' (Pss. 5.2(3); 44.4(5); 74.12); 'my Lord' (Ps. 16.2).

---

16 Brueggemann, *Message of the Psalms*, p. 78.
17 Mays, *The Lord Reigns*, p. 27.

Those who pray identify themselves as servant(s) of the Lord in a variety of ways. The most direct is the simple statement, 'I am your servant' (Pss. 116.16; 143.12) or the related confession, 'You are my Lord' (Ps. 16.2). To be a servant means to belong to another. The identity as servant in this case, however, is not oppressive or demeaning as that identity can be in other relationships. Indeed, the Lord is one who rules on behalf of those who call themselves servants: 'Great is the Lord, who delights in the welfare of his servant' (Ps. 35.27).

The main 'service' the servant gives is trust. The prayers sometimes promise to give sacrifice and fulfil vows (Pss. 54.6(8); 56.12(13)). All such promises, however, come from the fact that the servant puts himself – his life, his future, his whole being – into God's hands, and that is the nature of the servitude. The servant on an individual level lives out what Israel was supposed to be as a people. God called Israel out of Egypt to serve God in the wilderness (Exod. 8.1). The narratives about that service, however, are mainly about God feeding and protecting the people of Israel on the one hand, and their failure to trust God on the other hand (Exod. 16). The individual who prays in the Psalms claims to rely completely on God and thus follows the model Israel was supposed to provide.

The psalmist expresses trust in God, and thus shows herself to be God's servant, in a number of ways. The psalmist's prime illustration is that she seeks God for help: 'In the morning I plead my case to you, and watch' (Ps. 5.3b(4b)). For the psalmist, God is the only recourse, and her recognition of that fact is part of the expression of the servant relationship: 'I say to the Lord, "You are my Lord; I have no good apart from you"' (Ps. 16.2).

The psalmist expresses this dependence on God also with a host of metaphors:

Protect me, O God, for in you I take refuge.
(Ps. 16.1)

But you, O Lord, are a shield around me, my glory, and the one who lifts up my head.
(Ps. 3.3(4))

The Lord is my rock, my fortress, and my deliverer, my God, my rock in whom I take refuge, my shield, and the horn of my salvation, my stronghold.
(Ps. 18.2(3))

156

The psalmist also frequently declares trust in God as a reason God should hear and answer:

> [1] To you, O LORD, I lift up my soul.
> [2a] O my God,[a] in you I trust;
>   [β] do not let me be put to shame;
>   [2b] do not let my enemies exult over me.
> (Ps. 25.1–2)

In this and other cases, it seems clear that the initial declaration of trust and dependence (vv. 1–2aα) justifies the petitions not to be 'put to shame' and not to let the enemies exult (v. 2aβ–b). The request the psalmist makes to God assumes a 'therefore'. There are occasionally explicit connections of this sort, such as in Psalm 43:

> Vindicate me, O God, and defend my cause
>   against an ungodly people;
> from those who are deceitful and unjust
>   deliver me!
> For you are the God in whom I take refuge;
>   why have you cast me off?
> Why must I walk about mournfully
>   because of the oppression of the enemy?
> (vv. 1–2)

In cases like these, the psalmist pleads for help and expects to receive it based solely on her dependence on the LORD.

Those who pray the prayers in the Psalms also identify their trustful relationship with God by declaring themselves 'poor' (*'ebyon*). A number of other terms appear as synonyms of this one, such as needy (*dal*) and afflicted (*'ani*). As if to offer God's perspective on those who pray and speak of themselves this way, the Psalter calls such persons by another name: 'righteous' (*tsadiq*). This label and related terms for those who pray appears more often in the Psalter than in any other book. It is the primary identity of those who pray in the Psalter (see further Chapter 8). Thus, Christoph Levin describes the book of Psalms as the 'prayer book of the righteous'.[18] The theme of the righteous

---

18 Christoph Levin, 'Das Gebetbuch der Gerechten: literargeschichtliche Beobachtungen am Psalter', *Zeitschrift für Theologie und Kirche*, vol. 90, no. 4 (December 1993), pp. 355–81; see esp. pp. 375–6, 379.

one who calls out to God for help appears all over the Psalter, and the presence of Psalm 1 as an introduction to the book is evidence that psalm editors were thinking about the plight of the ones called righteous as they finalized the book. The psalm makes the claim that God who is judge over the universe hears the prayers of the righteous and protects them from harm.[19]

The elements of psalmic prayer

Typically the first movement in the Psalter's prayers is a direct address to God. This beginning point is important because it signals something crucial about these psalms. They begin a conversation with God. They are not pointless rants about the psalmist's troubles, but words directed to God in the belief that God hears and cares.

The address to God shows that the psalmist thinks of God as both majestic and powerful and near and personal. This is one of the remarkable assumptions of the prayers in the Psalms. The God who created heaven and earth, who sits above the earth, is also close at hand and ready to help the individual who prays. The labels for God help create this impression. They are often simple ('O Lord', 'O God'), which appeals to God's nearness. Some of the prayers do use expanded epithets such as 'Most High' (Ps. 47.2(3)), 'Lord of hosts' (Ps. 24.10) and 'Shepherd of Israel' (Ps. 80.1(3)). These labels appeal to God's majesty, but the psalmist often casts them in relational terms, as the last of these epithets illustrates.[20] Perhaps most important, the psalmist often addresses God in the most personal terms. God is 'my God' (Ps. 7.1(2)). The Lord is 'my shepherd' (Ps. 23.1). The prayers claim access to God, who is above and beyond this world.

With the vocative there is often also a description of God that assigns salvific qualities and energy to the Lord and enhances the expression of the psalmist's dependence on God. The one who prays uses various metaphors to illuminate this dependence: 'you . . . are a shield around me' (Ps. 3.3(4)). The same is true of the metaphors for God as protector, such as rock, refuge, fortress and shepherd.

'Deliver me from evil'

The individual prayers complain to God about a variety of troubles. Many of them speak of sickness as the problem, though they express the problem as

---

19 Levin, 'Das Gebetbuch der Gerechten', p. 373.
20 Miller, *They Cried to the Lord*, pp. 58–9.

more than mere physical malady. By 'more than' I mean first that the psalmist uses poetic language that crashes through ordinary expressions of illness. Psalm 6.2(3) declares:

> Be gracious to me, O LORD, for I am languishing;
>   O LORD, heal me, for my bones are shaking with terror.

Again, the psalmist declares in Psalm 31:

> My strength fails because of my misery,
>   and my bones waste away.
> (v. 10(11))

There is never in these prayers a narrow description of an ailment, as though the psalmist is working from a medical diagnosis. It is never 'I have colon cancer' or 'I am suffering from rheumatoid arthritis'. The psalmist describes the ailment as a failing of the whole self. The problem is in the 'bones' that shake or waste away. The bones have no health, and the flesh no soundness (Ps. 38.3(4)). Similar is the term 'soul' (*nephesh*) which 'is struck with terror' (Ps. 6.3(4)). The terms 'bones' and 'flesh' refer to the total person in his or her mortal weakness, and 'soul' connotes the life force within the human.[21]

The language is about more than sickness also because the greater problem is that the psalmist feels at a distance from God and, therefore, at a distance from the source of life. The complaint in Psalm 13.1b(2b) is typical: 'How long will you hide your face from me?' The feeling that God has turned away, has abandoned the psalmist, is a common sentiment (Ps. 22.1(2)). The prayers often point to two opposing realms, those of life and death. In God's presence there is life. Outside God's presence the psalmist moves towards the abode of the dead. Psalm 16's confident ending expresses the alternatives beautifully:

> For you do not give me up to Sheol,
>   or let your faithful one see the Pit.
> You show me the path of life.
>   In your presence there is fullness of joy;
>   in your right hand are pleasures for evermore.
> (vv. 10–11)

---

21 Janowski, *Arguing with God*, pp. 18–19.

The life the psalmist seeks comes directly from the Source of life, so to 'behold God's face' is the highest joy (see Ps. 17.15). Likewise, for God to be absent, or to seem absent, is the greatest problem (though see Ps. 39.13(14)). The ultimate separation comes in death. So the psalmist often prays to God to be delivered from Sheol, the abode of the dead, and claims the promise that 'you do not give me up to Sheol, or let your faithful one see the Pit' (Ps. 16.10).

The abode of the dead is a place of separation from God, but it is also a place of separation from the life of the community. The psalmist sometimes prays as one near death who already feels the final separation from life (Ps. 41.5(6)), but prays with confidence that God keeps the faithful in life (Ps. 41.2(3)).

The evil the psalmist confronts often comes from enemies who wish him harm (Ps. 41.8–9(9–10)) or act intentionally to bring harm (Ps. 35.4–8). Those who try to hurt others are called 'wicked'. One of the common themes in the prayers is that such people are at present prospering (Ps. 10.12–13). In all this trouble the psalmist prays with confidence that God notices the plight of the oppressed and acts for them:

> Rise up, O Lord; O God, lift up your hand;
>   do not forget the oppressed.
> Why do the wicked renounce God,
>   and say in their hearts, 'You will not call us to account'?
> But you do see! Indeed you note trouble and grief,
>   that you may take it into your hands;
> the helpless commit themselves to you;
>   you have been the helper of the orphan.
> (Ps. 10.12–14)

Giving thanks

Complaint is by no means the only type of prayer in the Psalms. Praise and thanksgiving are also crucial expressions and modes of addressing God. Nevertheless, these 'happier' modes of prayer must take their rightful place in relation to the petitions and complaints in the book. The individual prayers for help model this movement from complaint to praise and thanksgiving. Also, the prayers that highlight God's goodness and blessings typically respond to the fact that God has answered the prayer for help. An example is Psalm 30.1(2):

> I will extol you, O Lord, for you have drawn me up,
>   and did not let my foes rejoice over me.

The trouble is past, but there was trouble and it remains fresh in the mind of the one who prays. A similar movement and logic is evident in Psalm 136, the great communal thanksgiving hymn. It begins with a call to 'give thanks to the LORD for he is good, for his steadfast love endures for ever' (v. 1). The prayer then recalls God's mighty deeds in the past, especially God delivering the people of Israel from bondage in Egypt and protecting them on their trek through the wilderness (vv. 10–22). The prayer concludes by saying, 'It is he who remembered us in our low estate' (v. 23). Members of the community do not give thanks for abundance or for a life that is devoid of trouble. Indeed, the prayer simply acknowledges that God remembered their low position in the world and had mercy on them.

'Forgive us'

One of the striking features of the Psalms is that the psalmist often protests that he is right or innocent (Ps. 17.1). In such cases, however, the psalmist is speaking of a specific case in which he has been accused falsely of a particular crime against another person. He never makes the argument that he is morally pure or free from sin. The prayers for forgiveness are few in number when we compare them to the prayers for help from sickness or enemies. Nevertheless, there are a number of prominent prayers that confess sinfulness. At least by the sixth century, the early Church had identified seven 'penitential' psalms that have this element of prayer at the centre (Pss. 6; 32; 38; 51; 102; 130; 143).[22] Of the penitential psalms, Psalms 32, 51 and 130 stand out. We cited the opening line of Psalm 130 ('Out of the depths I cry to you, O LORD') as a thematic statement about prayer in general. The Church has recognized it specifically as a description of the sinful state from which we pray.

Psalm 51 appears in the Church's lectionary as the passage for Ash Wednesday, and it appears prominently in the rest of the season of Lent. As a result, Psalm 51 has had as much or more influence on Christian theology and worship as any psalm. The superscription presents the psalm as David's prayer 'when the prophet Nathan came to him, after he had gone in to Bathsheba'. The story emphasizes both David's heinous crime and his repentance and admission that 'I have sinned against the LORD' (2 Sam. 12.13). So also the psalm declares, 'Against you, you alone, have I sinned' (Ps. 51.4(6)). The metaphor in verse 5(7) makes one of the strongest confessions of sin in Scripture:

---

22 See the study of Clare Costley King'oo, *Miserere Mei: The penitential psalms in late medieval and early modern England* (Notre Dame, IN: University of Notre Dame Press, 2012), pp. 3–5.

'Indeed, I was born guilty, a sinner when my mother conceived me.' So the Church has seen in this psalm an example of confession it has urged on others.

Finally, Psalm 32 is foundational for a Christian understanding of forgiveness and grace with its opening lines:

> Happy are those whose transgression is forgiven,
>   whose sin is covered.
> Happy are those to whom the LORD imputes no iniquity,
>   and in whose spirit there is no deceit.
> (vv. 1–2)

Paul quotes Psalm 32.1–2 in Romans 4.7–8 to make the case that Gentiles can receive God's approval by faith just as Abraham did. The word in Psalm 32.2 that NRSV translates 'imputes' (Hebrew root *hashab*) appears also in Genesis 15.6, which declares that God 'reckoned' Abraham's faith as righteousness. In turn, Luther and Calvin focused on Psalm 32 to make the point that salvation comes to human beings through God's free gift.[23]

A broader identity in prayer

There are roughly 50 individual prayers for help in the Psalter, and scholars have rightly identified these as the backbone of the book. The content of these psalms and the history of praying them, however, encourages an identity in prayer that moves well beyond the personal and individual. Mays suggests that the nature of the prayers in the Psalms and the practice of using them in prayer throughout the ages encourage a broader application of them in three ways: they call us to an identity that is communal; they encourage us to pray in a way that is typical, not personal; and they urge us to remember that the Church prays Christologically.[24]

We find the first broader perspective immediately in the community prayers for help (see Chapter 4). The individual prayers themselves, however, also encourage a communal identity. A number of prayers in the Psalter that seem to be prayers by individuals have within them invitations for community members to pray as well. One of the most interesting is Psalm 129. It begins, 'Often have they attacked me from my youth' (v. 1a). This sounds like any number of

---

23 See Ellen Charry's extended discussion in *Psalms 1–50: Sighs and songs of Israel* (Brazos Theological Commentary on the Bible; Grand Rapids, MI: Brazos Press, 2015), pp. 166–7.

24 Mays, *The Lord Reigns*, p. 50.

the prayers for help in individual style that dominate the Psalter. After the first line, however, another voice enters. It seems to be a worship coordinator of sorts who invites the community to pray the same words: 'let Israel now say – "often have they attacked me from my youth"' (vv. 1b–2a). Psalm 131 is similar. It includes one of the most personal and moving expressions of trust in the Psalter:

> O LORD, my heart is not lifted up,
>   my eyes are not raised too high;
> I do not occupy myself with things
>   too great and too marvellous for me.
> But I have calmed and quieted my soul,
>   like a weaned child with its mother;
>   my soul is like the weaned child that is with me.
> (vv. 1–2)

As Patrick Miller points out, a more wooden (and straightforward) translation of verse 2 points clearly to a woman as the one who prays these words: 'Like a weaned child on its mother, like the weaned child on me is my soul.'[25] As personal and specific to a person as the prayer is, it also ends with a call for Israel to 'hope in the LORD' (v. 3).

The prayers in the Psalter also direct us to prayer that is typical and not just personal. The prayers are there for us to take with us when we pray publically or pray for someone else. We should recognize in the prayers the pain of humanity as well as our own individual pain. The rabbis declared, 'Whatever David says in his book pertains to himself, to all Israel, and to all times.'[26]

It is this feature of the prayers in the Psalms that makes them excellent resources for pastoral care.[27] Donald Capps presents the prayers for help as a framework for pastoral counselling with those in grief. Each stage of counselling represents a movement in prayer: complaint, petition, words of assurance, and promise of praise.[28] The prayers in the Psalms therefore show both a process and a model prayer in each stage. They provide a way to get from grief

---

25 Miller, *They Cried to the Lord*, pp. 239–40.

26 *The Midrash on Psalms* (trans. William G. Braude; Yale Judaica Series 13; New Haven, CT: Yale University Press, 1959), vol. 1, p. 230.

27 See Carol L. Schnabl Schweitzer, 'Psalms as resources for pastoral care', in *The Oxford Handbook of the Psalms* (ed. William P. Brown; New York, NY: Oxford University Press, 2014), pp. 583–95.

28 Donald Capps, *Biblical Approaches to Pastoral Counseling* (Eugene, OR: Wipf & Stock, 2003), pp. 77–80.

to praise, but they also allow for doubt and uncertainty. The honesty of the prayers gives language for each of these within the framework of faith.

Finally, Christians have traditionally read the prayers in the Psalter Christologically. They are Christ's prayers. As we will see further in the Conclusion, the Gospels report that Jesus' prayers on the cross came almost exclusively from the Psalms. The Church has gone beyond that direct evidence of Jesus' praying, however. It has read all the psalms as his prayers. This reading of the prayers is the natural outcome of Jesus' identity as the son of David, the Messiah (Matt. 1.18–25). It therefore turns the prayers into Jesus' intercessions for the Church and for the world. As it does, it reminds us that the prayers in the Psalter are also theology.[29] We will explore the implications of this kind of reading in the next chapter.

Conclusion

The prayers of the psalmists and the prayers we might pray when they inspire us are first and foremost prayers of honesty, as though we are talking with a friend and confidant. We might well say that psalmic prayers follow the advice in Rosanne Cash's song, 'Tell Heaven':

> When you're like a broken bird, tell heaven.
> Battered wings against the darkened day,
> when your worries won't let you sleep, tell heaven.
> When the tears won't ever go away,
> if you got no one to love, tell heaven.
> There's no one on the telephone today,
> when every story falls apart, tell heaven.
> Nothing good seems like it will come your way,
> tell heaven.[30]

As Cash instructs in this song, so the Psalms suggest that the one in pain bring all of it before God, openly and honestly. The designation 'heaven' here, however, does not do justice to the One to whom the psalmist prays. That One is the Lord God, the one the psalmist calls 'my God', 'my shepherd' and 'my refuge', the one the people of Israel seek as 'our God'.

29 Miller, *They Cried to the Lord*, p. 1.
30 Rosanne Cash, 'Tell Heaven', from the album *The River & the Thread*, Blue Note Records, 2014.

10

The tradition of psalmic prayer, Part 2: Psalms that pray for vengeance

Rise up, O LORD, in your anger; lift yourself up against the fury of my enemies.
(Ps. 7.6a(7a))

Repay them according to their work, and according to the evil of their deeds; repay them according to the work of their hands; render them their due reward.
(Ps. 28.4)

Let them be like chaff before the wind, with the angel of the LORD driving them on. Let their way be dark and slippery, with the angel of the LORD pursuing them.
(Ps. 35.5–6)

Let them be like the snail that dissolves into slime; like the untimely birth that never sees the sun.
(Ps. 58.8(9))

Of all the elements of prayer in the Psalms, these are surely not suited for Christian prayer! Or so the common judgement about prayer goes. The psalms we are considering here are 'psalms of vengeance'. They sometimes appear with the label 'imprecatory', which means 'cursing', because these psalms in one form or another curse or wish ill for an enemy. It is mainly that element that seems inappropriate for Christian prayer. Indeed, these psalms seem to run counter to Jesus' instructions to love and pray for one's enemies (Matt. 5.43–48) and to contradict his model prayer which calls on God to 'forgive us our debts, as we also have forgiven our debtors' (Matt. 6.12). The apostle Paul seems to speak directly against such prayers when he says, 'Bless those who curse you' (Rom. 12.14) and further 'Never avenge yourselves' (Rom. 12.19). The psalms that curse the enemy and call on God to bring vengeance seem to be illegitimate modes of prayer for the Church, and many have rejected them as such.

Despite these common impressions of the imprecatory psalms, the Church throughout the ages has insisted that 'these psalms are available and even appropriate for Christian prayer, and sometimes they are necessary'.[1] These angry, cursing psalms dispel yet another false idea about the purpose of prayer. There is a popular notion that prayer takes the one who prays into 'subliminal harmonies' and puts him or her in tune with the cosmos, into a sort of Zen-like state. Prayer can do that. The prayers of the Psalms, however, often take the one who prays into the inequities and injustices of the world, what the Psalms refer to as 'evil' or 'wickedness'. The Psalms make us aware of the prevalence of evil and its effect on God's creation and God's creatures. When we are aware of all of that, any harmony we may achieve in prayer is hard-won and may come only after much consternation and struggle with God. Indeed, when we enter into prayer with such consciousness, 'prayer is combat'.[2] For that reason, the psalms of vengeance are among the most important 'tools' for prayer, as Eugene Peterson says.

Why do we need prayers of vengeance?

What we have just said makes a case for the imprecatory psalms as resources for our prayers. Nevertheless, their harsh content continually strikes many who read them as 'sub-Christian'. For that reason, it is perhaps necessary to say more about the place these texts have in Christian prayer today.

In the last chapter we said that many of the psalms that complain to God are prayerful expressions of the Lord's Prayer petition, 'Your will be done, on earth as it is in heaven', and the psalms of vengeance fall into that category as well. Most, if not all, of the imprecatory psalms fit into the classification of 'prayers for help' (either by an individual or by a community). We noted concerning those psalms that the ones who pray them pray for God to address the inequities and injustices in the world, and the psalms we are discussing here are pointed examples of that same type of prayer. The particular extreme

---

1 Ellen F. Davis, *Getting Involved With God: Rediscovering the Old Testament* (Lanham, MD: Cowley, 2001), p. 23.

2 Eugene H. Peterson, *Answering God: The Psalms as tools for prayer* (San Francisco, CA: HarperSanFrancisco, 1989), p. 95.

expressions we encounter in the imprecatory psalms are important for the Church for at least three reasons.

First, and most generally, the imprecatory psalms are the primary tool we have for calling on God's help against 'the cosmic powers of this present darkness' and 'the spiritual forces of evil in the heavenly places' (Eph. 6.12).[3] This reading of the imprecatory psalms should not surprise us since the New Testament expresses the same concern for the problem of evil. The apostle Paul says directly in 1 Corinthians 16.22, 'Let anyone be accursed who has no love for the Lord.' Jesus also testifies to his opposition to evil by his exorcisms (e.g. Mark 1.21–28).

Second, the psalms that pray for vengeance are actually praying for God to address violence done to the poor and lowly. Therefore, imprecation is not extraneous to the Psalms or to the Bible; rather, it is a central part of the Bible's testimony to the faith of God's people.

Third, these psalms are important resources for the Church to help it speak out against violence, particularly the more subtle forms of violence done through economic injustice and the misuse of language. In other words, the imprecatory psalms are protests against violence, not texts that approve of violence. Therefore, we are not to avoid them. They are necessary for a robust life of faith and prayer.

Guidelines for praying psalms of vengeance

To say that the imprecatory psalms are necessary, however, still leaves open the question of how we should pray them or use them to inform our prayers. Because they are so extreme in their rhetoric and their petitions are so harsh, there is potential to misuse them. To extend Peterson's metaphor of the psalms as a tool, we must use these tools carefully and we need instruction in how to do so. Thankfully, the Church has preserved some profound reflection on the imprecatory psalms and how they might inform our prayers or even *be* our prayers.

1 As prayers for an end to evil, the psalms of vengeance are not personal or petty. They are essentially prayers for God's will to be done 'on earth as it is in heaven' (Matt. 6.10).

2 Despite their ardent opposition to victimization, the imprecatory psalms do not propose violent means of preventing victimization. To the

---

3 Peterson, *Answering God*, p. 95.

contrary, these psalms are prayers to God. Those who pray the psalms do not ask God to empower them to attack their enemies. Rather, they call on God as judge of the universe to deal with the enemies. Thus, the psalms of vengeance counter violence in two ways. First, they speak against those who are violent and call into question their actions. But second, they turn vengeance over to God. The psalmist does not claim vengeance for himself or herself.

3 The Psalter is concerned for violence done to the weak by the powerful and so directs its prayers more than any other part of Scripture to the problem of the suffering of those the Psalms call 'righteous' (see Chapter 8). Although this language appears throughout the Bible, it appears in its greatest concentration in the Psalms. There is much to suggest, in fact, that the entire book of Psalms is about the plight of the righteous who are continually plagued by those the Psalter calls 'wicked'. The imprecatory psalms are the prayers of the righteous as they plead for God to deliver them from the clutches of the wicked.

As we have noted, however, 'righteous' is not a label the psalmist claims for herself. It is essentially a divine perspective on those people who live in humility and depend on God. The psalmists call themselves 'poor' and 'needy'. This identity has led the Church to say that the Psalms, including the imprecatory psalms, are the prayers of Jesus. As the prayers of Jesus they are, in turn, prayers for those who suffer. When we embrace and pray the psalms of vengeance, we join Jesus in his work for God's kingdom, in the effort to establish justice and righteousness.

Three 'model' prayers

Petitions for God to act against an enemy run throughout the Psalms and appear in some of the most familiar and beloved psalms. Nevertheless, there are several imprecatory psalms that stand out for their harsh language and their sustained prayers for God to curse an enemy.

Psalm 109

Psalm 109 'contains the most vehement of the imprecations in the Psalter'.[4] The psalm contains prayers for God to kill an opponent, to leave his wife a

4 James Luther Mays, *Psalms* (Interpretation: A Bible commentary for teaching and preaching; Louisville, KY: Westminster John Knox Press, 1994), p. 348.

widow and his children orphans (vv. 8–10), and for creditors to ravage his possessions (v. 11).

The circumstances of the one who prays the psalm are relatively clear. This is not always the case since many of the 'complaint psalms' use language and imagery that make it nearly impossible to determine the circumstances of the one praying. Psalm 109, however, presents a clear situation: someone is accusing the psalmist falsely. Although verse 3 contains language related to war, this seems to be metaphorical ('they beset me' appears in parallel to 'words of hate'). The problem, from start to finish, is that the psalmist is the victim of false accusation. Hence, the psalmist complains that the wicked are violently attacking with words. The petition to God, in turn, is a plea to stop the abuse.

The psalm develops this complaint in three main sections. Verses 1–5 plead to God for help to stop the verbal assaults and accusations ('Do not be silent', v. 1). This section of the psalm abounds with references to aggression through words, thus making clear that the problem is public defamation. The psalmist complains that the opponents come at him with 'deceitful mouths' (v. 2a), 'lying tongues' (v. 2b) and 'words of hate' (v. 3a).

The most objectionable language of the psalm appears in the second part, verses 6–19, but the role of these verses in the psalm is not clear. The question is whether this section is the speech of the psalmist against opponents, or if the psalmist is quoting what the opponents have said about him. The second option is attractive because the speech is against an individual. This section may represent the accusation against the psalmist. For example, verse 6 states, 'Appoint a wicked man *against him*; let an accuser stand on *his right*.' A group is attacking the psalmist ('*They* beset me with words of hate', v. 3), so the singular references in verses 6–19 would make sense in the mouth of the psalmist's opponents.[5] NRSV adopts this position and clarifies it by adding 'They say' at the beginning of verse 6.

This understanding of the section would also seem to lessen the offensiveness of the language since it would represent the words of the wicked, not the psalmist. Despite the attractiveness of this position, however, there is good reason to think it is not correct. There is no break in the speech between verses 5 and 6. The words 'They say' do not appear in Hebrew (see NIV for a translation that shows the continuity between vv. 5 and 6). Furthermore, verses 16–19 characterize the opponents better than the psalmist.

Much of the second section of the psalm has language the Psalter uses to describe the wicked, which adds to the notion that here the psalmist is speaking

---

5   Emphasis added in the quotations from vv. 6 and 3.

about his enemies. Verse 16 is typical of the Psalter's description of the wicked: 'For he did not remember to show kindness, but pursued the poor and needy and the broken-hearted to their death' (see Ps. 10.9). The charge that the person in question loves to curse (vv. 17–19) sounds much like the description of the wicked in Psalm 10.7 ('Their mouths are filled with cursing and deceit and oppression'). Given the psalmist's opponents' deceitful and violent words, this section would make sense as the psalmist's speech against them. As McCann says, in verse 6 'the psalmist asks for redress, suggesting in effect that the accusers get a dose of their own medicine'.[6] Verses 8–19 essentially represent the sentence for the psalmist's enemies, who have tried to destroy him with their words.

The final main section of Psalm 109 (vv. 20–29) returns to prayer and petition. The first verse of this section declares that the opponents deserve the punishment that appears in verses 6–19. But the final portion of the psalm puts this prayer in perspective. The psalm does not end with hatred for the enemy, but with trust in God. Verses 28–29 capture what the psalmist is essentially asking throughout the psalm, that is, for God to prove the accusers wrong, to rebuff them publically. In a culture in which public opinion, honour and shame are paramount issues, the psalmist finally wants the community to know his own innocence and to recognize the lies of the opponents. Despite the extensive petitions of verses 6–19, the overall shape of the prayer suggests that those who use the psalm are not to dwell on the prospect of their opponents' suffering. Instead, the psalmist holds out the hope that God 'stands at the right hand of the needy, to save them from those who would condemn them to death' (v. 31).

This final line captures the essence of the psalm: the opponents are out for blood; they are merciless in their attacks on the psalmist; but the psalmist trusts in the protection of God, the only hope available for one powerless in the hands of the wicked. Hence, a careful reading of Psalm 109 indicates that the psalm is not ultimately a wish or call for violence. In fact, the psalm responds to a violent attack made up of words, false accusations. In the end the psalmist turns the need for justice over to God:

Help me, O Lord my God!
   Save me according to your steadfast love.
(v. 26)

---

6 J. Clinton McCann Jr, 'The book of Psalms', in *The New Interpreter's Bible* (ed. Leander E. Keck; Nashville, TN: Abingdon Press, 1996), vol. 4, p. 1125 (641–1280).

Most importantly, the psalmist trusts that God is the polar opposite of the enemies:

> They may curse, but you will bless;
>> when they attack they will be put to shame,
>> but your servant will rejoice.
> (v. 28 NIV 1984)

The psalm ends with another statement of trust that casts new light on the difficult words of verses 6–19:

> For he stands at the right hand of the needy,
>> to save them from those who would condemn them to death.
> (v. 31)

When we recognize the seriousness of the charges against the psalmist and the helplessness of the psalmist to rebuff the accusers, verses 6–19 become more understandable. What at first may sound like a yearning for vengeance, on closer examination is closer to a legal claim submitted to God who judges rightly.[7] The psalm is ultimately the prayer of one of the righteous who looks to God as the true arbiter of justice, the one the psalmist praises for acting with equity and steadfast love (vv. 21, 26).

Psalm 137

Psalm 137 is one of the most difficult and troubling psalms in the Psalter and one of the most problematic passages in the Bible. The problem is really the final verse (v. 9), which extols those who repay Babylon for its destruction of Jerusalem. The difficulty of the verse centres on its focus on Babylon's children, presumably innocent victims of the psalmist's rage:

> Happy shall they be who take your little ones
>> and dash them against the rock!
> (Ps. 137.9)

Hence, some readers naturally reject the conclusion to the psalm as sub-Christian.

---

7 Walter Brueggemann, 'Psalm 109: three times "steadfast love"', *Word & World* 5, no. 2 (1985), p. 154 (144–54).

The Church often ignores the most difficult parts of Psalm 137 while readily embracing verses 1–6. The psalm appears in the Revised Lectionary (Year C, Proper 22, Sunday between 2 and 8 October), but rarely does anyone read verse 9 and the larger section in which it appears (vv. 7–9). A common practice is to offer the psalm in a musical version that excludes the last three verses.[8] Indeed, hymns based on Psalm 137 typically include only the exiles' mourning for Zion: 'By the rivers of Babylon – there we sat down and there we wept' (v. 1), and the torment of the captors with their taunt, 'Sing us one of the songs of Zion' (v. 3). An example is the hymn 'By the Babylonian Rivers'.[9]

This illustrates, however, that Christians seem to accept the love of and lament over Jerusalem with great sympathy but they insist there be no expression of anger over the devastation of the holy city. Or perhaps those who reject verses 8–9 would like a response to Jerusalem's fall that is more thoughtful and forgiving. That perspective, however, misses the impact the final two verses are intended to make. As Erich Zenger says: 'The elimination of verses 8–9 would not only destroy the literary structure of the psalm, but would deprive it of an essential key to a correct and theologically acceptable (!) understanding of its perspective on violence.'[10]

Psalm 137 divides naturally into two parts. Verses 1–6 express the grief of those who held Jerusalem as their 'highest joy' (v. 6d). The first three verses recall the circumstances that produced such grief: as verse 1 indicates, the problem is that those who speak the psalm have 'remembered Zion' (v. 1c). The central subject of the psalm, in fact, may be the word 'remember'. In verses 1–6 the issue is that the memory of Zion produces intense pain and grief and yet the psalmist cannot forget Zion.

As we observed in Chapter 7, Zion was the place of God's presence, the place where the people of Israel gathered to worship and to celebrate God's goodness and justice. The psalmist's grief is brought on by separation. The mourners sat and wept over Zion while in Babylon (v. 1a–b). To make matters worse, the victorious Babylonians taunted the lovers of Zion by saying, 'Sing us one of the songs of Zion' (v. 3c). To this the mourners offer the reflection in verse 4, 'How could we sing the LORD's song in a foreign land?'

---

8 See Peter C. Bower, ed., *Handbook for the Revised Common Lectionary* (Louisville, KY: Westminster John Knox Press, 1996), p. 255.

9 In *Glory to God: The Presbyterian hymnal* (ed. David Eicher et al.; Louisville, KY: Westminster John Knox Press, 2013), number 72.

10 Erich Zenger, *A God of Vengeance? Understanding the psalms of divine wrath* (trans. Linda M. Maloney; Louisville, KY: Westminster John Knox Press, 1996), p. 48.

The problem these verses imply is the loss of what Zion represented for the captives in Babylon. The expression 'songs of Zion' likely refers to psalms we have called 'Zion songs' (see Chapter 4), psalms such as 46, 48, 84, 87, 122, 127 and 132. These psalms typically speak of God dwelling on Zion as king and protector of the city and its people. The taunt of the captors, therefore, includes ridicule of Israel's belief in the power of its God. But the belief that the LORD reigns in Zion is more than just a political conception of where Israel stands among the nations. Israel's belief in God's rule on Zion is a faith that God maintained the order of the world. That belief included faith that God protected the poor and helpless (Ps. 132.15). From an Israelite perspective, Babylon represented just the opposite: coercive imperial power, military might and oppressive force. Israel's experience with Babylon in the late seventh and early sixth centuries BCE shaped this impression. Babylon pressed Judah into vassal status, and when Judah rebelled, Babylon took measures to punish the small kingdom, culminating in Babylon's destruction of Jerusalem in 587 BCE. The role of Edom (v. 7) in the devastation is not completely clear. One theory is that Edom refused to participate in a rebellion against Babylon and thus left Judah to fend for itself. Jeremiah 40.11 indicates that some residents of Judah escaped to Edom, perhaps suggesting Edom had made itself safe from Babylonian attack.

Because of the trauma of the Babylonian attack, the destruction of Jerusalem at the hands of Babylon seemed to signal the onset of chaos. In verses 5 and 6 those who mourn over Jerusalem struggle to maintain hope that chaos has not returned for ever.

With this understanding of what Israel lost when it lost Jerusalem (vv. 1–6), the second part of Psalm 137 (vv. 7–9) becomes more understandable. In fact, it becomes essential to the theology of the psalm. Verses 7–9 address God concerning those who destroyed Jerusalem and they address the oppressive forces as well. The psalmist speaks verse 7 against the Edomites who cheered on the Babylonians and thus participated in the destruction of Jerusalem. Verse 7 uses again the word 'remember', but now it calls on God not to forget. Specifically, the psalmist calls on God to 'remember . . . against the Edomites'. The problem with Edom is that, as Israel's 'brother' (see Gen. 25.19–30), this neighbour state is heir to the promises to Israel and should understand the importance of Jerusalem for the stability of the world.

Then the psalm concludes with two beatitudes:

Happy shall they be who pay you back
    what you have done to us!

Happy shall they be who take your little ones
   and dash them against the rock!
(vv. 8–9)

Two points are crucial to put verses 8–9 in their proper theological context. First, it is important to recognize that verses 8–9 do not contain a petition or request of God. Although commentators sometimes refer to these verses as a curse, the only curse Psalm 137 contains is the self-curse in verses 5–6. Rather, verses 8–9 contains two statements of confidence that God will return to Babylon what it deserves.[11] This is the nature of statements introduced by the Hebrew term 'ashre ('happy', 'fortunate', 'blessed'), the word that begins two lines in verses 8 ('Happy shall they be who pay you back') and 9 ('Happy shall they be who take your little ones . . .'). The word, often translated 'happy' (NRSV; NIV), really means something like 'privileged'. That is, the word does not pronounce a blessing; it simply denotes what the speaker believes to be the state of affairs, at least the state that will surely come.

The second point is that the psalm speaks against the Edomites and the Babylonians because they fail to recognize the reign of God and, as such, they are doomed to failure. Isaiah and Jeremiah declared Babylon's fall in similar terms (Isa. 47.1; Jer. 50.42). The indictment against these two nations is essentially that the Babylonians imagined themselves to be in control of the world and the historical processes. Although Psalm 137 does not say this directly, many other Old Testament texts do. For example, Habakkuk 1 indicates that although God used Babylon to punish Israel, Babylon did not recognize God's control, but thought instead that it had accomplished Israel's defeat thanks to its own abilities. Therefore, God would put Babylon in its place as well.

The type of arrogance and the sense of autonomy Babylon displayed is how the Psalms characterize the wicked. As already noted, the wicked are not personal enemies and the evil they perpetrate is not petty; rather, they are the enemies of God. The main sign that they are against God is that they oppress the poor and powerless, those called 'righteous' in the Psalter. For that reason the Psalms rightly set God's righteousness over against wickedness, and God opposes the wicked directly: 'For you are not a God who delights in wickedness; evil will not sojourn with you . . .' (see Ps. 5.4–6(5–7)). Therefore, when the psalmist asks God to act against the Edomites or especially the Babylonians, it is a plea to protect the poor and to re-establish justice.

---

11 See John Goldingay, *Psalms, vol. 3: Psalms 90–150* (Baker Commentary on the Old Testament Wisdom and Psalms; Grand Rapids, MI: Baker Academic, 2008), pp. 608–9.

As Erich Zenger argues, the language and tone of verses 7–9 is really legal. It asks for God to repay the perpetrators of crime (Edom and Babylon) according to the severity of that crime.[12] Hence, the psalmist shows a limit in his request for vengeance, however harsh the request may seem. Most importantly, the legal overtones of verses 7–9 clarify that the psalmist is not asking for Israel to take on the place in the world order that Babylon previously occupied. Israel is not praying for God to empower it to be the devastator of Babylon. Rather, the prayer is for God to act as judge over Babylon and to set the world aright, to allow God's control to reappear.

The identity of those who speak the words of verses 8–9 is important. They are not terrorists or vigilantes asking for power to retaliate. They are in fact powerless to bring about any change in their circumstances. All they can do is plead with God to 'remember against Edom', and they speak rhetorically against Babylon. In other words, Psalm 137.7–9 is the prayer of the powerless. That means then that the psalmist offers the prayer to God in these verses instead of acts of violence. It places the request for justice where it belongs, in the hands of God.

Still, the beatitude that concludes the psalm is shocking and we must clarify it further. The reference to 'dashing your little ones against the rock' describes in the harshest language possible a reality of warfare. Conquerors often killed the children of those they defeated in order to cut off the future of those people. When the Babylonians destroyed Jerusalem in 587 BCE they killed the two sons of King Zedekiah to prevent a resurgence of the Davidic empire (2 Kings 25.7). This event may well have influenced the final line of Psalm 137 as the psalmist saw Babylonian invaders dash Jerusalem's children against the rocks.

Despite the reality of armies killing children in warfare, however, the Church has not traditionally read the end of Psalm 137 along these lines. Instead, it has read verse 9 in such a way that the 'little ones' were figures of evil thoughts and desires. Augustine understood the Babylonian little ones to be 'evil desires at their birth'. For Augustine, Babylon represented those forces that hindered the child of Jerusalem from reaching her true home. Therefore, he embraced Psalm 137.9 almost as an imperative to rid the soul of evil. He said:

> when lust is little, by no means let it gain the strength of evil habit; when it is little, dash it. But thou fearest, lest though dashed it die not; 'Dash it against the Rock; and that Rock is Christ' (1 Corinthians 10.4).[13]

---

12 Zenger, *A God of Vengeance?*, pp. 49–50.
13 Augustine, *Nicene and Post-Nicene Fathers of the Christian Church*, First Series, vol. 8: *Expositions on the book of Psalms* (ed. Philip Schaff; New York, NY: The Christian Literature Company, 1888), p. 632.

Augustine's interpretation of Psalm 137.9 may seem far removed from the historical situation behind the Psalms and it may seem to have nothing in common with the angry words of the psalmist. But this figurative reading has more to commend it than we might at first think. Babylon's destruction of Jerusalem produced such ire precisely because it disrupted the purpose of God that God administered from Mount Zion (Isa. 2.2–4). The psalmist's intense memory of Zion (vv. 1–6) was not due to personal or sentimental associations alone; rather, the psalmist remembered Zion as the place of worship, the place where Israel celebrated God's reign (note that the references to hand and tongue suggest worship leadership). Therefore, we may read the psalmist's wish for someone to dash the Babylonian 'little ones' as a wish for someone to quench the source of evil. We may understand this disturbing end to Psalm 137 under the psalm's overarching concern to remember. In verses 1–6 the psalmist declares it is impossible not to remember Zion. Though Zion is now in ruins, the psalmist pledges never to forget. To forget Zion would be to forget God's order and purpose for the world. The raw emotion at the end of the psalm comes from the psalmist's intense love for Zion. But the psalmist also speaks against those who destroyed Jerusalem because they represent and cooperate with the forces of evil. The psalmist calls for God to 'remember against' those who destroyed Zion. The psalmist casts these forces as enemies of Israel and enemies of God. They represent the evil that runs rampant in the world. In such a circumstance, for the victim of evil, 'to forget is to submit to evil'.[14]

We should not deny the raw emotion behind Psalm 137.9. The brutal imagery may have come from real experiences of the death of children during the Babylonian destruction of Jerusalem. But it is possible to interpret Psalm 137.9 symbolically without losing entirely the connection to historical Babylon and the event of the Babylonian exile. As Zenger suggests, given the larger issues of justice that lie behind the psalm, we may understand the Babylonian little ones on another more important level as the children of the Babylonian royal house who are poised to continue the brutality experienced in 587 BCE.[15] So Zenger proposes a helpful paraphrase of verses 8–9:

O daughter Babylon, you devastator!
Happy the one who brings you to judgment
Because of what you have done to us!

14 McCann, 'The book of Psalms', p. 1228.
15 Zenger, *A God of Vengeance?*, p. 50.

Happy the one who seizes you
And puts an end to your rule forever![16]

We must make one final point about the final verse of Psalm 137. The beatitude that seems ready to reward baby-killers appears as speech directed to Babylon, but the psalmist in reality speaks it to God. This is how we began the discussion of these psalms, with the problem of these words as prayer. But in the end the character of Psalm 137.9 as prayer may be what makes it acceptable and understandable. As a prayer this line is an act of faith. It assumes God hears and acts. It also assumes God knows how to deal with the likes of Babylon, but the psalmist can do nothing directly to respond to the injustices of Babylon. This identity of the psalmist, in turn, may provide an important guideline for anyone who would allow this psalm to shape his or her prayer. Indeed, we may embrace it fully and pray such words only if we are unarmed.

Another clue to how we may pray Psalm 137 is the brutal honesty with which verse 9 makes its point. The honesty makes the prayer authentic in that the one who prays does not need to worry about appearances before God. This honesty runs the risk of outsiders misunderstanding it and thus encouraging violence. But if we truly read *with* the psalmist, we must admit that similar feelings of anger and vengeance are within all people. The question then becomes: what will we do with such anger? Psalm 137 provides the answer: submit that sign of human frailty to God in prayer.[17] Such an act of prayer, though rough in its particular expression in this psalm, has two important effects that lead away from violence. It frees the one who prays from violence. It also has potential to lead to forgiveness and reconciliation. As McCann says, the one who prays this honestly to God 'begins a journey that transforms grief and anger into compassion'.[18]

Psalm 139

As troubling as Psalm 137.7–9 is, the concluding verses of Psalm 139 actually seem to contradict Jesus' teaching more directly. When the psalmist says, 'I hate those who hate you, O LORD' (see v. 21), the expressions of hatred seem, on the surface at least, to directly oppose Jesus' instructions to 'bless those who curse you, pray for those who abuse you' (Luke 6.28; cf. Matt. 5.44).

---

16 Zenger, *A God of Vengeance?*, p. 91.
17 See McCann, 'The book of Psalms', p. 1230.
18 McCann, 'The book of Psalms', p. 1230.

Psalm 139 is one of the most beloved psalms in the Psalter, which makes the concluding imprecation even more troubling. The psalm contains a beautiful testimony to God's presence in which the psalmist speaks of God knowing her completely. In Psalm 139.1–18 the psalmist emphasizes how intimately God knows her. The word 'know' appears five times in this section (vv. 1, 2, 4, 6, 14). The psalmist declares that God perfectly, intimately and graciously knows her. It is impossible to escape God's presence, she declares (139.7–12). Even in Sheol God is there (contrast Job 17.12–16). The nearness of God ties closely to God's acts of creating and recreating. God's Spirit is present always with the psalmist to bring order, purpose and beauty (vv. 7–12). Thus, the psalmist reflects on how God formed her in the womb (v. 13) and made all the days of her life purposeful (v. 16).

Although the psalmist's testimony to being known by God in verses 1–18 may seem incongruous with the prayer against enemies in verses 19–24, it actually connects quite strongly to it by the double appearance of the word 'know' in verse 23: 'Search me, O God, and know my heart; test me and know my thoughts.' In fact, we may read the prayer for God to destroy the wicked as the conclusion to which verses 1–18 logically lead. The prayer for God to 'test' and 'know' the psalmist's heart may have its origin in the psalmist's defence against false charges and may have been originally a request for hearing in the presence of temple personnel. Regardless of the original setting, however, the psalm in present form is a prayer for God to deal with the wicked, those who personify evil as they oppose the will of God. The prayer is based on the psalmist's confidence in God's justice and order on the one hand, and the problem of evil, represented by the wicked on the other hand. The psalmist here wants it to be known that she stands with God and God's purpose, which means she stands naturally against the wicked.

We should read the language of hate in Psalm 139 in this larger context of the psalmist aligning with God's intentions in creation. It is telling that the psalmist does not say, 'I hate those who hate me.' Rather, she says:

> Do I not hate those who hate *you*, O Lord?
>   And do I not loathe those who rise up against *you*?
> (v. 21)[19]

In other words, the wicked are not personal enemies or merely persons who have a grudge against the psalmist. As with Psalm 137, they are the very enemies of God, perpetrators of evil (v. 20). Regarding this stance against the

---

19 Emphasis added.

wicked, therefore, two points are important about the psalmist's 'hate' of them. First, the term 'hate', like the opposite word, 'love', is a term that often occurs in contexts that describe covenant making, or not making.[20] It communicates absolute loyalty to a covenant partner. For example, 1 Samuel 20.12–17 describes the love between David and Jonathan in the context of the covenant they enter with each other. In Deuteronomy the covenant into which Moses leads Israel is marked by Israel's love for and obedience to God (Deut. 29—30; see especially 30.6).[21] So, when the psalmist says 'I hate those who hate you', it means she refuses to engage in and formally support those who act against God's intentions.

Second, the declaration of hatred for the enemies of God is part of the psalmist's profession of being known by God and dependent on God. The psalmist demonstrates being 'with' God (v. 18) by the fact that she does not align with evil. A portion of Psalm 141, two psalms later, captures the intention of Psalm 139.19–24. The psalmist prays to be kept from evil and to be kept with the righteous, even though such an alliance is costly. Psalm 141.5 says:

Let the righteous strike me;
  let the faithful correct me.
Never let the oil of the wicked anoint my head,
  for my prayer is continually against their wicked deeds.

So, Psalm 139 is a testimony to God knowing the psalmist and God shaping and governing her will, rather than those the Psalms call 'wicked' influencing her life through their activities. The wicked, of course, are perpetrators of violence. They go against God's intentions for peace and reconciliation. So the psalmist's opposition to the wicked is another way of expressing concern for God's good order, that is, *shalom*. Moreover, this way of speaking is not intended to promote violence. Rather, it is a refusal to ally with those who *are* violent.

The imprecatory psalms and the meaning of 'vengeance'

Our discussion of the imprecatory psalms, and the three examples we have just explored, points to one clear point that has echoes throughout Scripture:

---

20 Ernst Jenni, 'אהב 'hb to love', in *TLOT*, vol. 1, p. 52.

21 See William Moran, 'Ancient Near Eastern background of love of God in Deuteronomy', *Catholic Biblical Quarterly* 25, no. 1 (1963), pp. 77–87.

vengeance belongs to God alone (Deut. 32.35; Ps. 94.1; Isa. 63.4; Rom. 12.19; Heb. 10.30). Vengeance is not the right or responsibility of humans. When humans take vengeance into their own hands it inevitably crosses over into violence. As Walter Brueggemann rightly says: 'to keep some vengeance for self and to withhold it from God is to mistrust God, as though we could do it better than God.'[22] Such a conclusion is liberating in one sense. It places retaliation outside the bounds of acceptable human behaviour and thus frees human beings to work at reconciliation and forgiveness.

This exclusive association of God with vengeance, however, may also be troubling. A God who is concerned with vengeance may not seem like a God we should love and seek after. If we look more closely, however, we may see that the Psalms' close affiliation of God with vengeance is theologically and ethically essential. Divine vengeance is the other side of divine compassion. If Scripture declared only that God shows compassion but did not also declare that God is involved in vengeance, it would then portray God as inept in expressing compassion in concrete ways. When God promises Israel or the righteous that his steadfast love to them is certain, God shows that steadfast love by punishing those who oppress them. This is how God 'right-wises' human life.[23]

The association of God with vengeance is essential also because it has to do with God defending a moral order in the world. It may be helpful to consider further the word 'vengeance' that sometimes appears in translations of certain psalms (e.g. Ps. 94.1). Erich Zenger points out that this English word, which is generally associated with retaliation and anger, may not express the Hebrew word adequately. Rather, the Hebrew term (*neqamot*) signals something like justice or fairness. Thus, in Psalm 94.1 the psalmist calls on the 'God of vengeance' to 'shine forth'. The word translated 'shine forth' (*hopiya‘*) in Psalm 50 speaks directly of God judging with righteousness (vv. 2–6). In Psalm 80 God shines forth to save God's people who have been ravaged by their neighbours (vv. 2, 7, 19(3, 8, 20)). Thus, the prayer in Psalm 94 is for the sovereign God to bring fairness and equity to the world by defending those who are powerless.[24] In fact, Psalm 94.2 continues, 'Rise up, O judge of the earth; give to the proud what they deserve.' The petition is not for irrationality or vengeance in the sense often used, but for the equity that only God can bring.

Nevertheless, we should not understand God's vengeance as something God expresses dispassionately. To the contrary, God has sided with those the

---

22 Walter Brueggemann, *Praying the Psalms* (Winona, MN: St Mary's Press, 1982), p. 72.
23 Brueggemann, *Praying the Psalms*, p. 74.
24 Zenger, *A God of Vengeance?*, pp. 70–1.

Psalms call 'righteous' and determined to defend them. God rises up as judge with a preference for certain people and groups to whom God offers special care. In the Old Testament Israel is the object of God's compassion. But Israel never possesses God's compassion exclusively and Israel never controls God's vengeance. Israel is the special object of God's care only because and to the extent that Israel is righteous, faithful and obedient. When people display these characteristics and they are also oppressed, then God's vengeance works in their favour. In other words, God's actions are actually on behalf of the 'poor and needy', of which Israel happens to be the primary example.[25]

The identification of God's vengeance with the poor appears strongly in the New Testament. The hymn in Luke 1.51–53 depicts a radical reversal of fortunes in which God raises up the poor, needy and hungry while God puts down the rich, proud and well-fed. Also in Luke, Jesus' inaugural appearance in the synagogue has him reading from Isaiah 61.1–2, which includes anticipation of 'the day of vengeance of our God' on behalf of the afflicted. Thus, this dimension of prayer in the Psalms does not oppose the teachings of Jesus. Rather, it is a cry for aspects of what Jesus calls the 'kingdom' of God (see Matt. 5.5).

What place then do the prayers of vengeance have in Christian prayer? They are important to Christian prayer ultimately because they plead for the end of evil. As we saw in the previous chapter concerning psalmic prayer in general, the imprecatory psalms are closely related to the Lord's Prayer and its petition for God's will to be done on earth as in heaven.

Brueggemann characterizes the Christian use of the imprecatory psalms by saying that when we pray them we are praying 'in Jewish territory'.[26] He describes the Psalms in terms of Jewishness first of all because the Psalms grew out of situations of suffering like those the Jews have experienced throughout their history. Hence the 'Jews are a paradigm of the deepest longings and yearnings of all of humanity'.[27] The first and perhaps most essential feature of praying the imprecatory psalms is to enter such prayer from the perspective of that deep longing of humankind. People who enjoy privilege and power must be cautious, therefore, when using these psalms lest they simply use them as yet another means of securing the privilege they already enjoy. For

---

25 See Joel Kaminsky, *Yet I Loved Jacob: Reclaiming the biblical concept of election* (Nashville, TN: Abingdon Press, 2007).

26 Brueggemann, *Praying the Psalms*, p. 43.

27 Brueggemann, *Praying the Psalms*, p. 47.

such persons the psalms of vengeance should evoke self-criticism, generosity, mercy – and, when warranted, repentance.

In each of our example psalms above, we noted that the plea to God against an enemy was appropriate because the enemy had far superior power and was arrogant and oppressive. Nevertheless, God's punishment of the enemies is not the full picture and does not give the last word. Declarations of God's mercy and the hope of including these recalcitrant powers in the kingdom of God temper the call for God to punish the enemy.

A rabbinic reflection on Psalm 104.35 provides an appropriate summary of the theological convictions behind the prayers of imprecation in the Psalms. The Babylonian Talmud tells a story of a certain rabbi who prayed for the death of a violent person who had attacked him (*b. Ber.* 10a). The rabbi prayed the words of Psalm 104.35, 'Let sinners be consumed from the earth, and let the wicked be no more.' But the rabbi's wife corrected her husband. She pointed out that the verse does not actually say 'Let *sinners* (*hote'im*) cease.' Instead, it reads 'Let *sins* (*hata'im*) cease.' Therefore, she argued, the psalm is a prayer for the end of evil, not an end for a particular wicked person.

The rabbi's wife was reading what appears in the Masoretic Text. Her husband, however, was apparently reading the verse as attested in a manuscript from Qumran that does say 'Let sinners cease' (which NRSV translates as well). His wife argued further that the verse's concluding comment, 'Let the wicked be no more', means that when sins cease there will be no one who is wicked.[28]

This story offers a very important perspective on this matter, namely that the righteous are not to entreat God to punish individuals. Rather, the righteous are to pray for the end of evil and its many expressions so that the reign of God might be evident in the world.

28 Louis Jacobs, 'Praying for the downfall of the wicked', *Modern Judaism* 2, no. 3 (1982), p. 297 (297–310).

Conclusion: The Psalms and Jesus Christ

The authors of the New Testament spoke in biblical sentences.[1] They constantly quoted from and alluded to Old Testament passages as they told their stories of Jesus and made their case that Jesus is the Messiah. The biblical sentences they spoke came from the Psalms more often than from any other Old Testament book. The books of Genesis and Isaiah were also crucially important for the early Church's understanding of Jesus, but the authors of the New Testament believed that the Psalms stand out as the place in the Old Testament that anticipates Jesus' life and ministry, and especially his suffering and death. Jesus speaks of this when he addresses his disciples after the resurrection in Luke's Gospel: 'Then he said to them, "These are my words that I spoke to you while I was still with you – that everything written about me in the law of Moses, the prophets, and the psalms must be fulfilled"' (Luke 24.44). Jesus' words are remarkable to many modern readers because he suggests that the Psalms, along with parts of the Law and the Prophets, are comprehensive in the ways they spoke ahead of time about him. His life, suffering, death and resurrection are all there. As we will see in the following pages, New Testament writers saw especially in the so-called royal psalms (see Chapter 4) a foreshadowing of Jesus. Psalms 2 and 110 are among the most important in this regard. They highlight the special place of the king in God's reign, and they anticipate Jesus' fulfilment of royal promises. The earliest Christians also saw the prayers for help as especially reflective of Jesus' suffering. Thus, Psalms 22, 31 and 69 have a special role in the Passion account. But Jesus' first followers saw him in more than select psalms or types of psalms. Indeed, they saw all the psalms as Jesus' prayers. The Psalms represented the full instruction in prayer that appears only in abbreviated form in the Lord's Prayer.[2]

---

1 This is a quote from Paul J. Achtemeier which, to the best of my knowledge, is not in print anywhere.
2 See Dietrich Bonhoeffer, *Psalms: The prayer book of the Bible* (Minneapolis, MN: Augsburg, 1970), p. 16.

Jesus' identity as Son of God and Messiah

Each of the Synoptic Gospels begins by introducing Jesus as the 'Son of God' and the 'Messiah', and these labels appear quite prominently in the Psalms, particularly in psalms we have labeled 'royal psalms' (see Chapter 4). Matthew, Mark and Luke vary in the ways they communicate Jesus' identity, but all are clear on this point. Matthew begins: 'An account of the genealogy of Jesus the Messiah, the son of David, the son of Abraham' (Matt. 1.1). The word 'Messiah' is an anglicized form of the Hebrew term NRSV translates 'anointed', which in the Old Testament is a clear reference to the king (see Chapter 7). 'Son of David' reminds us that God made a promise to David to establish his ruling house for ever (2 Sam. 7). Thus, Matthew begins with clear markers of Jesus' identity drawn from the Old Testament.

Mark opens more simply with 'The beginning of the good news of Jesus Christ, the Son of God' (Mark 1.1). The message is clear, however, about who Jesus is. 'Christ' is the Greek term that translates the Hebrew *meshiah*, 'Messiah'. 'Son of God' is how the Old Testament speaks of the king's special place in God's administration (see again Chapter 7).

Although Luke begins with a unique narrative of Jesus' birth, he never-theless goes to great pains to tell us that Jesus was descended from David (Luke 1—2). So, Luke also establishes Jesus' royal lineage. So also John's Gospel is most distinctive, and yet John also early on identifies Jesus by the same labels (John 1.41). The Gospels reinforce the identity of Jesus as Son of God and Messiah when they introduce Jesus' proclamation of and representation of the kingdom of God (Matt. 3.2; Mark 1.2–6; Luke 3.1–6).

Although the Gospels do not quote the Psalms directly in these initial state-ments about who Jesus is, they clearly envisage Jesus like the anointed in the Psalms, the one who represents God's reign on earth. As we noted in Chap-ters 6 and 7, the claim that 'the LORD reigns' is central to the Psalter's message. Furthermore, the Psalms begin by introducing God's reign with a report that God is carrying out divine rule through the king on Mount Zion, and God declares to the king, 'You are my son' (Ps. 2.7). The Gospels insist this is the identity of Jesus.

Baptism, Transfiguration and trial

The royal identity of Jesus and the influence of the Psalms on this identity is nowhere more clear than in the baptism of Jesus. Mark reports the baptism this way:

In those days Jesus came from Nazareth of Galilee and was baptized by John in the Jordan. And just as he was coming up out of the water, he saw the heavens torn apart and the Spirit descending like a dove on him. And a voice came from heaven, 'You are my Son, the Beloved; with you I am well pleased.'
(Mark 1.9–11)

Matthew is similar:

And when Jesus had been baptized, just as he came up from the water, suddenly the heavens were opened to him and he saw the Spirit of God descending like a dove and alighting on him. And a voice from heaven said, 'This is my Son, the Beloved, with whom I am well pleased.'
(Matt. 3.16–17)

The voice from heaven affirms Jesus' identity by calling him 'my Son', a clear allusion to Psalm 2.7. The Gospel writers seem to conceive Jesus' baptism as a coronation and so they draw from the Psalter's language that originally signified the king's installation on Zion. Luke 3.22 reports the heavenly voice just as Mark does. Matthew alters it only slightly by changing the second-person address 'You are . . .' to a third-person declaration, 'This is . . .' It is clear, however, that Matthew has Psalm 2.7 in mind.

Psalm 2.7 also figures prominently in the account of Jesus' Transfiguration (Matt. 17.1–13; Mark 9.2–8; Luke 9.28–36). Again the Synoptic Gospels report it as a coronation, with a voice from heaven echoing Psalm 2.7: 'This is my Son.' As in the baptism scene, the Transfiguration portrays Jesus as God's Son in a way that interprets Psalm 2.7. The Synoptics add other designations as well. 'Beloved' is perhaps an allusion to Isaac in Genesis 22, and 'well pleased' likely comes from Isaiah's description of the servant of the LORD (Isa. 42.1). The writers perhaps intended these additions to hint at the suffering Jesus would endure, that his kingship would be marked by his death. If that is their intention, they are simply making clear the identity of the anointed already in the Psalms, namely as one who suffers persecution and humiliation at the hands of the nations (see Acts 4.25–26).

Psalm 2 also seems to play an important role in Matthew's account of Jesus' trial and the judgement that leads to his death. The Gospels report that Pilate charges Jesus with the treasonous identity, 'King of the Jews' (Matt. 27.37; Mark 15.12, 18; Luke 23.38; John 18.34; 19.19). Matthew reports the charge in a way that is distinctive, however, in two details. He states that the charge read 'This is . . . the King of the Jews' and that the charge appeared 'over his head'. Tucker Ferda makes the interesting observation that here Matthew is reporting the charge against Jesus in a way that brings the crucifixion scene in line with the baptism and Transfiguration. In both of those accounts the voice from heaven began with the words 'This is . . .' Furthermore, in both accounts something significant appears over Jesus' head, a dove in the baptism and a cloud in the Transfiguration. Thus, Ferda argues that Matthew is presenting Jesus' death as another coronation scene and intends the charge against Jesus to echo Psalm 2.7.[3] By doing this, Matthew highlights the irony of Jesus' death and Jesus' kingship: he rules by dying, and those who kill him actually acknowledge his kingship. In turn, the centurion's confession, 'This man was God's Son' (Matt. 27.54), begins the proclamation of Jesus' death among the Gentiles.

Suffering and death

As we just noted, the Gospel writers saw in Jesus' death a sign of his coronation. They also recognized in Jesus' identity as the anointed his identity with the suffering righteous in the Psalms. We see this particularly in the way the Passion story quotes from and alludes to the prayers for help (see Chapter 4).

The literary connections between the Passion account and the Psalms are numerous. In the story of Jesus' suffering and death the Gospels quote or allude to the Psalter eight or nine times (depending on how one counts allusions), more than any other portion of the Old Testament. The important point, however, is that all of these references draw from psalms in which the righteous cry out to God in their suffering, or in which their suffering is described. According to Luke, for example, Jesus' last words on the cross come from Psalm 31.5a(6a): 'Father, into your hands I commend my spirit' (Luke 23.46). Matthew and Mark seem to draw from Psalm 69.21(22) (the righteous being given 'vinegar to drink') when they portray those who crucify Jesus giving him 'sour wine' (Matt. 27.48; Mark 15.36) or wine 'mixed with gall' (Matt. 27.34). The latter is particularly close to Psalm 69. It depicts a righteous person suffering at the hands of evildoers and being taunted by them. The offering of wine that contained a sedative was apparently common practice before crucifixion.[4] But in Matthew 27.34 the wine contains a poison or

3 Tucker S. Ferda, 'Matthew's *titulus* and Psalm 2's king on Mount Zion', *Journal of Biblical Literature* 133, no. 3 (2014), pp. 561–81.

4 See the discussion in W. D. Davies and Dale C. Allison, *A Critical and Exegetical Commentary on the Gospel According to Saint Matthew* (ICC; Edinburgh: T&T Clark, 1988–1997), vol. 3, pp. 612–13.

harsh-tasting substance. It signifies the mocking Jesus endures at the hands of the soldiers.[5] With these allusions the Gospel writers portray Jesus like the righteous in the Psalms who suffer at the hands of the wicked. This connection is perhaps most explicit, however, in the use of Psalm 22 in Matthew and Mark.

The writers of the Passion story in the first two Gospels shaped the account largely around the portrait of and response to suffering in Psalm 22. Neither Matthew nor Mark cites the psalm in order to suggest a pattern of prophecy and fulfilment. Rather, both seem to understand Jesus as one who embodied the type of suffering the psalm describes, or they saw the suffering of the righteous in Psalm 22 as paradigmatic of Jesus' suffering.[6]

The most obvious use of Psalm 22 is in Jesus' cry on the cross, 'My God, my God, why have you forsaken me?' (Matt. 27.46; Mark 15.34). Jesus' words are an exact quote from Psalm 22.1(2), but scholars debate about what the cry to God indicates about the experience of Jesus on the cross. Some believe the cry is a genuine expression of God-forsakenness that simply uses the first verse of the psalm to communicate the feeling of abandonment.[7] Others argue that Jesus' use of the first verse of the psalm indicates that he had the whole psalm in mind since first lines of poems were sometimes used to indicate the entire work.[8] The second opinion reads too much into the citation from Psalm 22. Indeed, the fact that the cry is absent in Luke and John may indicate that some in the early Church were embarrassed by the tradition that Jesus complained of God abandoning him. Moreover, Matthew particularly emphasizes Jesus' abandonment, first by his own country (Matt. 13.53–58), then by his disciples (26.56, 69–75), then by the crowds (27.15–26) and finally by God (27.46).[9] The two positions do not have to be mutually exclusive, however, since, as we have

---

5 Davies and Allison point out, however, that some think this verse has an act of compassion in view and that the women at the cross are the ones who offer the wine (*Matthew*, vol. 3, p. 613, n. 26); *b. Sanh.* 43a and Matt. 27.55–56 both mention the women; the context, nevertheless, suggests the offering of wine is an act of mocking.

6 See the discussion of J. Clinton McCann Jr, *A Theological Introduction to the Book of Psalms: The Psalms as Torah* (Nashville, TN: Abingdon Press, 1993), pp. 169–75.

7 Numerous exegetical stretches may be cited: for example, L. P. Trudinger ('*Eli, Eli, lama sabachthani? A cry of dereliction? or victory?*', *Journal of the Evangelical Theological Society* 17 (1974), pp. 235–8) argues that Jesus' cry is actually a cry of victory since God has handed him over to be a sacrifice for sin; E. Best, in *The Temptation and the Passion: The Markan soteriology* (Cambridge: Cambridge University Press, 1965), pp. lxiv–lxviii, suggests that Jesus is aware he is bearing God's judgement for the sins of others (based on Mark 10.38–39; 14.35–36); Jürgen Moltmann's extensive use of Ps. 22.1, though immensely helpful theologically, should not be confused with historical analysis (which Moltmann, of course, acknowledges it is not); see *The Crucified God: The cross of Christ as the foundation and criticism of Christian Theology* (New York, NY: Harper & Row, 1974), esp. pp. 150–3.

8 Davies and Allison, *Matthew*, vol. 3, pp. 624–5.

9 Davies and Allison, *Matthew*, vol. 3, p. 623.

observed, complaint grows out of faith. The fact that Psalm 22 ends with assurance – as do almost all individual complaint psalms – itself suggests that complaint (even of being abandoned by God) and faith belong together in the life of the righteous.

The so-called cry of dereliction is not the only part of Psalm 22 Matthew and Mark used. In fact, the whole account of Jesus' crucifixion seems to mirror the experience of the one who cries out in Psalm 22. The mocking of Jesus by those who pass by (Mark 15.25–32; Matt. 27.38–44) reflects the mocking of the one who suffers in Psalm 22.6–8(7–9) (note the shaking of the heads in both texts). It is possible that the taunting 'Aha!' of Mark 15.29 has another psalm in mind, but if so, it is surely a psalm that reflects the suffering of the right-eous (perhaps Ps. 40.15(16)//70.3(4)). All four Gospels link Jesus on the cross to Psalm 22.18(19) when the soldiers cast lots for his clothes (Matt. 27.35; Mark 15.24; Luke 23.34b; John 19.24). There are no direct statements about what this use of Psalm 22 means, but the collective weight of references in all four Gospels suggests that the early Christians understood Jesus as the prime example of a righteous one who suffered at the hands of the wicked. Jesus' association with David may provide additional evidence of this point.

Resurrection of the 'son of David'

As we have just observed, the identification of Jesus with David, or more gen-erally the expectation that Jesus would be a royal figure, may seem ironic in the light of Jesus' suffering. Kings may make others suffer, but they do not suffer themselves, the reasoning goes. Therefore, the crucifixion of Jesus is unexpected and causes the kingship of Jesus to be reinterpreted in terms of suffering and self-giving. This traditional view makes sense in the light of the expectations for the Messiah to rein in God's foes, rebuild the Temple and usher in the kingdom of God. But the notion that the suffering of the LORD's anointed is totally unexpected is hard to square with the portrait of David in the Psalms. We have observed that David in the Psalms is mainly one who suffers. He is the model righteous one who responds to suffering by trusting in God. Some ancient Jewish interpretation of the Psalms recognized this point. Thus, the rabbis concluded that tribulation would precede the Messiah's vic-torious work.[10] The early Church inherited this idea and saw the same pattern in Jesus' suffering and death.

---

10 See *b. Sanh.* 97a on Ps. 89.51(52).

David Moessner argues that the writer of Luke–Acts is relying precisely on this view of David in the Psalter when he presents the suffering and death of Jesus as a fulfilment of Scripture.[11] Moessner focuses on Luke 24.44–48 in which Jesus informs his disciples that his suffering, death and resurrection were foretold 'in the law of Moses, the prophets, and the psalms' (v. 44). He suggests that what Jesus argued from the Psalter seems to be revealed in Peter's Pentecost speech in Acts 2.14–36.

In Acts 2.14–36 Peter quotes from Psalms 16 and 110 (Pss. 15 and 109 in the Greek version) in order to 'prove' that the Old Testament foretold Jesus' Passion and resurrection. The two psalms connect in their references to the 'right hand': God is at David's right hand in Psalm 16.8 and David is at God's right hand in Psalm 110.1. Both psalms refer to God protecting the anointed and God not giving him over to death. Psalm 16.10 declares, 'For you do not give me up to Sheol, or let your faithful one see the Pit' (Acts 2.31). Peter understands David as speaking prophetically about his descendant, Jesus, since David did die and decompose. But David and Jesus had in common that they were the LORD's anointed, that the wicked opposed them and that they suffered at the hands of the wicked (Acts 2.23). Hence, David in his suffering was a type of Christ, who also suffered, but God delivered David from the hands of his enemies, and God delivered Jesus from death, the ultimate enemy.

---

11 David P. Moessner, 'Two lords "at the right hand"? The Psalms and an intertextual reading of Peter's Pentecost speech (Acts 2:14–36)', in *Literary Studies in Luke-Acts: Essays in honor of Joseph B. Tyson* (ed. Richard P. Thompson and Thomas E. Phillips; Macon, GA: Mercer University Press, 1998), pp. 215–32.

Works cited

Alter, Robert. *The Art of Biblical Poetry*. New York: Basic Books, 1985.

Anderson, Bernhard W. *Out of the Depths: The Psalms speak for us today*. Revised and expanded edition. Philadelphia, PA: Westminster Press, 1983.

Athanasius. 'Letter to Marcellinus.' In *Athanasius: The life of Antony and the Letter to Marcellinum*. Ed. Robert C. Gregg. Classics of Western Spirituality. New York, NY: Paulist Press, 1980.

Augustine. *Nicene and Post-Nicene Fathers of the Christian Church*. First Series. Vol. 8: *Expositions on the book of Psalms*. Ed. Philip Schaff. New York, NY: The Christian Literature Company, 1888.

Bellinger, W. H., Jr. *Psalms: A guide to studying the Psalter*. 2nd edn. Grand Rapids, MI: Baker Academic, 2012.

Best, E. *The Temptation and the Passion: The Markan soteriology*. Cambridge: Cambridge University Press, 1965.

Biblia Hebraica Stuttgartensia. Ed. A. Alt, O. Eissfeldt, P. Kahle et al. Stuttgart: Deutsche Bibelgesellschaft, 1967.

Bonhoeffer, Dietrich. *Psalms: The prayer book of the Bible*. Minneapolis, MN: Augsburg, 1970.

Bower, Peter C., ed. *Handbook for the Revised Common Lectionary*. Louisville, KY: Westminster John Knox Press, 1996.

Brettler, Marc Zvi. 'Jewish theology of the Psalms.' In *The Oxford Handbook of the Psalms*. Ed. William P. Brown. New York, NY: Oxford University Press, 2014, pp. 485–98.

——. 'Psalms and Jewish biblical theology.' In *Jewish Bible Theology: Perspectives and case studies*. Ed. Isaac Kalimi. Winona Lake, IN: Eisenbrauns, 2012, pp. 187–97.

Briggs, Charles Augustus and Emily Grace. *A Critical and Exegetical Commentary on the Book of Psalms*. Vol. 1. ICC. Edinburgh: T&T Clark, 1906.

Brown, William P. *Psalms*. Interpreting Biblical Texts. Nashville, TN: Abingdon Press, 2010.

——. *Seeing the Psalms: A theology of metaphor*. Louisville, KY: Westminster John Knox Press, 2002.

Brueggemann, Walter. 'The costly loss of lament.' *Journal for the Study of the Old Testament* 36 (1986), pp. 57–71.

——. *The Message of the Psalms: A theological commentary*. Minneapolis, MN: Augsburg, 1984.

——. *Praying the Psalms*. Winona, MN: St Mary's Press, 1982.

——. 'Psalm 109: Three times "steadfast love".' *Word & World* 5, no. 2 (1985), pp. 144–54.

Burgess, John P. *Why Scripture Matters: Reading the Bible in a time of church conflict*. Louisville, KY: Westminster John Knox Press, 1998.

Calvin, John. *Commentary on the Book of Psalms*. Vol. 1. Edinburgh: Calvin Translation Society, 1845.

——. *Institutes of the Christian Religion*. Ed. John T. McNeill. Trans. Ford Lewis Battles. Library of Christian Classics 20. Philadelphia, PA: Westminster Press, 1960.

Capps, Donald. *Biblical Approaches to Pastoral Counseling*. Eugene, OR: Wipf & Stock, 2003.

Charry, Ellen T. *Psalms 1–50: Sighs and songs of Israel*. Brazos Theological Commentary on the Bible. Grand Rapids, MI: Brazos Press, 2015.

Childs, Brevard S. *Introduction to the Old Testament as Scripture*. Philadelphia, PA: Fortress Press, 1979.

——. 'Psalm titles and Midrashic exegesis.' *Journal of Semitic Studies* 16, no. 2 (Fall 1971), pp. 137–50.

The Constitution of the Presbyterian Church (U.S.A.), Part I: Book of Confessions. Louisville, KY: Geneva Press, 1999, 7.001 and 7.111.

Creach, Jerome F. D. 'Like a tree planted by the temple stream: portrait of the righteous in Psalm 1:3a.' *Catholic Biblical Quarterly* 61, no. 1 (January 1999), pp. 34–46.

——. 'The Psalms and the cult.' In *Interpreting the Psalms: Issues and approaches*. Ed. Philip S. Johnston and David G. Firth. Leicester: Apollos, 2005, pp. 119–37.

——. 'The shape of Book Four of the Psalter and the shape of Second Isaiah.' *Journal for the Study of the Old Testament* 80 (1998), pp. 63–76.

——. *Yahweh as Refuge and the Editing of the Hebrew Psalter*. JSOTSup 217. Sheffield: Sheffield Academic Press, 1996.

Crenshaw, James L. *Old Testament Wisdom: An introduction*. 3rd edn. Louisville, KY: Westminster John Knox Press, 2010.

Cross, Frank Moore, Jr. *Canaanite Myth and Hebrew Epic*. Cambridge, MA: Harvard University Press, 1973.

Cross, Frank Moore, Jr and David Noel Freedman. *Studies in Ancient Yahwistic Poetry*. Biblical Resource Series. Grand Rapids, MI: Eerdmans, 1997.

Crossan, John Dominic. *The Birth of Christianity: Discovering what happened in the years after the execution of Jesus*. San Francisco, CA: HarperSanFrancisco, 1998.

——. *The Greatest Prayer: Rediscovering the revolutionary message of the Lord's Prayer*. New York, NY: HarperOne, 2010.

Crow, Loren D. *The Songs of Ascents (Psalms 120–134): Their place in Israelite history and religion*. SBLDS 148. Atlanta, GA: Scholars Press, 1996.

Davies, W. D. and Dale C. Allison, *A Critical and Exegetical Commentary on the Gospel According to Saint Matthew*. 3 vols. ICC. Edinburgh: T&T Clark, 1988–1997.

Davis, Ellen F. *Getting Involved with God: Rediscovering the Old Testament*. Lanham, MD: Cowley, 2001.

deClaissé-Walford, Nancy, Rolf A. Jacobson and Beth LaNeel Tanner, *The Book of Psalms*. New International Commentary on the Old Testament. Grand Rapids, MI: Eerdmans, 2014.

Delekat, L. *Asylie und Schutzorakel an Zionheiligtum*. Leiden: Brill, 1967.

Diodore of Tarsus. *Commentary on Psalms 1–51*. Trans. Robert C. Hill. Atlanta, GA: Society of Biblical Literature, 2005.

Dobbs-Allsopp, F. W. *On Biblical Poetry*. Oxford: Oxford University Press, 2015.

Eaton, John. *Kingship and the Psalms*. Cambridge: SCM Press, 1976.

——. 'The Psalms and Israelite worship.' *Tradition and Interpretation: Essays by members of the Society for Old Testament Study*. Ed. G. W. Anderson. Oxford: Clarendon Press, 1979, pp. 241–72.

Ferda, Tucker S. 'Matthew's *titulus* and Psalm 2's king on Mount Zion.' *Journal of Biblical Literature* 133, no. 3 (2014), pp. 561–81.

Feuer, Avrohom Chaim. *Tehillim: A new translation with a commentary anthologized from Talmudic, Midrashic and rabbinic sources*. New York, NY: Mesorah, 1985.

Frost, Robert. 'Stopping by Woods on a Snowy Evening.' In *The Norton Anthology of American Literature*. Shorter edition. Ed. Ronald Gottesman et al. New York, NY: Norton, 1980, pp. 1294–95.

Gerstenberger, Erhard S. *Der bittende Mensch*. Neukirchen-Vluyn: Neukirchener Verlag, 1980.

——. 'The lyrical literature.' In *The Hebrew Bible and Its Modern Interpreters*. Ed. Douglas A. Knight and Gene M. Tucker. Chico, CA: Scholars Press, 1985, pp. 419–21.

——. 'Non-temple psalms: the cultic setting revisited.' In *The Oxford Handbook of the Psalms*. Ed. William P. Brown. Oxford: Oxford University Press, 2014, pp. 338–49.

——. 'Psalms.' In *Old Testament Form Criticism*. Ed. John H. Hayes. San Antonio, TX: Trinity University Press, 1974, pp. 179–88.

——. 'Theologies in the book of Psalms.' In *The Book of Psalms: Composition and reception*. Ed. Peter W. Flint. Vetus Testamentum Supplements 99; Leiden: Brill, 2005, pp. 603–25.

Gillingham, Susan E. *A Journey of Two Psalms: The reception of Psalms 1 and 2 in Jewish and Christian tradition*. Oxford: Oxford University Press, 2013.

——. 'The Levites and the editorial composition of the Psalms.' In *The Oxford Handbook of the Psalms*. Ed. William P. Brown. Oxford: Oxford University Press, 2014, pp. 201–13.

Glory to God: The Presbyterian hymnal. Ed. David Eicher et al. Louisville, KY: Westminster John Knox Press, 2013.

Goldingay, John. *Psalms, vol. 3: Psalms 90–150*. Baker Commentary on the Old Testament Wisdom and Psalms. Grand Rapids, MI: Baker Academic, 2008.

Goulder, Michael. *The Prayers of David (Psalms 51–72): Studies in the Psalter II*. JSOTSup 102. Sheffield: Sheffield Academic Press, 1990.

Gunkel, Hermann with Joachim Begrich. *An Introduction to the Psalms: The genres of the religious lyric of Israel*. Trans. James D. Nogalski. Macon, GA: Mercer University Press, 1998 (German original 1933).

Hensley, Adam D. *Covenant Relationships and the Editing of the Hebrew Psalter*. Library of Hebrew Bible/Old Testament Studies 666. London: T&T Clark, 2018.

Holladay, William L. *The Psalms through Three Thousand Years: Prayerbook of a cloud of witnesses*. Minneapolis, MN: Fortress Press, 1993.

Hossfeld, Frank-Lothar and Erich Zenger. *Psalms 2: A commentary on Psalms 51–100*. Trans. Linda M. Maloney. Hermeneia. Minneapolis, MN: Fortress Press, 2005.

——. *Psalms 3: A Commentary on Psalms 101–150*. Trans. Linda M. Maloney. Hermeneia. Minneapolis, MN: Fortress Press, 2011.

Howard, David M., Jr. 'Psalm 94 among the kingship-of-Yhwh psalms.' *Catholic Biblical Quarterly* 61, no. 4 (1999), pp. 667–85.

——. *The Structure of Psalms 93–100*. Biblical and Judaic Studies 5. Winona Lake, IN: Eisenbrauns, 1997.

Jacobs, Louis. 'Praying for the downfall of the wicked.' *Modern Judaism* 2, no. 3 (1982), pp. 297–310.

Jacobson, Rolf A. 'Christian theology of the Psalms.' In *The Oxford Handbook of the Psalms*. Ed. William P. Brown. New York, NY: Oxford University Press, 2014, pp. 498–512.

Janowski, Bernd. *Arguing with God: Theological anthropology of the Psalms.* Trans. Armin Siedlecki. Louisville, KY: Westminster John Knox Press, 2013.

——. 'Die "Kleine Biblia": zur Bedeutung der Psalmen für eine Theologie des Alten Testaments.' In *Der Psalter in Judentum und Christentum.* Ed. Erich Zenger. Herder's Biblical Studies 18. Freiburg: Herder, 1998, pp. 381–420.

Jenni, Ernst. 'אהב *'hb* to love'. In *Theological Lexicon of the Old Testament* (hereafter *TLOT*). Ed. Ernst Jenni and Claus Westermann. Trans. Mark E. Biddle. Peabody, MA: Hendrickson, 1997. Vol. 1, p. 52.

Jerome. Letter 28. *Nicene and Post-Nicene Fathers of the Christian Church.* Second Series. Vol. 6: *Jerome: Letters and Select Works.* Ed. Philip Schaff and Henry Wace. Buffalo, NY: The Christian Literature Company, 1893.

Kaminsky, Joel. *Yet I Loved Jacob: Reclaiming the biblical doctrine of election.* Nashville, TN: Abingdon Press, 2010.

Keel, Othmar. *The Symbolism of the Biblical World: Ancient Near Eastern iconography and the book of Psalms.* Trans. Timothy J. Hallet; Winona Lake, IN: Eisenbrauns, 1997 (1978).

King'oo, Clare Costley. *Miserere Mei: The penitential psalms in late medieval and early modern England.* Notre Dame, IN: University of Notre Dame Press, 2012.

Knight, Douglas A. 'The Pentateuch.' In *The Hebrew Bible and Its Modern Interpreters.* Ed. Douglas A. Knight and Gene M. Tucker. Chico, CA: Scholars Press, 1985, pp. 263–96.

Knohl, Israel. *The Sanctuary of Silence: The Priestly Torah and the Holiness School.* Minneapolis, MN: Fortress Press, 1995.

Kraus, Hans-Joachim. *Psalms 1–59: A continental commentary.* Trans. Hilton C. Oswald. Minneapolis, MN: Fortress Press, 1993.

——. *Psalms 60–150: A continental commentary.* Trans. Hilton C. Oswald. Minneapolis, MN: Fortress Press, 1993.

Kugel, James. *The Idea of Biblical Poetry.* New Haven, CT, and London: Yale University Press, 1981.

LeMon, Joel. *Yahweh's Winged Form in the Psalms: Exploring congruent iconography and texts.* Orbis Biblicus et Orientalis 242. Göttingen: Vandenhoeck & Ruprecht, 2010.

Levenson, Jon D. 'The sources of Torah: Psalm 119 and the modes of revelation in Second Temple Judaism.' In *Ancient Israelite Religion: Essays in honor of Frank Moore Cross.* Ed. Patrick D. Miller Jr, Paul D. Hanson and S. Dean McBride Jr. Philadelphia, PA: Fortress Press, 1987, pp. 559–74.

Levin, Christoph. 'Das Gebetbuch der Gerechten: literargeschichtliche Beobachtungen am Psalter'. In *Zeitschrift für Theologie und Kirche*, vol. 90, no. 4 (December 1993), pp. 355–81.

Lewis, C. S. *Reflections on the Psalms*. London: Geoffrey Bles, 1958.

Liedke, G. 'שפט špt to judge.' In *TLOT*, Vol. 3, pp. 1392–9.

Liedke, G. and C. Petersen. 'תורה tôrâ instruction.' In *TLOT*, Vol. 3, pp. 415–22.

Lowth, Robert. *Lectures on the Sacred Poetry of the Hebrews*. 2 vols. New York, NY: Garland, 1971 (original 1787)

Luther's Works, vol. 11: First Lectures on the Psalms II, Psalms 76–126. Ed. Hilton C. Oswald. St Louis, MO: Concordia, 1976.

McBride, S. Dean, Jr. 'Polity of the covenant people.' *Interpretation: A journal of Bible and theology* 41 (1987), pp. 229–44.

McCann, J. Clinton, Jr. 'The book of Psalms.' In *The New Interpreter's Bible*. Ed. Leander E. Keck. Nashville, TN: Abingdon Press, 1996. Vol. 4, pp. 641–1280.

——. 'The single most important text in the entire Bible: toward a theology of the Psalms.' In *Soundings in the Theology of the Psalms: Perspectives and methods in contemporary scholarship*. Ed. Rolf A. Jacobson. Minneapolis, MN: Fortress Press, 2011, pp. 63–75.

——. *A Theological Introduction to the Book of Psalms: The Psalms as Torah*. Nashville, TN: Abingdon Press, 1993.

——, ed. *The Shape and Shaping of the Psalter*. JSOTSup 159. Sheffield: Sheffield Academic Press, 1993.

McCarter, P. Kyle. *II Samuel: A new translation with introduction, notes and commentary*. Anchor Bible 9. New York, NY: Doubleday, 1984.

McKenzie, Steven L. *King David: A biography*. Oxford: Oxford University Press, 2000.

Mays, James Luther. 'The God who reigns.' In *The Forgotten God: Perspectives in biblical theology. Essays in honor of Paul J. Achtemeier on the occasion of his seventy-fifth birthday*. Ed. A. Andrew Das and Frank J. Matera. Louisville, KY: Westminster John Knox Press, 2002, pp. 29–38.

——. *The Lord Reigns: A theological handbook to the Psalms*. Louisville, KY: Westminster John Knox Press, 1994.

——. *Psalms*. Interpretation: A Bible commentary for teaching and preaching. Louisville, KY: Westminster John Knox Press, 1994.

The Midrash on Psalms. Trans. William G. Braude. Yale Judaica Series 13. New Haven, CT: Yale University Press, 1959.

Miller, Patrick D. 'The beginning of the Psalter.' In *The Shape and Shaping of the Psalter*. JSOTSup 159. Ed. J. Clinton McCann, Jr. Sheffield: JSOT Press, 1993, pp. 83–92.

——. *The God You Have: Politics, religion, and the first commandment*. Facets. Minneapolis, MN: Fortress Press, 2004.

——. *Interpreting the Psalms*. Philadelphia, PA: Fortress Press, 1986.

——. *The Lord of the Psalms*. Louisville, KY: Westminster John Knox Press, 2013.

——. 'The Psalter as a book of theology.' In *Psalms in Community: Jewish and Christian textual, liturgical, and artistic traditions*. SBL Symposium Series 25. Ed. Harold W. Attridge and Margot E. Fassler. Atlanta, GA: Society of Biblical Literature, pp. 87–98.

——. *They Cried to the Lord: The form and theology of biblical prayer*. Minneapolis, MN: Fortress Press, 1994.

——. *The Way of the Lord: Essays in Old Testament theology*. Grand Rapids, MI: Eerdmans, 2007.

Moessner, David P. '*Two* lords "at the right hand"? The Psalms and an intertextual reading of Peter's Pentecost speech (Acts 2:14–36).' In *Literary Studies in Luke-Acts: Essays in honor of Joseph B. Tyson*. Ed. Richard P. Thompson and Thomas E. Phillips. Macon, GA: Mercer University Press, 1998, pp. 215–32.

Moltmann, Jürgen. *The Crucified God: The cross of Christ as the foundation and criticism of Christian theology*. New York, NY: Harper & Row, 1974.

Moran, William. 'Ancient Near Eastern background of love of God in Deuteronomy.' *Catholic Biblical Quarterly* 25, no. 1 (1963), pp. 77–87.

Mowinckel, Sigmund. *The Psalms in Israel's Worship*. Trans. D. R. Ap-Thomas. 2 vols. Oxford: Blackwell, 1962.

Neale, J. M. and R. F. Littledale. *A Commentary on the Psalms: From primitive and mediaeval writers and from the various office-books and hymns of the Roman, Mozarabic, Ambrosian, Gallican, Greek, Coptic, Armenian, and Syriac rites, vol. 1: Psalms 1–38*. 3rd edn. London: Joseph Masters, 1874.

Norris, Kathleen. 'Incarnational language.' *Christian Century* 114, no. 22 (30 July–6 August 1997), p. 699.

Peterson, Eugene H. *Answering God: The Psalms as tools for prayer*. San Francisco, CA: HarperSanFrancisco, 1989.

Pritchard, James B., ed. *Ancient Near Eastern Texts Relating to the Old Testament*. 3rd edn. Princeton, NJ: Princeton University Press, 1969.

Roberts, J. J. M. *The Bible and the Ancient Near East: Collected essays*. Winona Lake, IN: Eisenbrauns, 2002.

——. 'The religio-political setting of Psalm 47.' *Bulletin of the American Schools of Oriental Research* 221 (1976), pp. 129–32.

Robinson, J. H., ed. and trans. *Petrarch: The first modern scholar*. New York, NY: Putnam's, 1907.

Sanders, James, ed. *The Dead Sea Psalms Scroll*. Ithaca, NY: Cornell University Press, 1967.

Schmid, Hans Heinrich. 'Creation, righteousness, and salvation: "creation theology" as the broad horizon of biblical theology.' In *Creation in the Old Testament*. Ed. Bernhard W. Anderson and Dan G. Johnson. Issues in Religion and Theology 6. Philadelphia, PA: Fortress Press, 1984, pp. 102–17.

Schmidt, Hans. *Das Gebet der Angeklagten im Alten Testament* (Giessen: Alfred Töpelmann, 1928)

Schweitzer, Carol L. Schnabl. 'Psalms as resources for pastoral care.' In *The Oxford Handbook of the Psalms*. Ed. William P. Brown. New York, NY: Oxford University Press, 2014, pp. 583–95.

Seybold, Klaus. *Introducing the Psalms*. Trans. Graeme Dunphy. Edinburgh: T&T Clark, 1990.

Smith, Mark S. 'The Levitical compilation of the Psalter.' *Zeitschrift für die alttestamentliche Wissenschaft* 103 (1991), pp. 258–63.

Soskice, Janet. *Metaphor and Religious Language*. Oxford: Clarendon Press, 1985.

Sperber, H. *Einführung in die Bedeutungslehre*. 2nd edition. Leipzig: de Gruyter, 1930.

Stamm, J. J. 'Ein Vierteljahrhundert Psalmenforschung.' *Theologische Rundschau* 23 (1955), pp. 48–9.

Starbuck, Scott R. A. *Court Oracles in the Psalms: The so-called royal psalms in their Ancient Near Eastern context*. SBLDS 172. Atlanta, GA: Society of Biblical Literature, 1996.

Stolz, Franz. *Psalmen im nachkultischen Raum*. Theologische Studien 129. Zurich: Theologischer Verlag, 1983.

Tate, Marvin E. *Psalms 51–100*. Word Biblical Commentary 20. Waco, TX: Word Books, 1990.

Toorn, Karel van der. 'Ordeal.' In *Anchor Bible Dictionary*. Ed. David Noel Freedman. Garden City, NY: Doubleday, 1992. Vol. 5, pp. 40–2.

Trudinger, L. P. '*Eli, Eli, lama sabachthani?* A cry of dereliction? or victory?' *Journal of the Evangelical Theological Society* 17 (1974), pp. 235–8.

Upper Room Worship Book: Music and liturgies for spiritual formation. Comp. and ed. Elise S. Esliger. Nashville, TN: Upper Room Books, 2006.

Wellhausen, Julius. *Prolegomena to the History of Israel*. Trans. J. Sutherland Black and Allan Menzies. Cambridge: Cambridge University Press, 2014 (German original 1878).

Westermann, Claus. *Praise and Lament in the Psalms*. Atlanta, GA: John Knox Press, 1981.

——. *The Psalms: Structure, content and message*. Minneapolis, MN: Augsburg, 1980.

Williams, Ronald J. *Hebrew Syntax: An outline*. 2nd edition. Toronto: University of Toronto Press, 1976.

Wilson, Gerald H. *The Editing of the Hebrew Psalter*. SBLDS 76. Chico, CA: Scholars Press, 1985.

——. 'The use of royal psalms at the "seams" of the Hebrew Psalter.' *Journal for the Study of the Old Testament* 35 (1986), pp. 85–94.

Wright, N. T. *A Case for the Psalms: Why they are essential*. San Francisco, CA: HarperOne, 2013; UK edn: *Finding God in the Psalms*. London: SPCK, 2014.

Yarchin, William. 'Is there an authoritative shape for the book of Psalms? Profiling the manuscripts of the Hebrew Psalter.' Paper presented at the Sixteenth World Congress of Jewish Studies, Hebrew University, Jerusalem, 2013.

Zenger, Erich. 'The composition and theology of the fifth book of Psalms, Psalms 107–145.' *Journal for the Study of the Old Testament* 80 (1998), pp. 77–102.

——. *A God of Vengeance? Understanding the psalms of divine wrath*. Trans. Linda M. Maloney. Louisville, KY: Westminster John Knox Press, 1996.

Copyright acknowledgements

Index of Scripture references and ancient authors

OLD TESTAMENT

Genesis
1—2 *2, 135*
1.1 *122*
1.1—2.4a *72*
1.1–14 *72*
1.6–8 *72*
1.9–10 *39*
1.9–13 *72*
2.7 *135*
2.15–17 *46*
6—9 *122*
15.6 *162*
20 *53*
22 *185*
25.19–30 *173*
26.1–16 *53*
49.5–7 *57*

Exodus
3.7 *152*
3.9 *152*
3.13–15 *121*
12.49 *131*
14.1 *129*
15 *152*
15.1–8 *11*
15.1–21 *84*
15.20 *84*
16 *156*
20.7 *142*
20.17 *142*

23.16 *92*
32 *113–14*
32.10 *113*
32.11 *113*
32.12 *113*
34.22 *92*

Leviticus
3.1–17 *64*
7.11–18 *64, 84*
7.12 *74*
9.22 *83*
9.22–24 *83*
23 *88*
23.4–8 *88*
23.9–14 *88*
23.16 *88*
23.33–43 *92*

Numbers
5.11–31 *95*
6.22–26 *83*
10 *84*
10.35 *84*
10.35–36 *84*
10.36 *84*
21 *83*
21.17–18 *83–4*

Deuteronomy
4.8 *131*
5.21 *142*
17.8–13 *94–5*

17.14–20 *76, 109*
21.1–8 *95*
27.3 *132*
27.17–19 *127*
29—30 *179*
30.6 *179*
32.8–9 *126*
32.35 *180*
33 *11*
33.8 *57*

Judges
9.7–15 *43*
11.34 *84*

1 Samuel
2.1–10 *11*
2—3 *57*
8 *130*
10.1–8 *130*
16.1–13 *130*
16.7 *76*
16.11 *42*
16.14–23 *12*
17.15 *42*
17.20 *42*
17.28 *42*
17.34–37 *42*
18.6–9 *84*
20.12–17 *179*
21.10–15 *53*
24 *130*
24.6 *75*

24.10 *75*
26 *130*
26.9 *75*
26.11 *75*

2 Samuel
5.6–10 *128*
6 *73, 87*
7 *184*
11—12 *18*
11.27b *18*
12 *95*
12.1–15 *51*
12.11 *51*
12.13 *18, 161*
15 *50, 107*
15—18 *48*
15.12 *50*
15.25–28 *50*
16.8 *50*
16.14 *50*
17.22 *50*
22 *50*
23.1 *52*

1 Kings
4.31 *18*
8.31–32 *94*
17.17–24 *83*
22.49 *129*

2 Kings
4.18–37 *83*

18.13—19.37 *129*
25.7 *175*

1 Chronicles
9.33–34 *57*
15—16 *57, 96*
15.1—16.36 *87*
15.16 *12*
15.17 *18*
15.19 *18*
15.20–21 *85*
15.21 *12*
15.28 *12, 87*
16 *18*
16.4 *18*
16.4–5 *57*
16.5 *12*
16.7 *87*
16.7–42 *18*
16.8–34 *87*
16.41–42 *18*
22 *1*
25.1 *18*
25.1–31 *18*
26 *57*
26.1–19 *18*

2 Chronicles
32.25 *138*
36.23 *18, 23*

Ezra
2.41 *57*
3.8 *15*
4 *62*

Nehemiah
8 *57, 92*
8.5–8 *92*

Job
1.1 *143*

6.24 *131*
7.17–18 *136*
17.12–16 *178*
33 *85*
33.26 *85*
33.27–30 *85*
34.6 *135*
42.3 *138*

Psalms
1 *24, 47, 78, 91, 97, 102, 106, 133, 158*
1—2 *24, 26, 103, 105, 107*
1—41 *25, 104*
1.1–3 *136*
1.2 *47, 103, 105, 133, 143*
1.2–3 *8*
1.3 *45, 46, 47, 133*
1.3a *24*
1.3b *24*
1.4–6 *24, 136*
1.6 *106, 110, 118*
1.6b *97*
2 *2, 24, 75, 93, 97, 104, 106, 124, 130, 183*
2.1–2 *124, 144*
2.1–3 *130*
2.1–6 *106*
2.4 *24, 43*
2.7 *76, 184, 185–6*
2.7–9 *75–6*
2.10–12 *97*
2.11 *24*
2.12 *24, 106, 107–8, 119, 144, 154*
2.12a *97*
3 *17, 48–51, 53, 55, 107, 107–9, 144*

3—41 *22, 23, 26, 54, 102, 149, 153*
3.1(2) *50, 53, 107*
3.1a(2a) *107*
3.1b(2b) *107–8*
3.2(3) *50, 107–8*
3.3(4) *107, 156, 158*
3.3–4(4–5) *50*
3.5(6) *55*
3.5–6(6–7) *50*
3.6(7) *53*
3.7(8) *55*
3.7a(8a) *108*
3.8(9) *108*
4 *62, 85*
4.1(2) *62*
4.2(3) *62*
5 *85*
5.2(3) *43, 155*
5.3b(4b) *156*
5.4–6(5–7) *174*
6 *14, 15, 16, 17, 21, 22, 85, 161*
6.1 *19*
6.2(3) *15, 22, 153, 159*
6.3(4) *8, 22, 159*
6.6(7) *153*
6.6a(7a) *19*
6.6a–b(7a–b) *19*
6.6–7(7–8) *19*
6.7(8) *19*
7 *16, 17, 22*
7.1(2) *44, 158*
7.6a(7a) *165*
8 *2, 16, 71, 72, 108, 135–6*
8.1–2(2–3) *71*
8.4(5) *135*
8.5(6) *135*
9 *16*
9—10 *13, 91*

9.5(6) *106*
9.7–9(8–10) *126*
9.17(18) *106, 144*
9.18(19) *126*
10 *22*
10.2–11 *105*
10.5 *106*
10.7 *170*
10.9 *170*
10.12–13 *160*
10.12–14 *160*
10.13 *107*
10.15 *94*
10.15–16 *106, 144*
10.16 *43*
10.17–18 *126*
11.1 *44*
11.6 *95*
11.7 *95*
12 *85*
13 *66*
13.1b(2b) *159*
13.1–2(3–4) *66*
13.2–3(3–4) *66–7*
13.3b(4b) *67*
13.3–4(4–5) *66*
13.4(5) *67*
13.5(6) *66*
13.5–6(6–7) *67*
13.6(7) *66*
14 *13, 24*
14.1 *105*
15 *27, 79, 109, 141–4*
15—24 *26, 109*
15.1 *79, 141*
15.1b *143*
15.2 *143*
15.2–4 *79*
16 *16, 17, 27, 109, 159, 189*
16.1 *67, 106, 156*

16.2 *155–6*
16.5 *95*
16.9–11 *27*
16.10 *160, 189*
16.10–11 *159*
17 *17, 95, 109*
17—18 *27*
17.1 *161*
17.1–2 *95*
17.13 *95*
17.15 *137, 160*
18 *17, 50, 53, 109, 144*
18.1–2(2–3) *106*
18.2(3) *44, 156*
18.50(51) *145*
19 *2, 72, 91, 109*
19.11b(12b) *133*
20 *76, 108*
20—21 *109*
20.3 *57*
20.6 *131*
20.7 *35–36*
20.8 *35–36*
21 *76, 108*
21—22 *27*
22 *85, 109, 153, 183, 187–8*
22.1(2) *146, 153, 155, 159, 187–8*
22.6–8(7–9) *188*
22.18(19) *188*
22.22(23) *153*
22.27–28(28–29) *154*
23 *27, 67, 109, 127*
23.1 *14, 42, 158*
23.3a *67–8*
23.4 *27*
23.4–5 *67*
23.5 *95*
23.5a *68*

23.6 *27, 53, 95*
24 *79, 109, 141–4*
24.1 *141*
24.3 *79, 141*
24.3–6 *27*
24.4 *79, 141–2*
24.4a *141*
24.7–10 *84, 88*
24.10 *109, 158*
25 *20, 91*
26.1 *36*
25.1–2 *157*
25.1–2aα *157*
25.2aβ–b *157*
26.1 *36*
26.6 *1*
27.4 *53*
28.4 *165*
29 *71, 127*
30 *18, 74, 85, 96*
30.1(2) *160*
30.1–3(2–4) *74–5, 96*
30.4–5(5–6) *75*
30.6–12a(7–13a) *75*
30.11(12) *96*
30.12(13) *96*
30.12b(13b) *75*
31 *159, 183*
31.1(2) *106*
31.5a(6a) *186*
31.6(7) *142*
31.10(11) *159*
32 *16, 139, 161*
32.1–2 *139, 162*
32.2 *162*
32.2–3 *140*
32.3–7 *139*
32.10 *139*
32.10–11 *139–40*
32.11 *140*
33 *22, 72, 91, 139*

33.1 *139*
33.2 *140*
33.3 *140*
33.4 *140*
33.4–5 *140*
33.5b *140*
34 *17, 53, 68, 78, 91, 144*
34.6(7) *137*
34.8(9) *1*
34.11(12) *78*
34.13–18(14–19) *105*
34.19(20) *106*
35.2 *40*
35.4–8 *160*
35.5–6 *165*
35.27 *156*
37 *78, 91*
37.39–40 *105, 131*
38 *85, 161*
38.3(4) *159*
38.18(19) *137*
39 *67, 91, 155*
39.13(14) *160*
40 *4, 75, 155*
40.1–3(2–4) *3*
40.1–10(2–11) *68, 75*
40.6(7) *2, 58*
40.11–17(12–18) *155*
40.12(13) *155*
40.13–17(14–18) *13, 24, 75, 155*
40.15(16) *188*
40.17(18) *58, 108*
41 *22, 25, 58, 104*
41.1(2) *144*
41.1–3(2–4) *104*
41.2(3) *160*
41.5(6) *160*

41.8–9(9–10) *160*
41.9(10) *60*
41.13(14) *25, 104*
42 *16, 44*
42—43 *13, 45*
42—49 *18, 23, 102*
42—72 *25, 26, 104*
42—83 *24*
42.1 *44*
42.1–2a *45*
42.2b *45*
42.3 *45*
42.4 *45*
42.6 *45*
43 *157*
43.1–2 *157*
43.2 *44, 106*
43.2a *45*
44 *16, 68*
44.4(5) *43, 155*
45 *16, 76, 85, 108*
45.2(3) *76*
45.6(7) *76*
46 *16, 73, 85, 108, 128, 173*
46.1(2) *130*
46.4(5) *47, 73*
46.8–11(9–12) *130*
46.11a(12a) *73*
47 *72, 92, 121, 123*
47.1(2) *86*
47.2(3) *43, 158*
47.2–7(3–8) *128*
47.3–4(4–5) *124*
47.5(6) *128*
47.8–9(9–10) *125*
48 *73, 108, 128–9, 173*
48.1(2) *128*
48.1b *129*
48.1b–2(2b–3) *129*
48.2a(3a) *129*

48.2b(3b) *129*
48.3(4) *73*
48.4–8(5–9) *129*
48.7(8) *129*
48.9(10) *128–9*
48.12–14(13–15) *73*
49 *58, 78, 91*
49.1(2) *78*
49.3–4(4–5) *78*
50 *18, 23, 90, 180*
50.2–6 *180*
50.7–11 *90*
50.8 *57*
50.8–15 *2*
51 *17, 144, 161*
51—72 *21, 22, 23,
   54, 149, 153*
51.4(6) *18, 161*
51.5(7) *41, 161*
51.10–12(12–14)
   60
51.18–19(20–21)
   53, 56
51.19(21) *57*
52 *17, 144*
52.7(9) *107*
52.8(10) *45, 46,
   47, 53*
53 *13, 24*
54 *17, 85, 144*
54.6(8) *156*
55 *85*
55.6–8(7–9) *40–1*
55.12–14(13–15)
   60, 107
56 *17, 85, 144*
56—60 *16*
56.12(13) *156*
57 *13, 43, 54, 144*
57.1(2) *44, 106, 128*
58.8(9) *165*
59 *17, 144*

59.1(2) *33, 34*
59.2(3) *34*
59.5(6) *37*
60 *13, 17, 144*
61 *85*
61.3(4) *38*
61.4(5) *38, 44*
62 *68, 144*
62.2(3) *128*
63 *17*
63.7 *44*
65—68 *17*
65.9(10) *47*
65.9–13(10–14) *89*
67 *85*
68 *71*
68.4(5) *20*
68.1(2) *84*
68.7(8) *84*
68.7–18(8–19) *87*
68.24–27(25–28)
   87–8
69 *85, 183, 186*
69.2(3) *40*
69.21(22) *186*
69.33(34) *58*
70 *13, 24, 155*
70.3(4) *188*
70.5(6) *22*
71 *22, 52*
71.1(2) *22*
72 *2, 18, 22, 25,
   54, 58, 76, 104,
   107–8, 110, 131,
   144*
72.1–4 *131*
72.4 *131*
72.5 *131*
72.6 *131*
72.6–7 *108*
72.12–14 *108*
72.18–19 *26, 104*

72.20 *21, 54–5, 59,
   109, 110*
73 *17, 58, 91, 110*
73—83 *18, 23*
73—89 *25, 26, 104,
   110*
73.1 *110*
73.2–3 *110*
73.3 *110*
73.8–9 *105*
73.17 *110*
73.18 *110*
74 *68, 110*
74.3 *111*
74.12 *155*
75 *17, 87, 111*
75.1(2) *87*
75.2–10 (3–11) *87*
76 *73, 85, 111, 128*
76.1–2(2–3) *130*
77 *111*
77.20(21) *112*
78 *2, 58, 73–4, 91,
   111, 114*
78.1–3 *78*
78.1–4 *74, 91–2*
78.5 *78*
78.12–16 *73*
78.17–19 *73*
78.20–37 *73*
78.39 *73–4, 114*
78.52 *42*
78.70 *145*
79 *68, 111*
80 *111, 127, 180*
80.1(2) *158*
80.2(3) *180*
80.7(8) *180*
80.19(20) *180*
81 *90, 111*
81.1–2(2–3) *86*
81.1–5a(2–6a) *87*

81.2–3(3–4) *86*
81.5(6) *90*
81.5b(6b) *87*
81.6–7(7–8) *91*
81.6–16(7–17) *87,
   90*
82 *43, 111, 125–7*
82.1 *126*
82.1b *127*
82.2 *126*
82.2–4 *126*
82.2–6 *126*
82.3–4 *126*
82.5 *126*
82.5b *127*
82.6–7 *126*
82.7 *126*
83 *111*
84 *18, 23, 73, 82,
   128, 130, 173*
84—85 *23*
84.1–4(2–5) *73,
   82*
84.3–4(4–5) *130*
85 *18, 23, 111*
86 *17, 111*
87 *18, 23, 73, 87,
   128, 173*
88 *18, 23, 67, 111,
   155*
89 *18, 25, 104, 111*
89.1–37(2–38) *93*
89.3(4) *115, 145*
89.20(21) *145*
89.30–32(31–33)
   111
89.33(34) *111*
89.34(35) *111*
89.35(36) *145*
89.47–48(48–49)
   113, 136
89.49(50) *111, 145*

89.50(51) *111*
89.51(52) *115, 188*
89.52(53) *25, 104*
90 *17, 18, 112–15*
90—106 *25, 26, 104, 111*
90.1–2 *112, 114*
90.3–6 *113*
90.5–6 *45, 46, 114*
90.5–10 *136*
90.7 *113, 115*
90.7–8 *113*
90.9 *113, 115*
90.11 *113, 115*
90.12 *113*
90.13 *113, 115*
90.14 *114*
90.14–17 *113*
90.17 *34–35*
91 *30*
91.1 *30–1*
91.1–2 *30*
91.2 *31*
92 *17, 18, 85*
92.12–15 *45, 47*
92.13 *46*
93 *72, 92, 116, 121, 123*
93—99 *116–17, 121*
93—100 *23, 43, 116*
93.1 *5, 23, 93, 112*
93.1b *72*
93.1b–4 *23*
93.3 *122*
93.3–4 *123*
93.4 *122*
93.5 *23, 116*
94 *180*
94.1 *180*
94.1–2 *125*

94.2 *116, 180*
94.12–15 *116*
94.23 *116*
95 *51, 70, 72, 87, 90*
95—99 *92*
95.1–2 *86*
95.1–7 *23*
95.3 *43, 123*
95.4 *39, 40*
95.4–5 *23, 123*
95.5 *39, 40*
95.5–7 *123*
95.6–7 *23*
95.8–11 *91*
95.19 *116*
96 *32, 52, 70, 72*
96.1 *31, 32, 33*
96.1–2 *32*
96.1–3 *86*
96.1–6 *32*
96.3 *32*
96.4–5 *72*
96.7–9 *32*
96.10 *23, 43, 72, 112, 123*
96.10a *72*
96.10–12 *23*
96.10–13 *32*
96.13 *23*
97 *72*
97.1 *23, 93, 112*
97.2 *43, 140*
97.2b *125*
97.2–5 *23*
97.4–5 *72*
97.6–7 *72*
97.9 *43*
97.10–11 *23*
98 *70, 72*
98.1 *86*
98.1–2 *43*

98.7–8 *23*
98.9 *125*
99 *72, 116*
99.1 *93, 112*
99.4 *116*
99.6 *112, 116*
99.7 *23, 117*
98.9 *23*
99.1 *23*
99.4 *23*
100 *70, 116*
100.1 *86*
100.1–4 *70*
100.3 *23*
100.4 *82*
100.5 *70*
101 *112*
102 *18, 161*
103 *17, 75, 112*
103.7 *112*
103.15–16 *136*
104 *2, 70, 72*
104.1a *70–1*
104.2 *5*
104.2b *70–1*
104.3 *72*
104.5 *72, 122*
104.5b *70*
104.9 *72*
104.10a *71*
104.30 *122*
104.35 *182*
105 *74, 87*
105—106 *2, 114–15*
105.1–2 *86*
105.6 *115*
105.8–10 *115*
105.15 *115*
105.23–25 *41*
105.26 *41, 112*
105.26–45 *114*

105.36 *41*
105.37–45 *41*
106 *25, 74, 87*
106.6–33 *114*
106.7 *114*
106.16 *112, 114*
106.19 *114*
106.20–23 *114*
106.23 *112, 114*
106.32 *112, 114*
106.47 *115*
106.48 *26, 104*
107—145 *26*
107—150 *25, 104, 117*
107.1 *117–18*
107.8 *118*
107.15 *118*
107.21 *118*
107.31 *118*
107.41–42 *118*
107.43 *118*
108 *13*
108—110 *23*
109 *168–71*
109.1 *169*
109.1–5 *169*
109.2a *169*
109.2b *169*
109.3 *169*
109.3a *169*
109.5–6 *169*
109.6–19 *169–71*
109.6 *169–70*
109.8–10 *169*
109.8–19 *170*
109.11 *169*
109.16 *170*
109.17–19 *170*
109.20–29 *170*
109.21 *171*
109.26 *170–1*

109.28 *171*
109.28–29 *170*
109.31 *170–1*
110 *2, 51, 93, 183, 189*
110.1 *189*
111 *19, 20*
111—118 *23*
111.1a *19*
111.1b *20*
112 *20, 91*
113.1 *86*
114 *13*
114.1–6 *20*
115 *13*
115.2 *36*
115.9–11 *86*
115.16 *72*
116 *13*
116.1–2 *23*
116.1–9 *13*
116.10–19 *13*
116.16 *156*
116.17 *74*
117 *69*
117.1 *69*
117.2 *24, 69*
118 *2, 69, 86, 88*
118.1 *23*
118.1a *86*
118.1b *86*
118.1–4 *64, 88*
118.2 *86*
118.3 *86*
118.4 *86*
118.8–9 *24*
118.22 *14*
118.26–27 *88*
118.27 *86*
118.27–28 *117*
118.28–29 *23*
118.29 *86*

119 *20, 91, 118, 132–4*
119.26–29 *133*
119.33–35 *132*
119.77 *134*
119.80 *134*
119.89–91 *133*
119.94 *134*
119.99–100 *133*
120—134 *18, 23, 86*
121 *23, 79, 86*
121.1 *79*
121.2 *79*
122 *23, 128, 173*
122.5 *145*
124 *75*
124.1 *75*
125 *23, 73*
126 *23, 128*
127 *173*
127.11 *18*
128 *23*
129 *23, 75, 96, 162*
129.1 *75*
129.1a *96, 162*
129.1b *96*
129.1b–2a *163*
129.2–3 *96*
130 *152, 161*
130.1 *152*
131 *138–9, 163*
131.1–2 *138, 163*
131.2 *138, 163*
131.3 *163*
132 *23, 73, 128, 173*
132.1 *145*
132.5 *84*
132.7 *86*
132.8 *84*
132.10 *145*

132.11–12 *145*
132.15 *173*
132.17 *145*
133 *23*
134 *23*
134.1–2 *86*
135 *90*
135.19–20 *86*
136 *2, 71–2, 74, 86, 90, 161*
136.1 *64, 84–5, 161*
136.5 *122*
136.5–9 *122*
136.6 *72, 122*
136.7 *122*
136.8 *122*
136.9 *122*
136.10–15 *89–90*
136.10–22 *161*
136.23 *161*
137 *52, 54, 90, 171–8*
137.1 *172*
137.1a–b *172*
137.1c *172*
137.1–6 *172–3, 176*
137.3 *172*
137.3c *172*
137.5 *173*
137.5–6 *174*
137.6 *173*
137.6d *172*
137.7 *173*
137.7–9 *172–3, 175, 177*
137.8 *174*
137.8–9 *172–6*
137.9 *171, 174, 176–7*
138 *17*

138—145 *23*
138.1 *64*
139 *177–9*
139.1 *178*
139.1–18 *178*
139.2 *178*
139.4 *178*
139.6 *178*
139.7–12 *178*
139.13 *178*
139.14 *178*
139.16 *178*
139.18 *179*
139.19–24 *178–9*
139.20 *178*
139.21 *177–8*
139.23 *178*
140.12(13) *58*
141 *179*
141.2 *58*
141.5 *179*
142 *17, 54, 144*
143 *137, 161*
143.12 *156*
144 *53*
144.3 *136*
144.3–4 *53*
144.4 *136*
144.9 *86*
144.10 *53, 145*
144.11 *53*
145 *26*
145.8 *118*
145.18–20 *118*
145.20 *118*
145.21 *26*
146—150 *12, 25, 26, 103, 118*
146.1 *103*
146.3 *38*
146.3–4 *25, 119*
146.4 *39*

146.5–6 *39*
146.9 *119*
146.10 *103*
147 *13, 71*
147.1 *103*
147.1–11 *13*
147.7 *86*
147.12–20 *13*
147.20 *103*
148 *22*
148.1 *103*
148.14 *103*
149.1 *103*
149.3 *86*
149.9 *103*
150 *103*
150.3–5 *86*
151 *13, 51*

Proverbs
1.7 *35*
2.7 *143*
3.5 *105*

Isaiah
2.1–4 *130*
2.2–4 *176*
23.1 *129*
23.14 *129*
38 *95*
38.20 *16*
40—55 *116*
40—66 *94*
40.1–11 *42*
40.10 *94*
42.1 *185*
44.23 *11, 94*
47.1 *174*
49.13 *94*
55.12 *94*
59.19 *94*
60.1 *94*

61.1–2 *181*
62.11 *94*
63.4 *180*

Jeremiah
8.18—9.3 *11*
17.5–8 *47*
17.6 *47*
17.8 *47*
18.5 *142*
33 *85*
33.10–11 *64, 74, 84, 96*
33.11 *85*
40.11 *173*
50.42 *174*

Ezekiel
6.3 *45*
27.25 *129*
28 *138*
28.2 *138*
28.5 *138*
28.17 *138*
47.12 *47*

Hosea
12.7 *142*

Amos
6.1–6 *154*

Jonah
2 *11*

Micah
4.1–4 *130*
6.11 *142*

Habakkuk
1 *174*
3.19 *21*

NEW TESTAMENT

Matthew
1.1 *184*
1.18–25 *164*
3.2 *184*
3.16–17 *185*
5.3–11 *105*
5.5 *181*
5.21–48 *142*
5.43–48 *165*
5.44 *177*
6.9–10 *151*
6.10 *151–2, 154, 167*
6.12 *165*
10.29 *30*
13.53–58 *187*
17.1–13 *185*
18.1–5 *139*
21.6–11 *88*
22.41–45 *51*
26.39 *151*
26.56 *187*
26.69–75 *187*
27.15–26 *187*
27.34 *186*
27.35 *188*
27.37 *185*
27.38–44 *188*
27.46 *149, 152, 187*
27.48 *186*
27.54 *186*

Mark
1.1 *184*
1.2–6 *184*
1.9–11 *185*
1.21–28 *167*
9.2–8 *185*
11.7–11 *88*

9.33–37 *139*
12.35–37 *17, 51*
14.36 *151*
15.12 *185*
15.18 *185*
15.24 *188*
15.25–32 *188*
15.29 *188*
15.34 *146, 149, 151, 187*
15.36 *186*

Luke
1—2 *184*
1.51–53 *181*
3.1–6 *184*
3.22 *185*
6.28 *177*
9.28–36 *185*
9.46–48 *139*
19.35–38 *88*
20.41–44 *51*
22.42 *151*
23.34b *188*
23.38 *185*
23.46 *149, 186*
24.44 *11, 183, 189*
24.44–48 *189*

John
1.41 *184*
4.24 *141*
12.12–13 *88*
18.34 *185*
19.19 *185*
19.24 *188*
19.28 *149*

Acts
1.16 *51*
1.20 *11*

2.14–36 *189*
2.23 *189*
2.31 *189*
4.25–26 *17, 185*

Romans
4.7–8 *162*
12.14 *166*
12.19 *166, 180*

1 Corinthians
10.4 *175*
16.22 *167*

Ephesians
6.12 *167*

Hebrews
4.7 *51*
10.30 *180*

ANCIENT AUTHORS

The Instruction
of Amenemope
47
Midrash on
Psalms 25, 48,
86, 101, 104, 163

Talmud
b. Ber. 7b *49, 51*
b. Ber. 10a *182*

b. Sanh. 97a *188*

Dead Sea Scrolls
11QPsᵃ *21, 51*

Albertus Magnus
55

Athanasius of
Alexandria
'Letter to
Marcellinus' *3*

Augustine
Expositions on the
book of Psalms

54–5, 59, 101,
175–6

Bonaventure *55*

Diodore of Tarsus
101

Jerome
Letter 28 *20*

John Chrysostom
1

Venerable Bede
55

Index of modern authors

Alter, Robert 19, 32, 37, 40, 190
Anderson, Bernhard W. 17, 143, 190, 197

Bellinger, William H., Jr 6, 71, 190
Best, E. 187, 190
Bonhoeffer, Dietrich 149, 183, 190
Bower, Peter C. 172, 190
Brettler, Marc Zvi 120, 190
Briggs, Charles Augustus and Emily
    Grace 20, 62, 190
Brown, William P. 6, 27, 28, 30, 44, 56,
    109, 120, 163, 190, 193, 194, 197
Brueggemann, Walter 79, 103, 150, 153,
    155, 171, 180–1, 190–1
Burgess, John P. 29, 191

Calvin, John 3, 7, 30, 48, 59–60, 61, 162, 191
Capps, Donald 163, 191
Charry, Ellen T. 3, 162, 191
Childs, Brevard S. 49–50, 102, 144, 191
Creach, Jerome F. D. 43, 47, 80, 107, 112,
    116, 134, 191
Crenshaw, James L. 78, 91, 191
Cross, Frank Moore, Jr 5, 121, 192
Cross, Frank Moore, Jr and David Noel
    Freedman 5, 192
Crossan, John Dominic 126, 151, 192
Crow, Loren D. 86, 192

Davies, W. D. and Dale C. Allison 146,
    186–7, 192
Davis, Ellen F. 150, 153, 166, 192
deClaissé-Walford, Nancy, Rolf A.
    Jacobson and Beth LaNeel Tanner 13,
    14, 192

Delekat, L. 95, 192
Dobbs-Allsopp, F. W. 31, 192

Eaton, John H. 76, 93, 192

Ferda, Tucker S. 186, 192
Feuer, Avrohom Chaim 49, 192
Frost, Robert 34, 192

Gerstenberger, Erhard S. 62, 80, 83, 92–3,
    96, 120, 192–3
Gillingham, Susan E. 47, 56–8, 193
Goldingay, John 174, 193
Goulder, Michael 21, 193
Gunkel, Hermann 6, 63–5, 75, 79–80, 83,
    92, 94, 102, 193

Hensley, Adam D. 116, 193
Holladay, William L. 2, 193
Hossfeld, Frank-Lothar and Erich Zenger
    89, 102, 124, 127, 193
Howard, David M. 116, 193

Jacobs, Louis 182, 193
Jacobson, Rolf A. 120, 194
Janowski, Bernd 103, 152, 159, 194
Jenni, Ernst 179

Kaminski, Joel 181, 194
Keel, Othmar 42, 194
King'oo, Clare Costly 161, 194
Knight, Douglas A. 62, 194
Knohl, Israel 81–2, 194
Kraus, Hans-Joachim 39, 141, 143, 194
Kugel, James 19, 29, 31–2, 36–7, 41, 194

7

7
7
7

LeMon, Joel 38, 44, 194
Levenson, Jon D. 20, 132–3, 194
Levin, Christoph 157–8
Lewis, C. S. 29, 80, 194
Liedke, G. 125, 195
Liedke, G. and C. Petersen 131, 195
Lowth, Robert 33, 36–7, 195
Luther, Martin 1, 127, 195

McBride, S. Dean, Jr 132, 195
McCann, J. Clinton, Jr 6, 102, 126–8, 170, 176–7, 187, 195
McCarter, P. Kyle 50, 195
McKenzie, Steven L. 52–3, 195
Mays, James Luther 6, 43, 45, 68–9, 74–5, 103, 117, 121–2, 135, 137–9, 142–5, 151, 154–5, 162, 168, 195
Miller, Patrick D. 8, 20, 28, 33, 102–3, 109, 121, 137–8, 142, 151, 158, 163–4, 195
Moessner, David P. 189, 196
Moltmann, Jürgen 187, 196
Moran, William 179, 196
Mowinckel, Sigmund 81, 93–4, 196

Neale, J. M. and R. F. Littledale 1, 55, 196
Norris, Kathleen 29, 196

Peterson, Eugene H. 4, 28–9, 30–1, 33, 149, 151, 166–7, 196

Pritchard, James B. 47, 196

Roberts, J. J. M. 76, 97, 129, 196

Sanders, James 21, 51, 196
Schmid, Hans Heinrich 143, 197
Schmidt, Hans 94, 197
Schweitzer, Carol L. Schnabl 163, 197
Seybold, Klaus 6, 12, 22, 54, 197
Smith, Mark S. 56, 197
Soskice, Janet 42, 197
Sperber, H. 41, 197
Stamm, J. J. 93, 197
Starbuck, Scott R. A. 77, 197
Stolz, Franz 83, 197

Tate, Marvin E. 89, 91, 197
Toorn, Karel van der 95, 197
Trudinger, L. P. 187, 197

Wellhausen, Julius 61–2, 197
Westermann, Claus 12, 103, 197
Williams, Ronald J. 16, 198
Wilson, Gerald H. 102–3, 111, 198
Wright, N. T. 1–4, 198

Yarchin, William 14, 198

Zenger, Erich 117, 172, 175–7, 180, 198

Index of subjects

Abimelech 53

Absalom 48–9, 53

'according to The Gittith': meaning as part of psalm headings 16

'according to Muth-labben': meaning as part of psalm headings 16

'according to The Sheminith': meaning as part of psalm headings 16

accusation: as setting for psalms 95, 169; *see also* enemy

Achish 53

acrostic psalms 19–20

anointed: David as 107, 130; as instrument of God's kingship 108, 130–1; Saul as 130; as title for king 75, 119; *see also* king, human

antithetical parallelism 33, 35–6, 37; common in Proverbs 35; features of 35

Aramaic version 16

ark of covenant 44, 57, 84, 87–8, 92; *see also* cult; LORD of hosts

Asaph 23

Augustine 149; interpretation of Psalm 137 by 175–6; as interpreter of Psalms 54–5; on Psalms as a book 101

authorship, Davidic 48–60, 101; Calvin's interpretation of 49–50, 59–60; Dead Sea Scroll evidence of 51; inquiry influenced by documentary hypothesis 62; modern questions about 52–3, 101–2; New Testament references to 51; in pre-modern interpretation 54–6, 59, 101; rabbinical interpretation of 49–51; *see also* David; rabbis

Babylonian exile 53; and end of monarchy 131, 134; and loss of Jerusalem 134, 172–4; and shape of Psalter 119

Bathsheba 18

'blessed' 24

book, Psalms as: modern questions about 10–12; pre-modern views of 101; Psalms 90—106 as key to 115; recovery as trend in biblical studies 102–3; signs in literary features of Psalter 103–5; *see also* Psalms, book of

Calvin, John 61: as interpreter of Psalms 48–9, 59; as refugee 59

canon, canonical 13

chiasm, chiastic 26, 109

Church: use of Psalms to teach prayer 5; worship of 31

Codex Alexandrinus 12

Codex Vaticanus 12

collections of psalms 22–4, 102; of Asaph 23; Davidic 22–3, 26; as 'growth rings' of Psalter 22; of Korahites 23

colon (plural cola): as segment of poetic line 19, 32–41

colophon 21, 54–5

Common English Bible (CEB) 16, 67

complementarity: as type of parallelism 39–40; *see also* parallelism, semantic

consequential statements: narrative-like 40, 41; as type of parallelism 40–1; *see also* parallelism, semantic

Contemporary English Version 22

covenant, Davidic 111–12, 115; relation to Abrahamic 115–16; *see also* David

creation: as central feature of divine kingship 123–4; conception of 72; hymns about 71–2; as sign of God's majesty 71–2; *see also* king, God as

cult 81; and ancient Israelite worship 81–3; and ark of covenant 84; evidence of in narratives 83–4; evidence of in psalm headings 85–6; evidence of within psalms 86–7; and healing rituals 95–6; and Israel's festivals 88–90; and Israel's kings 93, 96–7; Jerusalem Temple 81–3; Levites as musicians in 85; and national ceremonies 81; prophets' involvement in 90–1; relation to doctrine and ethics 81; and rituals of individuals 94–5; role of education in 91–2; role of lyrics in 83–7; and sacrifice 81–2; as setting for Psalms 81; theories concerning 87–97; *see also* Temple, Jerusalem

Cush: in heading of Psalm 7 49

David: as author of Psalms 7, 8, 17, 48–60, 101; covenant with 111; as example in prayer 60, 118; God's choice of 74; as one of the poor/righteous 58, 107–8, 144–6; in psalm headings 16–18, 48–51, 52–3; questionable character of 59–60; as 'son of Jesse' 54; story of 21; as type of Jesus Christ 54, 55; *see also* king, human

Dead Sea Scrolls 21, 51

documentary hypothesis: focus on authorship and date of documents 62; as precursor to study of psalms' genre 61–2

doxologies: and fivefold division of Psalms 25–6, 104; *see also* Psalms, book of; book, Psalms as

earth: as part of creation 39

Elohim: as name for God in Psalms 42—83 24

enemy: of David 107–8; in prayers for help 67; in psalms of vengeance 169–70; as the wicked 160

enthronement: of God as subject of hymns 72, 92–4, 123, 128

'entrance liturgy' as type of psalm 26 7

Ethan: temple musician 18

festivals: agricultural origins of 88–9; and Israel's worship 88–90; as settings for hymns of praise 69

form criticism 7, 61–4; development in twentieth century 61–4; limitations of 65, 77–9; and scholarship of Hermann Gunkel 63–5; *see also* genre; Gunkel, Hermann

fortress, metaphor for God 44, 112, 158; *see also* refuge

Gath 16

genre 7; labels for psalms in headings as ancient expression of 61; modern examples identified by patterns of speech and structure 63; Psalms' transcendence of 65; *see also* form criticism; Gunkel, Hermann

God: administration of kingdom of 128–34; claims about in Psalms 7; as creator 71–2, 121–4; 155; honour of as basis for petition 68; as judge 125–8, 167–8, 177, 180–2; praise of 8, 68–73; reign of 24, 92–3, 111–16, 120–5; relation to in prayer 149–52; *see also* enthronement

golden calf 113–14

Greek version 13, 16, 51, 52; *see also* Septuagint

Gunkel, Hermann: formulated genre labels for psalms 63–79; recognized generic language in Psalms as interpretive key 63–4; revolutionized Psalms study 63; and rise of form criticism 63–5, 80; *see also* form criticism; genre

Hallelujah: as key expression in hymns of praise 69

Hannah 11

'happy' 24

heading, of psalms 15–18; and Davidic authorship 48–51, 52–4; elements of 15; evidence of Israel's cult in 85–6; historical notes in 17–18, 48–51; relationship to David narrative 50; and versification 15; *see also* cult

healing, as part of Israel's cult 82–3; *see also* cult; sickness

heavens: as part of creation 39

Heman 18

hemistich, as alternative to colon 32; *see also* colon

Hezekiah 62

human being: categories of righteous and wicked 136–7; in relation to God's reign 135–6; as weak creature 135–6

hymn(s): as descriptive title for psalms 12; Psalms as inspiration for 1

hymn of praise: about creation 71–2; description of God's mighty deeds as dominant feature in some 70–1, 74; about God's enthronement 72; about God's salvation of Israel 73–4; imperative call to worship as dominant feature in some 69–70; as type of psalm 65, 68–74; about Zion 73

hymnal 12

intensification: as feature of parallelism 37–8; as having 'seconding' effect 38; *see also* parallelism, semantic

Jerusalem *see* Zion; Temple, Jerusalem

Jeshua 62

Jesus Christ: Christian interpretation of psalms concerning resurrection of 188–9; New Testament appeal to psalms for identity as Messiah 184; psalms and royal identity of in baptism and transfiguration 184–6; psalms as background for Passion account 186–8; and royal psalms 77, 183

Josephus 12

Josiah 62

justice: as feature of God's reign 125–6, 167–8, 177, 180–2

king, God as 43; as centre of Book IV of Psalter 116–17; as centre of theology of Psalms 121–2; characteristics of 122–7; and establishing justice 125–7; and God as creator 123–4; as root metaphor 43; as subject in enthronement psalms 23, 43, 72, 116–17; *see also* God

king, human 27; celebrated in royal psalms 75–7; as conduit of blessings 76; promoted himself through royal psalms 77; under authority of Torah 109; weakness of 109–11; *see also* royal psalms; Torah

Korahites 18

lament: as element of prayers for help 65; as main feature of psalmic prayer 152–5; as main feature of Psalms 4, 12

Leningrad Codex 13, 21, 35; *see also* Masoretic Text

Levites: as authors and collectors of Psalms 56–8; as leaders of music in Jerusalem Temple 15, 18, 57–8; as 'poor and needy' 58; relationship to David 57; role in teaching Torah 58 line(s): as basic unit in Hebrew poetry 18–19, 20, 31, 32, 41

liturgy: at gate of Temple 79; Psalms as 12; as type of psalm 78–9

LORD of hosts, association with ark of covenant 73, 84, 87–8, 92; *see also* ark of covenant

lyre 12, 16

Maccabean period 81

manuscripts, Hebrew: edition of Psalms 13, 15, 21; medieval 13; *see also* Leningrad Codex; transliteration of 8; versification in Psalms 8

Maskil 16–17

Masoretic Text 35; *see also* Leningrad Codex

measure(s): as division of poetry in body of Psalms 18–19; *see also* strophe

metaphor 32, 41; elements of 42

metre 32

Miktam 16–17

mizmor 12, 16, 17; *see also* psalm(s)

monotheism 123–4, 126

mortality: as metaphor for failure of monarchy 114; as symbol of human weakness 113–14

Moses 11, 62; books of 25, 62; prayer of 112–14; in psalm headings 18, 112–13

mountain: location of Temple 47; as part of creation 39

Nathan 18

nations: God's rule over 72, 124–5; as opposed to God's reign 75

New Revised Standard Version (NRSV) 16, 21, 76

new year festival: role of enthronement psalms in 92–3; role of Israel's king in 93; theory of 92–4

'of David' (*ledawid*) 17, 49, 52; *see also* headings

parallelism, semantic: as basic element of Hebrew poetry 19, 32; categories of 33–41; nature of 32–3; *see also* antithetical parallelism; synonymous parallelism; synthetic parallelism

penitence, psalms of 161–2; David's prayer of 161–2; use of in New Testament 162

Pentateuch 62

Philo 12

pilgrimage: to Jerusalem 23, 79; liturgy for 79

poetry 28, 32–3; in body of psalms 18–19; expressive of depths of human condition 30, 31; and meaning of texts 28–9; as mode of theological expression 29–30; power of figurative language in 30–1; relation to prose 28

poor, as objects of God's care 125–7; as subject of prayers for vengeance 167; *see also* vengeance

praise, and content of Psalms 12; appearance in complaints 68; as characteristic of hymns 68; at conclusion of Psalms 12, 103, 118–19; *see also* hymn of praise

prayer(s): as characteristic of righteous 157; Christological character of in Church 162, 164; of David 11, 23, 110; elements of 158–62; as genre label in psalm headings 17; and identity as God's servants 155–7, 162–4; of Jesus 149; and the Lord's Prayer 151–2, 183; of Moses 112–14; neglect of Psalms in Christian tradition of 150–1; out of the depths 152–5; psalmic prayer and pastoral care 163–4; in Psalms 7; Psalms as 8, 12; Psalms as our 11; Psalms as tools for 149; and sickness 158–9; *see also* lament; righteous

prayer for help by community: as type of psalm 64, 68

prayer for help by individual: as backdrop for passion of Jesus 186–8; as type of psalm 64, 65–7

procession: as part of Israel's worship 87; role of ark of covenant in 87–8; *see also* cult

prophets: as part of Israel's worship 90–1; and sacrifice 90

'a Psalm of David': meaning as part of psalm headings 16–18; *see also* David

psalm(s): as genre label in psalm headings 16–17; number of 13–14; order of 14; as part of book of Psalms 11; as religious poem 11; translation of Greek *psalmos* 11–12; translation of Hebrew *mizmor* 12, 16, 17

Psalms, book of: accent on complaint in 4; book of, as title 11; as centre of Bible 1; in Christian life and worship 1, 4; as compendium of Scripture 2; contribution to Christian theology 1–2; complexity of 5; difficult content of 5; distinctive place in Bible of, 11; express depths of human emotion 2–3; influence on popular culture 3–4; order or shape of 27, 101–19; as poetry 28–31; role of, in Church 1; scholarship concerning 5–6, 48–60, 61–4; as spiritual resource 11; strangeness to modern readers 5; as tools for prayer 4; as witness to Jesus Christ 1–2; *see also* David; Jesus Christ; poetry

Psalter, as title for book of Psalms 12; *see also* Psalms, book of

rabbis 25; interpretation of psalms of vengeance by 182; reading of Davidic headings by 48–51

refuge: in expression 'take refuge' 24, 44; as metaphor 38; as sub-metaphor of king 43, 127; origins of metaphor 43; related expressions 44, 112; under God's 'wings' 44; *see also* rock; fortress

repetition: as feature of parallelism 33; verbatim 34, 35

righteous: behaviour of 141–4; David as 107–8, 144–5; as Israel 110–11; as obedient to Commandments 142–3; praise as characteristic of 139–41; prayer as activity of 137–9; as primary category of human beings 136; relation to wicked 105–6, 136–7; subject of Psalms 1–2; subject of psalms that instruct 78; suffering of 110, 168; synonyms for 136; as those who trust in God 137–40; way of 24, 105–6

rock: metaphor for God 44

royal psalms: and coronation rituals 76; and court language 76; difficulty of identifying 76–7; and Jesus Christ 77, 105, 184–6, 188–9; in Psalms 15—24 109; at 'seams' of Psalter 104; setting in life of king 75; as type of psalm 75–7; *see also* Jesus Christ; king, human

sacrifice 57–8; *see also* cult

Saul 12

scribes 8, 15, 20, 26, 27, 52, 56, 101

selah 20–1

Sepher tehillim: as title for book of Psalms 12

Septuagint 13; *see also* Greek version

'setting in life' (*Sitz im Leben*): of Psalms 7, 80–1; as recurring event in life 63–4; relation to genre 63, 65; thanksgiving offering as ancient example of 64; wedding as modern example of 63–4; *see also* form criticism

shepherd 23, 127; image of monarch in Ancient Near Eastern iconography 42;

metaphor for God 42, 43; origins in
Israel's national life 42; sub-metaphor
for God as king 127

Sheminith, The 5–16, 49; *see also*
headings

Shiggaion 16–17; *see also* headings

Sheol: as abode of dead 159–60; and
petitions for deliverance 160

sickness: and Israel's cult 82–3, as subject
in prayer for help by individual 67,
158–9; as subject in Psalms 22; *see also*
cult; prayer

simile 32, 44–5

Solomon 18, 22

song: as genre label in psalm headings
16–17; Psalm in popular 4; Psalms as
12

'a Song of Ascents': as part of psalm
headings 18, 23

song of trust: Psalm 23 as example of
67–8; as subtype of prayer for help by
individual 67–8

steadfast love (*hesed*), sought after in
prayer 113

'with stringed instruments': as part
of psalm headings 15, 16; *see also*
headings

strophe(s): as division of poetry in body
of Psalms 18–19, 32

synonymous parallelism 33–5, 37, 40, 41

synthetic parallelism 33, 36; limitations
of category 36–7

Temple, Jerusalem 12, 15, 18, 21, 23, 53,
57, 62; destruction of 68; entry into 79;
gates of 27, 79; as location of Israel's
cult 81–3; location of righteous person
47; as refuge 31; source of security and
fruitfulness 47, 113

Temple Mount 27

tenor: as element of metaphor 42; *see also*
metaphor

tent, as place of God's protection 38

thanks (*todah*): as central feature of
thanksgiving songs 74; as general
feature of prayer 160–1; *see also*
thanksgiving songs of individual

thanksgiving songs of individual: as
liturgy for thanksgiving offering 74;
as type of psalm 74–5; *see also* genre

thanksgiving songs of Israel: as type of
psalm 68, 75; *see also* genre

theology (of Psalms) 7–8; in Christian
interpretation 120; God's kingship
as centre of 121–2; in Jewish
interpretation 120

theology, Christian 4; and the Psalms 7,
8, 120–1; *see also* God

thirst: as image of desire for God 45

titles: of book of Psalms 11–12

'to the leader' 15; *see also* headings

Torah 131–3; in enthronement psalms
116–17; as God's instruction 20, 27;
and human king 109; instrument
of God governing the world 118,
131; Moses and 117, 132; as object of
meditation 24, 47; in Psalm 119 133–4;
in Psalms 1—2 103; Psalms as 25;
relation to Temple and Zion 47, 128,
134

translation 21–2; and book divisions in
Psalms 26; and descriptive labels for
Psalms in 21–2; relation to chapter
and verse numbers 21

tree: image of permanence and
fruitfulness 45–6; part of Ancient
Near Eastern gardens 46; simile of
righteous 45–6; *see also* simile

trust: as characteristic of righteous
105–8; as element of prayer for help
67; as feature of psalms of vengeance
170; as main feature of song of trust
67–8; *see also* righteous

types of psalms 61–79; *see also* genre

vehicle: as element of metaphor 42; *see also* metaphor

vengeance, prayers for: Church's tradition regarding 165–6; and Church's work against violence 167; as expression of trust in God 175, 177; expressions of hatred in 178–9; guidelines for praying 167–8; meaning of vengeance in 179–81; necessity of prayer for 166–7; and prayer on behalf of poor and lowly 167; and quest for justice 170–1, 175–6; relation to Lord's Prayer 166; *see also* prayer(s)

verset: as alternative to colon 19, 32; *see also* colon

warrior: God as 127; sub-metaphor for God as king 127

water: in enthronement psalms 72; as representative of chaos 72, 123–4

wicked: Babylon as 174; as primary category of human beings 136; relation to righteous 105–6, 126; as subject of Psalms 1—2 24–5, 105–6; as subject of psalms that instruct 78; way of 24, 105–6; *see also* righteous

wisdom psalms: difficulty of identifying 78; as type of psalm 77–8

Yahweh: as name for God 24; translated 'LORD' 24

Zadokite priesthood 82

Zerubbabel 62

Zion: and ark of covenant 73; as centre of Davidic monarchy 128; as centre of God's kingship 128–30; as city of God 128; loss of in Babylonian attack 172–3; name for Jerusalem 73; physical features of 129; as place of God's presence 73, 129

Zion songs: praise Zion as city of God 129–30; as subtype of hymns of praise 73; *see also* genre

Printed and bound by CPI Group (UK) Ltd, Croydon, CR0 4YY

09/06/2025

14685962-0002